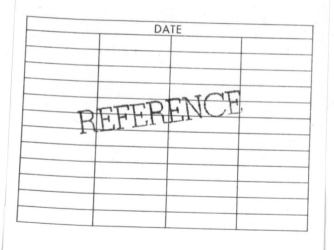

FORM 125 M

Human Behavior in Educational Administration

CLARENCE A. NEWELL
University of Maryland

PRENTICE-HALL, INC. Englewood Cliffs, New Jersey 07632

Library of Congress Cataloging in Publication Data

Newell, Clarence Albert (date).
  Human behavior in educational administration.

  Includes bibliographies and index.
  1. School management and organization.
  2. Organizational behavior. I. Title.
  LB2806.NN42   1978   371.2   77–16376
  ISBN 0-13-444638-0

© 1978 by Prentice-Hall, Inc., Englewood Cliffs, N.J. 07632

Printed in the United States of America

10 9 8 7 6 5 4 3 2 1

Prentice-Hall International, Inc., *London*
Prentice-Hall of Australia Pty. Limited, *Sydney*
Prentice-Hall of Canada, Ltd., *Toronto*
Prentice-Hall of India Private Limited, *New Delhi*
Prentice-Hall of Japan, Inc., *Tokyo*
Prentice-Hall of Southeast Asia Pte. Ltd., *Singapore*
Whitehall Books Limited, *Wellington, New Zealand*

TO

THE MEMBERS OF MY FAMILY—
ELOISE, PAUL, MARGIE AND JOHN, NANCY AND STEVE
AND ALEXANDER AND NATHANAEL—

From Whom I Have Learned at Least as Much
as They Have Learned From Me

This Book Is Affectionately Dedicated

CONTENTS

PREFACE

In this book I have drawn upon theories and research findings in the behavioral sciences and upon the literature in organizational behavior. I have attempted to identify major areas in which concepts and research findings pertinent to organization have emerged, and to present the thrust of the discoveries in each of these areas. In each instance, implications for educational administration are then indicated.

I believe that the schools will improve only as administrators and teachers grow in their understanding of human behavior. Such understanding is needed as it pertains to students, faculty, and the community. The human qualities of individual persons are often lost in the routines of running schools and in the crises which inevitably occur in educational organizations. While administration and organization are essential, they should be consistent with the central task of the schools, which is a human task concerning the development of human beings.

Of the many persons who have influenced my thinking over the years, I should like especially to mention Willard S. Elsbree and Paul R. Mort; my students and colleagues at the University of Maryland;

and my co-workers in the school systems in Maryland and the Washington, D.C., area. My wife, Eloise, worked with me in editing the manuscript. The manuscript was typed by Faith Bange.

Clarence A. Newell
College Park, Maryland

INTRODUCTION 1

If you think about your major concerns of the past week, you will discover that many of them center on your relationships with people. Administrators in particular are involved with people, for coordination of human effort is the essence of administration, and the resolution of human problems is administration's lifeblood.

Actually, administration includes both a task dimension and a human dimension; that is, there is the work of the organization which must be done if the organization is to be successful; and there are the human beings for whom the organization provides varying degrees of satisfaction and upon whom it must rely in order that the work will be done. An effective administrator needs to understand both dimensions and develop the necessary competence in both. Competence in the task dimension alone is not sufficient. If administrators are to function responsibly in providing educational programs which are effective in relation to needs, if they are to help appreciably in strengthening the staff, if they are to exercise strong leadership for the community and its representatives on the board of education, they need to develop an understanding of human behavior together with the requisite competence in interpersonal relationships.

Administration is an exciting vocation. In the field of education, it is especially rewarding because it concerns the growth and development of people. Administrators in education may face trying circumstances, they may feel alone or discouraged, but invariably their encounters with life will be rich, for they will experience the joys, frustrations, and challenges of working with people.

Many teachers and administrators are becoming acutely aware of the importance of human relationships. Some of their concerns are illustrated by the following statements, all actually made by teachers, supervisors, or administrators.

A School Superintendent

Why is it that teachers so often feel so far from the Central Office (of the school system)? We do all we can for them: work nights to improve their salaries, hire the best school principals and supervisors we can, give them opportunities for professional growth, and do all we can to help them. Yet we hear so often that teachers feel neglected, that they think the administration is not with them, and that they are disgruntled with the whole profession. We are doing all we can, and the community is exerting a genuine effort to support education. What is wrong?

A Supervisor

I wish more of our teachers could work with the superintendent in a small-group situation. He works very effectively in small groups. If the teachers could really see him in action, they might get some understanding of his depth of understanding of education. And he has such a wide range. He speaks so articulately about education, all the way from the kindergarten through the junior college. But he has lost the teaching staff. I don't understand why the teachers are so suspicious. He is really a fine educator.

A Teacher

From lengthy experience I have learned to do what I am told. If they (the administration) tell me to come in the door, I walk in. If they tell me to walk out the door, I walk out. I have learned that it does not pay to exercise initiative, but that the key to success in this school system is the willingness to follow orders.

A Teacher

We feel very fortunate in having our school principal. The thing I like most about him is that when I go in to talk with him in his office, he leans back and relaxes as if he is pushing all his other problems aside, as if he has all the time in the world, and then he gives me his full attention.

A School Principal

The superintendent, with my agreement, transferred me from a school where things were going well, to a school which was so chaotic that he felt an experienced administrator was needed. Now he has asked for the location of every child's home in order that this information can be used for planning school building locations. As I believe in democratic administration, I have always submitted such matters to the faculty for action. But if I submit this matter to the faculty in this school, I know they will vote not to prepare the information. What should I do?

An Assistant School Principal

I am in charge of discipline in a secondary school (grades 7-12, incl.) with an enrollment of over 1,000 students. During the first four weeks of school, only five students were sent by teachers to my office for disciplinary reasons. Then on Tuesday of the fifth week, one teacher sent seven students to the office for disciplinary action. Late in the day, acting on a hunch, I said to the principal: "Did you chew out that teacher today?" The principal answered: "Yes, I did. The first thing this morning."

A Teacher

In our school system we have a curriculum council on which every school is represented by an elected representative. This council can consider any problem that the teacher representatives want to consider, and the recommendations of the council go from the associate superintendent, who serves as chairman of the council, to the superintendent. Any teacher or any school faculty can ask a school representative to take any matter before the council. We thus have channels so that any idea for constructive improvement can have a fair hearing. Just knowing that our ideas will be seriously considered has been a powerful factor in the maintenance of high morale among the teachers.

A School Principal

A few years ago parents who were angry about some aspect of their child's school experience used to show up at my office periodically, and we would then discuss the problems involved. Today, however, parents who are angry are much more likely to circulate a petition. They don't come to my office and don't even go to see the school superintendent. Instead they take a petition directly to the board of education.

A Vice Principal

As a vice principal who was new in the high school, I decided to attend a community social affair sponsored by the local recreation department for newcomers in the community. At the party I soon became engaged in a discussion with a group of newcomers who were talking about the high school but did not know that I was one of the school's administrators. I was shocked to hear an openly stated opinion that the best way to improve high school education in the community would be to use dynamite or other explosives to blow up the school building. These men appeared outwardly to be ordinary citizens, but some of them favored violent "solutions" to societal problems.

IMPORTANCE OF HUMAN RELATIONSHIPS

Although problems of human relationships are as old as mankind, such problems have become exacerbated as technology has developed. Especially since World War II, these problems have become manifest in the form of high crime rates, deteriorating family life, greater incidence of emotional illness, racial confrontations, international tensions, corruption and general irresponsibility, and widespread loss of confidence in "the system." Although the human problems in society are of unprecedented severity, the self-correcting capacity of a democratic society gives hope that societal problems can be utilized to develop a better, more humane way of life.

Like the rest of society and its organizations, the schools also are troubled by upheavals. Students are restless, and some even come to school with knives, guns, and other lethal weapons. Some are using drugs or alcohol, and many are dropping out of school and out of society. Teachers, through stronger associations and collective bargaining, are demanding better schools, better working conditions, and greater material rewards. Parents are actively criticizing the schools, some insisting that schools change more rapidly and others opposing change. The financing of schools has become a heated political issue, involving not only questions relating to racial integration but disagreements over aid to nonpublic schools.

The education of the children in the schools is embedded in all these tensions, for the systems of interpersonal relationships which develop in each school reflect the tensions of the larger society. If tensions are dealt with constructively, the boys and girls in a school can develop coping patterns of interpersonal behavior, but if the tensions are allowed to become destructive, they have a debilitating influence. Thus, in school organizations as well as in the society, attention to the human as well as the task dimension is urgently needed.

Actually, the human and the task dimensions can never really be separated any more than one can separate psychology and physiology. On the one hand, mental processes cannot be separated from the brain and its physiological processes. Conversely, physiology is not separate from mental processes, for thoughts and feelings always trigger biochemical reactions in the body. The interrelationships between psychological and physiological processes are recognized in the designation of a whole series of maladies as psychosomatic illnesses.

Similarly, the human and task dimensions of organizations are inseparable. Because human relationships affect the ways in which individuals function, human relationships are central to task achievement in administration. And conversely, because the extent of task achievement affects the ways that people feel about themselves and others, task achievement affects human relationships. Yet attention can usefully be directed to one dimension at a time provided that the interrelationships between the two dimensions are not forgotten.

An administrator's relationships with other people are crucial to success in achieving the goals of any enterprise and especially in achieving the goals of education. There are three reasons why administrative relationships have such far-reaching effects in education.

First, an administrator in a school or school system helps to achieve the goals of the educational enterprise through other people. School principals or superintendents do not ordinarily undertake directly the work that needs to be done: they do not teach the children, kindle the fire, lay bricks, sweep the floors, or prepare lunch in the cafeteria. Instead, administrators plan, stimulate, coordinate, direct, and evaluate the work of other people. It is of paramount importance, therefore, that an administrator work well with people if he or she is to be effective.

The second reason runs deeper. Human relationships are the stuff out of which personality develops. Within the limits of an inherited organism, a person becomes what he is largely as a result of the meanings which he attaches to his relationships with other people.

It has long been recognized that relationships with other people have profound effects upon tiny babies. Even before babies can talk, they enter an active world of nonverbal communication with the people around them. Through this experience, a baby begins to infer meanings which have profound effects upon his or her whole development as a person.

Except for the family, the school is the institution which has the most powerful effect upon the development of children. A child spends a substantial amount of time in school each year—typically five or more hours each day for 180 or more days each year. If anyone doubts the intensity and importance of these relationships, he need only think back on his own school career. Most people can remember a number of their teachers, some of their fellow students, and even specific happenings that occurred during their school experiences. The vividness and emotional quality of these memories reveal the importance of school experiences to the individual. Both direct and indirect evidence seem to indicate that the school is indeed a powerful influence in the personality development of each child.

Human relationships are important for a third reason: they are not merely a means; they are an end in themselves. We human beings possess infinite value because we need each other. We need not only one another's services; we need each other as persons. Even a hermit writing a book on the top of a mountain is isolated only physically. From a psychological standpoint, the isolation is more apparent than real. The book is being written for the purpose of communicating with others; and it could not have been written had it not been for the hermit's relationships with others in past experience.

Because we need each other, no one is replaceable. For those people who know and care about us, no one else can take our place.

The fact that people need one another does not imply that an administrator should tolerate incompetence, avoid conflict, defer decisions, or always be "nice." The relationships of administrators to other people, however, are not only for the purpose of providing competent teachers, devising educational programs, constructing and maintaining school buildings, and obtaining the necessary funds. Important as these ends are, the human relationships themselves are an essential aspect of life — both to the administrator and to the people with whom he or she relates.

People must feel that their relationships with others are meeting their basic needs if they are to be healthy and productive. Children must experience relationships with adults whose basic needs are being reasonably well met if they are to develop satisfying concepts about themselves, concepts which will enable them to relate successfully to other people and to the world in which they live.

DEVELOPMENT OF SCIENTIFIC FINDINGS AND THEORY

One of the bitter ironies of our time is that we have learned so much about human nature and about interpersonal relationships, but seem able to do so little about changing them.

As has been frequently pointed out, the discoveries in the sciences dealing with human behavior lag far behind those in the physical sciences. Yet it is easy to underrate what is known about human nature. In fact, one of the important findings is that individuals will defend themselves against dangers perceived to be threatening, whether these dangers are physical or psychological; and hence, if they do not understand behavioral science findings and feel threatened by them, will say that they do not exist or are erroneous.

Although it is true that the behavioral sciences are still in their infancy, we have already learned a great deal. The main thing which has been learned about human nature is, I think, that human personality is more capable of change than was previously thought.

When Freud began his studies, it was thought that people are as they are because of heredity, that a person is born to be a certain way and that there is nothing anybody can do about it. Although Freud continued to stress the importance of heredity, he began to move away from the idea that human nature is determined by heredity and to place greater emphasis on the importance of early childhood experiences. He gave us some reason to believe that if such experiences could be improved, an individual would be able to lead a more constructive life.[1] More recently, the Neo-Freudians — such as Erich Fromm,[2] Karen Horney,[3] and Harry Stack Sullivan[4] — and phenomenological psychologists such as Allport,[5] Maslow,[6] and Combs and Snygg[7] —have placed increasing emphasis upon interpersonal relationships. Whether a person becomes a responsible, productive citizen or fails to develop the capacity for constructive relationships depends, according to these authorities, upon the sum total of the interactions between the human organism and the environment. Still more recently, the intensive studies of families, carried on at the National Institute of Mental Health and elsewhere,[8] seem to indicate that at any given time the behavior of an individual may

[1] Sigmund Freud, *A General Introduction to Psychoanalysis* (Garden City, N.Y.: Permabooks, A Division of Doubleday & Company, Inc., 1920, 1935, Permabooks Edition, 1953).

[2] Erich Fromm, *Escape from Freedom* (New York: Rinehart & Company, Inc., 1941, 1969). *Man for Himself* (New York: Rinehart & Company, Inc., 1947). *The Art of Loving* (New York: Harper & Brothers Publishers, 1956).

[3] Karen Horney, *The Neurotic Personality of Our Time* (New York: W. W. Norton & Company, Inc., 1937). *Self Analysis* (New York: W. W. Norton & Company, Inc., 1942). *Our Inner Conflicts* (New York: W. W. Norton & Company, Inc., 1945).

[4] Harry Stack Sullivan, *Conceptions of Modern Psychiatry* (Washington, D.C.: The William Alanson White Psychiatric Foundation, 1947). *The Meaning of Anxiety in Psychiatry and in Life* (New York: William Alanson White Institute of Psychiatry, 1948). *The Interpersonal Theory of Psychiatry* (New York: W. W. Norton & Company, 1953).

[5] Gordon W. Allport, *Becoming* (New Haven, Conn.: Yale University Press, 1955).

[6] Abraham H. Maslow, *Toward a Psychology of Being* (Princeton, N.J.: D. Van Nostrand Company, Inc., 1962).

[7] Arthur W. Combs and Donald Snygg, *Individual Behavior. A Perceptual Approach to Behavior* (New York: Harper & Brothers, 1959).

[8] Murray Bowen and others, "The Family as the Unit of Study and Treatment," *American Journal of Orthopsychiatry*, 31 (1961), 40-86. James L. Framo, *Family Interaction. A Dialogue Between Family Researchers and Family Therapists* (New York: Springer Publishing Company, Inc., 1972).

be symptomatic of what is going on at that time in the family. These psychologists do not deny the importance of individual experiences, but argue that self functioning is not as rigid and changeless as has been assumed. They have found that if real change takes place in the family, real changes take place also in the functioning of the individual family members. They have discovered that personality does not consist of unchanging attitudes and values. Rather it can be understood at any time only in terms of those interpersonal relationships which an individual is currently experiencing and which are charged with a high degree of emotional intensity.[9]

To summarize, we thought at first that human nature was determined by heredity; then, that environment played a part; then, that an individual's self was primarily the result of his interpersonal experiences; and now, that self functioning is symptomatic of the relationships which the individual helps to initiate and which he is currently experiencing.

Thus, the discoveries about behavior have given us reason to hope — reason to believe that humankind is beginning to make the most exciting discoveries ever, that at long last human beings may be able to learn how to live with their fellows through improving their own nature.

As has already been indicated, however, even though we have learned a great deal about human nature and human relationships, we have not been very successful in attempts to improve them. Their improvement is possible only through new educational applications of what has been learned about human behavior. The development of creative educational applications of behavioral science findings is an urgent necessity if the schools are to achieve their mission of preparing students to live responsibly and zestfully in the modern world.

THEORY, RESEARCH, VALUES

The development of any field of endeavor involves three aspects: theory, research, and values.

Theory is a comprehensive explanation of behavior (including the activity of inanimate matter) in any field. Theory concerns actual behavior, and thus, contrary to popular belief, does not consider what *should* happen. Instead, theory is helpful in predicting what kinds of behavior *will* occur under given conditions. A theorist develops theory on the basis of research findings and observations,

---

[9] W. R. Bion, *Experiences in Groups* (New York: Basic Books, Inc., 1959).

and utilizes powers of inference and intuition in order to formulate several consistent concepts which together comprise a comprehensive explanation of behavior. Because human understanding of the universe is always inexact and incomplete, and because human beings continue to learn, theories are never final but are always subject to change and revision. Theory affects what one will perceive when he views behavior, for it directs attention to certain aspects of behavior.

Research is the pursuit of truth through carefully systematized observation. Through the use of sophisticated methods and techniques, research makes possible the discovery of complex relationships which make facts more comprehensible and provide a basis for inferences about behavior. Research, like theory, focuses upon what *does* happen rather than what *should* happen. Research findings are never entirely accurate because the universe is so complex that man has never been able to grasp all the relationships in the intricate phenomena which he encounters, and so "the facts" discovered through research "change" from time to time. Research findings provide a basis for concepts and hence for theory; and conversely, a theory provides a basis for the identification of research problems, for there are aspects and implications in every theory and its concepts which need to be tested.

In contrast to theory and research, *values* concern what *should* be done. Theory and research become useful as guides to action only when linked to values, and thus values are an important part of any applied field (such as educational administration). Without values, action is impossible. An administrator may thoroughly understand personality and learning theories, and may be knowledgeable about current research findings relative to child development; however, an administrator can make decisions only with a commitment to values, whether it be to the development of children as freedom-loving and responsible citizens, or as automatons conforming to the dictates of the state, or to other values.

Similarly, behavior may be viewed on the basis of either of two quite different frameworks: as a scientific phenomenon or as social action.

When behavior is viewed as a scientific phenomenon, specific behaviors can be explained on the basis of scientific findings. Science is nonjudgmental and does not indicate whether specific behavior is good or bad. However, science can be helpful in formulating an *explanation* of why certain behaviors have occurred, for the role of scientific theories is to make such explanations possible.

Behavior can be viewed also on the basis of a different framework, that of social action. When behavior is viewed as social action, values are taken into account, and the behavior can be assessed as good or bad. In this context, the *consequences* of the behavior rather than an *explanation* of the behavior are of paramount importance.

Thus, if a child has been throwing rocks through school windows, the behavior can be explained on the basis of scientific findings, and on this nonjudgmental basis, the behavior is neither good nor bad. The actions can be explained on the basis of the child's inherited organism and life experiences. Viewed as a social act in which the *consequences* rather than the *causes* of behavior are taken into account, however, the action would be viewed by the great majority of citizens as bad.

In reacting to behavior, whether on the part of a child or on the part of a staff member, some administrators emphasize the scientific dimension while others emphasize the social-action dimension. Both bases are legitimate, and a wise administrator will use them alternately and in conjunction with one another, being aware of the relative emphasis given to each and the reasons for his or her choices between the bases at a particular time.

ROLE OF THE ADMINISTRATOR

Schools in a democratic society are maintained to help assure a productive and competent citizenry, and school administration has developed to assist in the accomplishment of this mission. To facilitate achievement of the educational mission, a school administrator helps in the formulation of broad policies and superintends their implementation. In the whole educational undertaking, the administrator has a major responsibility for obtaining both human and material resources, for putting them together in a desirable fashion, and for helping to focus energies on the major educational problems at hand.

Resources are inevitably limited, and various groups and organizations, both public and private, compete with the schools for them. Differing perceptions and value judgments mean that individuals and groups are often in disagreement, which is expressed in active conflict over educational programs. Rapid changes in the society result in confusion, frustration, and strife over the directions to be taken by the schools. The demands of blacks and of women and other groups for equality must be taken into account.

In all these matters, the administrator is responsible for taking those actions which will be effective through time. The best human relationships are those which, in the long run, result in the most productive organization. When people feel that an organization really cares about them, they tend to respond by caring about the organization. An administrator who develops sound human relationships can help a community to develop a sense of educational purpose, can enable a board of education to develop better policies, can help a school system to attract more competent staff, and can provide for successful implementation of school policies.

In influencing the learning climate of the school, no other individual is potentially as powerful as the school administrator. Because administrators have a pervasive influence throughout their organizations, it is important that they relate to others effectively. Their relationships, whatever they may be, are reflected in the lives and the human relationships of those with whom they associate. Whether an administrator is a school superintendent, school principal or some other official in a school system, especially if in the line of authority, the administrator's relationships are reflected in the effectiveness of the organization, in the ways in which teachers work with children, and ultimately in the personalities of the children themselves.

Because of their far-reaching effects, administrative relationships have an important bearing upon all social problems, and unless these relationships receive attention, the schools will continue to fall far short of their great potential in helping to alleviate social problems. Unfortunately, many of the current efforts to improve school experiences for children in particular, and to improve social conditions in general, neglect consideration of the administrator's relationships. There seems to be a failure to realize that money, although admittedly important, is not the complete answer to all problems. A different type of administration is needed in many communities if the schools are to make their maximum contribution toward improving social conditions and resolving social problems.

NATURE OF THIS BOOK

The development of effective administrative relationships necessitates the deepest kinds of insights into human nature and the ways in which people live with and relate to each other. People need to be able to pursue their own purposes and interests, and they need also to learn the meaning of hard work and to become toughened to the realities of adversity. In his relationships an administrator often may be understanding and pleasant, but there are times also when he may find that he is angry and irritable. The problem for an administrator is to understand as fully as possible what he should do, what he is doing, how his feelings affect what he is doing, and what the full implications of his behavior are.

To be effective in interpersonal relationships, administrators must combine the scientific findings made available through painstaking scientific research with their own insight and intuition. Successful action in human relationships depends upon reasonable congruence between an individual's actions and feelings, for a person can often sense whether or not another's action is authentic, and action which is taken by one person successfully may be unsuccessful if taken by another.

In considering the problems of human relationships, this book is primarily descriptive in nature rather than prescriptive; that is, the book attempts to describe human behavior and to indicate some of the considerations which need to be taken into account in meeting the human problems of school organization. The area of human relationships is not without its competencies and skills, however, and this book seeks to provide knowledge which is basic to the development of competence (including attitudes, factual information, skills, and procedures) in this area. The day is past when an administrator can expect to develop professional relationships through the sheer charm and force of his or her personality. A scientific basis is a necessity for competent administrative behavior. On the basis of scientific findings, skills and procedures for working with specific kinds of problems can be developed. Although detailed explanation of skills and procedures is beyond the scope of the present book, such skills and procedures are implicit throughout the discussion, and where appropriate, they are explained explicitly.

It is the viewpoint of this book that administrators need deliberately to develop the competencies of effective human relationships and to utilize these competencies in ways which are right for them, in ways which are consistent with their own feelings, perceptions, and defense patterns. An effective school administrator needs to be a creative artist in human relationships, one who develops an artistry freed from the shackles of ignorance and prejudice by competence in utilizing in an authentic way the great scientific findings which concern the nature of humankind.

SUGGESTED READINGS

Ackoff, Russell L., *Redesigning the Future. A Systems Approach to Societal Problems*, chaps. 1–5. New York: John Wiley & Sons, Inc., 1974.

Buchen, Irving H., "Humanism and Futurism: Enemies or Allies?" in *Learning for Tomorrow: The Role of the Future in Education*, ed. Alvin Toffler. New York: Random House, 1974, pp. 132–43.

Dreikurs, Rudolf, *Social Equality: The Challenge of Today*. Chicago: Henry Regency Co., 1971.

Gorney, Roderic, *The Human Agenda*. New York: A Bantam Book, Simon & Schuster, Inc., 1972.

Gross, Beatrice and Ronald Gross, eds., *Radical School Reform*. New York: A Clarion Book, Simon & Schuster, Inc., 1969.

Halpin, Andrew W., ed. *Administrative Theory in Education*, chaps. 1, 2 and 8. New York: The Macmillan Company, 1958.

Kaplan, Abraham, *The Conduct of Inquiry. Methodology for Behavioral Science*, chaps. 1, 8 and 10. Scranton, Pa.: Chandler Publishing Co., 1964.

Owens, Robert G., *Organizational Behavior in Schools*, chap. 2, "About Theory and Research." Englewood Cliffs, N.J.: Prentice-Hall, Inc., 1970.

Sergiovanni, Thomas J. and Fred D. Carver, *The New School Executive: A Theory of Administration*, chap. 1, "Applied Science and the Role of Value Judgments." New York: Dodd, Mead & Company, 1973.

Silberman, Charles E., *Crisis in the Classroom. The Remaking of American Education*. New York: Vintage Books, A Division of Random House, 1970.

Willower, Donald J., "Schools, Values and Educational Inquiry," *Educational Administration Quarterly*, 9, no. 2 (Spring 1973), 1–18.

BASIC PRINCIPLES
OF HUMAN
RELATIONSHIPS

2

Human relationships appear in such variety that one is likely to assume that there are no common elements which provide a basis for analyzing them. If we read a book or hear a lecture about human relationships and then try to apply specifically what we have learned, we are often baffled by the fact that our own situation is sufficiently different from what we have been told to vitiate the advice. Human relationships consist of the interplay between personalities, and since personalities are unique, so human relationships are endlessly varied and always changing.

This problem is highlighted by the maxims which have developed over the years as guides to behavior. These maxims, which may sound convincing when heard singly, are often inconsistent. Thus, "He who hesitates is lost" contradicts "Look before you leap." "Too many cooks spoil the broth" is not consistent with "Many hands make light work."

The inconsistencies in these maxims illustrate the dangers of trying to set forth specific guides to human relationships. Accordingly, rather than suggesting specific guides, we will now turn our attention to some principles which grow out of scientific findings concerning human personality.

A principle is a basic rule of action or conduct. Both principles and concepts are scientific generalizations based upon research findings and other observable fact, but their purposes are different. The purpose of a concept is to explain behavior or activity in a particular field, whereas the purpose of a principle is to provide a guide to action. A principle may be in the nature of a concept but has more direct implications for practice. Principles and concepts sometimes overlap, but they are by no means synonymous.

Principles are included in this chapter to provide general guides for administrative action in all aspects of human relationships. It is hoped, on the one hand, that they will help readers to recognize their responsibility for creating the kinds of interpersonal relationships desired and, on the other, that they will dispel some commonly held misconceptions about how people behave if they value human personality.

These principles are an outgrowth of many psychological theories including Neo-Freudian, phenomenological, and human systems theories. They are stated explicitly here in order that they may be of practical use to the reader.

1. *Basic to a consideration of all human relationships is the fact that each of us substantially affects his or her own relationships with others.* Each of us functions in ways which affect in large measure the kinds of situations in which we find ourselves.

Emphasis upon the part which each individual plays in his own destiny does not deny the importance of other factors, such as the people with whom he relates or the situations in which a person finds himself. Research has demonstrated that the situation does affect the way in which a person functions at a particular time. However, according to clinical evidence, the individual himself is an important causal factor in his human relationships. If a person wants a fight, sooner or later he or she will run across someone else who wants a fight. If a person wants friends and responds to others with positive feelings, he or she will find friends. If an administrator provides opportunities for the staff to share in the responsibilities and opportunities inherent in the functioning of a school, the staff will usually respond with healthy enthusiasm, if not immediately, then over a period of time.

Although events and the personalities of others affect us, there is a continuing factor running through all human relationships. This factor is the individual himself. In ways of which we are often unaware, in ways which may be ever so subtle, we indicate our feelings toward and expectations of other people, and thus provoke their responses to us. When someone has a problem in human relationships, he or she is usually contributing to the problem. Others may also be responsible for the problem, but if a person can find out what he is contributing to it and can change this aspect of his behavior, the problem will usually be less severe and often will be on the way to solution.

For example, consider a hardworking administrator who is the principal of a large urban junior high school. From his viewpoint, this administrator is highly competent. He puts in long hours at his job. However, he is having many difficulties. During the day he makes frequent trips around the school, for unless he is seen frequently in all parts of the building, discipline disintegrates. He seldom calls group meetings as he prefers to relate to teachers individually. The assistant principal, whom he selected, functions largely on a clerical level. The teachers do not take initiative or responsibility but are dependent on him. The principal complains that although he wants to develop an innovative school, the staff is phlegmatic. Staff members neither carry normal responsibility nor move ahead creatively. The principal is worn-out simply trying to keep the school operating. What the principal does not seem to realize is that his own actions — including staff selection and his relationships to staff and students — are a major factor in creating the problems.

As another example, a school superintendent in a major city took a courageous stand in furthering racial integration in the schools even when such a position was unpopular in the community. When he was later accused of racism, the superintendent felt hurt and unjustifiably demeaned. A former teacher of English literature, this administrator favored a highly structured curriculum. Such a curriculum was considered acceptable by many college-bound students from the upper socioeconomic groups but was unsuited to students from the lower socioeconomic groups, which included many black children. A track system that grouped children homogeneously was instituted in the school system with the result that most of the black children were placed in the lower tracks with the poorest teachers. Subsequently, the administrator was charged with being a racist. The administrator was not a racist in the usual sense of the term. Still, the charge of racism was a response to his administrative bias which worked against the provision of educational opportunities for black children.

Clinical psychologists report that juvenile delinquents often complain of their bad luck. If they get a job, they soon have "bad luck" and are fired. Occasionally they know someone who has kept a job over a long period of time because the individual has been "lucky." They tend to regard a person's capacity to keep a job as being a matter of luck rather than of reliability and competence.

In more subtle ways, many of us tend to ascribe to luck or to the disagreeableness of our fellows many behaviors which are affected by our own actions. When a person has a long run of misfortune, the person himself is almost certainly playing an important role in the "bad luck" which he is having.

Most problems of human relationships which administrators encounter have their origins both in the administrator and in the external situation. A balanced view takes both aspects into account. Administrators who typically blame themselves for problems which arise in their interpersonal relationships are doing themselves an injustice, while those who typically blame others for these problems are simply shifting responsibility. In both instances such individuals would be functioning poorly. A more effectively functioning person would recognize the problems in the situation and would also monitor his or her own behavior in coping with them.

When an administrator encounters human problems in an organization, he or she needs to view thoughtfully the social system as a whole in order to deepen and extend his or her understanding of the situation, and then needs to identify the ways in which the administrator's own behavior may be contributing to the problems. Often an administrator can begin by identifying a single type of behavior which he wants changed in the system, can see how his own behavior contributes to the problem, and can then modify this behavior so that the desired change comes about. In such a process an administrator needs to see himself not as a victim of the system but rather as an important participant in and, to some extent, a creator of the system.

2. *Strength of self is central in effective human relationships.* Each person needs to develop in terms of his or her own individuality and uniqueness in order to be effective in human relationships.

The word "self" might be defined as that which one really is. Sullivan believed that a human being is concerned with pursuing two goals: the pursuit of satisfaction, which concerns chiefly biological needs; and the pursuit of security, which pertains to cultural processes. He believed that in the pursuit of goals, a child encounters both approval and disapproval, and that in an effort to obtain approval and avoid disapproval, self is finally formed from the reflected appraisals of significant others.[1] While emphasizing the importance of the interaction between the individual and the culture, Erich Fromm extended the concept. According to Fromm, self con-

---

[1] Harry Stack Sullivan, *Conceptions of Modern Psychiatry* (Washington, D.C.: The William Alanson White Psychiatric Foundation, 1947), pp. 6–11. See also Patrick Mullahy, "A Theory of Interpersonal Relations and the Evolution of Personality," *Ibid.*, pp. 119-20.

sists of individuality resulting from the development of emotional and intellectual potentialities, and strength of self is shown by active expression of this individuality in behavior.[2]

The development of self is affected most by the family and next by the school. If the parents and teachers accept a child's feelings, establishing firm boundaries for their expression, the individual will tend to develop a strong self through learning to respect his or her own uniqueness. In our culture, however, normal expressions of feelings on the part of children are often met with punitive action, with the result that the development of self is stultified, and the individual learns to feel unworthy and revengeful. If self is not allowed to develop, if people's feelings and desires are frequently put down, they will express less joy, spontaneity, and uniqueness in their interpersonal relationships.

The development of self inevitably involves a certain amount of isolation. If an administrator is to be himself, his decisions must be his own. To be effective, administrators need to be in continuous communication with others in order that there may be an interchange of ideas, perceptions, and opinions. However, they must be free at the same time to act as individuals and to make those decisions which (whether popular or not) they believe will best accomplish educational purposes. The development of self does not come through consensus; it is possible only through individual identity and decision.

The development of self includes growth in the capacity to be responsible. The popular misconception that a person who is developing as a self becomes self-centered and irresponsible in his or her relationships with others results from a misunderstanding of the processes involved. Since an administrator who is developing as a self is learning to satisfy his own emotional needs through the realization of his potentialities, personal needs are less likely to be exaggerated in relationships with others, and he is therefore more capable of responding to others' needs in ways which are responsible and helpful.[3]

The development of self is closely related to the concept of authenticity, which has been discussed by a number of authors

---

[2] Erich Fromm, *Escape From Freedom* (New York: Rinehart & Company, Inc., 1941 © 1969 by Erich Fromm), pp. 256–62.

[3] For a discussion of congruence, which is closely related to the development of self, see Carl R. Rogers, *On Becoming a Person* (Boston: Houghton Mifflin Company, 1961), p. 339.

including Halpin,[4] Argyris,[5] Seeman,[6] and Rinder and Campbell.[7]

In studying the organizational climates of schools, Halpin became interested in finding explanations which would account for the differences between open and closed climates. "The Open Climate depicts a situation in which the members enjoy extremely high Esprit," work is done effectively, the organization is "moving," and the administrator "clearly provides leadership for the staff."[8] By way of contrast, "the Closed Climate marks a situation in which the group members obtain little satisfaction in respect to either task-achievement or social-needs," and in which "the principal is ineffective in directing the activities of the teachers."[9] After a number of variables had been taken into account, the only way in which the remaining differences between open and closed climates could be explained was through reference to the concept of authenticity (or genuineness).[10] Halpin goes on to say, "These observations [of authenticity and inauthenticity] fitted neatly with the climate data, for the Open Climate appeared to reflect authentic behavior, whereas the Closed Climate reflected inauthentic behavior. The OCDQ* subtests, and in particular those for Thrust and Esprit, provided indexes of this very quality of authenticity."[11]

The concept of authenticity helps to explain the ways in which a strong self comes into play in administration. Individuals who behave authentically do things in their own way within the requirements of their professional role. Role expectations are implicit in the concept of role. People expect that an administrator will behave in certain ways, and these expectations (including the expectations of the administrator and professional colleagues) define the role. Because some of the expectations are nebulous, are not strongly demanded, or are inconsistent with each other, the role boundaries typically

*Organizational Climate Description Questionnaire.
[4] Andrew W. Halpin, *Theory and Research in Administration* (New York: The Macmillan Company, 1966), pp. 203-24.
[5] Chris Argyris, *Interpersonal Competence and Organizational Effectiveness* (Homewood, Ill.: The Dorsey Press, Inc., 1962).
[6] Melvin Seeman, *Social Status and Leadership: The Case of the School Executive* (Columbus, Ohio: Bureau of Educational Research and Service, The Ohio State University, Monograph no. 35, 1960). See also Melvin Seeman, "The Meaning of Inauthenticity," unpublished paper.
[7] Irwin D. Rinder and Donald T. Campbell, "Varieties of Inauthenticity," *Phylon*, 13 (December 1952), 270-75.
[8] Halpin, *Theory and Research*, pp. 174-75.
[9] *Ibid.*, p. 180.
[10] *Ibid.*, p. 204.
[11] *Ibid.*, p. 205.

leave room for discretionary action. Within the general limits of these role boundaries, administrators with a strong sense of self will behave in ways which are valid for them.

An administrator who is developing as a self is one who is searching for ways in which his or her potentialities and those of the staff can be more fully realized. An administrator will be most effective, not if he tries to be a carbon copy of someone else, but rather if he acts independently and utilizes his own strengths and potentialities in the administrative role.

While striving to develop as a self, an administrator is also responsible for providing the conditions which enable the persons over whom he or she has power to develop as selves. It is inevitable that schools, like other organizations, exert pressures toward conformity. Because individual personality is unique, however, the development of self results in nonconformity. If administrators are to encourage the development of self, they need to learn to accept nonconformity and to cherish it. Such acceptance is difficult because the nonconformist so often seems to complicate problems in an organization. The easiest solution to a problem is usually to issue a mandate and require that everyone conform to it. When I have asked educational administrators what traits in people create the greatest problems for them in human relationships, I have found that they usually include "nonconformity" in their answers. Such a response is to be expected because a person who does not conform to expected patterns of behavior can be upsetting to the individual responsible for an institution's operation, but it does not indicate administrative encouragement of the development of self.

An educational administrator who is developing a strong self, who is aware of his or her own uniqueness and individuality, is in the best position to prize the uniqueness of someone else. The development of a strong self on the part of each administrator—and indeed of each faculty member—is the best assurance that children will be supported by the school in attempts to identify and develop their own unique potentialities.

3. *Good human relationships are those which are functional.* They are appropriate for the performance of necessary tasks.

Good human relationships exist when work is done effectively, and by the same token, optimum work accomplishment is possible only when good human relationships are experienced. Relationships of this type are not soft. They may and often do involve toughness. They demand that an individual take the consequences for his or her own acts, and at times necessitate administrative action which an individual may see as punishment. They involve vigorous disagreements. They certainly involve aggressive action.

Teachers and administrators who are sensitive to human needs have approached human relationships in two ways: 1) trying to placate students in the hope that they will want to learn; and 2) recognizing that learning is essential to human development. If you visit a classroom of the first type, in which the teacher is trying to please everyone without setting any limits or taking a definite position, you will be likely to find a situation in which the behavior of the children is either overaggressive or listless and in which little work is done. If you visit a classroom in which a teacher who cares about students is committed to the importance of learning, however, you are much more likely to see eager and active students. Work is essential, and the interpersonal relationships which result in the accomplishment of needed work are, in the long run, the best for people.

Although many school administrators have found that most school secretaries have better morale when they are doing necessary work than when they do not have enough work to do, they sometimes forget that the same principle holds for teachers and others as well. When staff members believe that they are part of an effective organization and that hard work on their part is necessary to enable the school to function well, their morale is considerably higher than when genuine effort seems unnecessary.

It is to be remembered, however, that functional relationships are those which promote the accomplishment of purposes over a period of time. A short-term view may sometimes be misleading.

This point is well illustrated by some research studies on leadership conducted by psychologists in small military groups.[12] In a study of army training, forty-eight squads were divided into two groups. Twenty-four squads were trained in regular army fashion. The other twenty-four were trained by psychologists who

> . . . set out early to impress trainees that the success and the very lives of combat-unit members are interdependent, that teamwork is required, that the careless mistake of one man can lead to disaster for the whole group. . . . that . . . the leadership *function* must be properly performed. . . .
>
> In this study . . . squad members were designated as responsible for suggesting an order to the leader if he did not notice the occasion for it or remember to give it. . . .
>
> At the conclusion of the training program one test was administered which involved a mission in which the leader and his assistant were both "killed." The problem of the unit was to complete its mission.

[12] M. Dean Havron and Joseph E. McGrath, "The Contributions of the Leader to the Effectiveness of Small Military Groups." From: *Leadership and Interpersonal Behavior* by Luigi Petrullo and Bernard M. Bass. Copyright © 1961 by Holt, Rinehart and Winston, Inc. Reprinted by permission of Holt, Rinehart and Winston.

The experimenters

> . . . encountered a finding that is rare in socio-psychological data. There was *no* overlap in performance scores between the two groups. All of the squads [trained by experimental methods] scored higher than any of the 24 Army-trained squads. It was obvious to those who umpired both groups that in the Army-trained squads the members depended entirely upon the leader to take the initiative. . . . On the other hand, in the squads trained by experimental methods, although both leader and assistant leader were removed and no one had been specifically designated as third leader, someone inevitably took over and the unit's performance on the mission was almost as good as the performance of those same squads when the leaders were present.

This study calls attention to the fact that the long-term view must be taken in determining whether or not relationships are functional. Many people believe that the best way for an army squad to operate is to center the responsibility in one man, yet the research study just cited indicates otherwise when a long-term view is taken. The best administrative decisions in terms of human relationships are those which contribute to task achievement through time.

School administrators are often so impatient to get results that they take a short-term view resulting in pseudo progress rather than any real improvement. For example, an administrator discussed with several staff members the need for improving instruction. The administrator was insistent that all staff members be required to develop daily lesson plans in accordance with a specified outline. In contrast, the staff members suggested that the administrator work with individuals and with the staff as a whole in developing individual and group goals, and that the specific actions taken be those agreed upon as flowing from the desired goals. In requiring daily lesson plans, the administrator was taking action which at best would result in a little quick improvement rather than substantial gains over a period of time.

One of the problems in attempts to improve administrative relationships is that as administrators become more sensitive to human relationships, they sometimes come to feel that their own relationships should achieve perfect harmony. Such a concept can be paralyzing, for it can prevent an administrator from taking needed action which may be unpleasant. An administrator who is to meet his or her responsibilities may, as a last resort, have to fire somebody. If an administrator is to be effective in working with people, he must feel free to act in a manner reasonably consistent with his own feeling system; he needs to feel free to take the action which is appropriate even though it may be unpleasant or may stir up negative feelings in others.

One implication of functional relationships is that administrators must be able to control some part of their own time. No one can function at a professional level without time to think and to plan. Wiles recommends that a school administrator or supervisor "keep an 'open door' to all staff members."[13] This recommendation is sound if taken in spirit rather than literally. Although an administrator needs to be available and at times may literally keep an "open door," he needs to reserve time to consider the major dimensions of the job, or he will get lost in detail and lose the perspective which is the hallmark of a true professional. Such reservation of time for thinking and planning need not make an administrator inaccessible.

Functional relationships suggest also that an administrator should require that staff members and students be held responsible for their actions. Such an approach is desirable simply because things work better that way: people learn to function more effectively through being held responsible, and at the same time, necessary work gets done. An administrator holds a person responsible for himself when he requires him to experience the consequences of his own acts. The most effective penalty is often that which grows out of the act itself. Thus, if a boy or girl mars a desk, the logical consequence is for the student to refinish the desk in order to put it in its former condition.

Holding individuals responsible for their own actions goes beyond penalties, however; it should encompass an individual's right to learn from his or her own experiences and errors. For example, an intern in educational administration recommended that a high school boy be suspended from school until his parents could come in for a discussion of the boy's behavior. On the morning that the parents came to school, the intern rushed into the school principal's office. "Here come Dan's parents," he exclaimed. "What are we going to do?" "You're the one who wanted the parents in here," answered the principal. "You go talk to them." This principal was providing an opportunity for the intern to learn from experience and to take responsibility for the consequences of his own action.

If administrators value human beings, they will not confuse the person with the person's behavior. A person is of great value; his behavior may be intolerable. If an administrator really values another person, he or she will not assign penalties lightly, but rather will carefully weigh an administrative decision in order that any action taken will, insofar as possible, result in a learning situation for the other.

Individual growth and task achievement can be mutually supportive. Work, in addition to being a necessity, can also provide individuals with a sense of worth resulting from the realization of

---

[13] Kimball Wiles, *Supervision for Better Schools*, 2nd ed. (Englewood Cliffs, N.J.: Prentice-Hall, Inc., 1955), p. 49.

self-imposed discipline, of sound achievement, and of having made valuable contributions to the life of the group.

4. *Good human relationships acknowledge the importance of reality — of people, things, and relationships as they are.* Good human relationships are based upon life as it is, not upon an idealized vision of nice people who are always good. Although the world contains much beauty and goodness and joy, it also includes sordidness, meanness, and unhappiness. The administrator's task is to function effectively in the world as it is.

Facts must be faced as facts even though one may prefer that they go away. People in good faith often strongly disagree with administrative actions which have been taken and, when their own children are involved, may experience such strong feelings that they become obstreperous. Furthermore, in looking closely at the subtleties of human behavior, one finds that people often behave destructively toward one another. Sometimes they will want to destroy an administrator or harm a school system. Some of the officers in the Army have a slogan called CYA (Cover Your Ass). They maintain that you should CYA at all times, that it is not a crime for someone to attack you, because the only crime consists of being taken by surprise. Effective administrators must maintain their position by being aware of threats to programs or to their status and by fighting back when necessary.

Among the facts which need to be taken into account in interpersonal relationships are those which have been discovered by the behavioral sciences. Like all "facts" which are perceived, these findings are never any more than an approximation of reality, and because truth is never perceived with complete accuracy, behavioral science findings change from time to time. This is not to say that the facts themselves change, although facts do sometimes become outdated, and persons and groups are always in the process of changing. However, perceptions of the facts change. These contradictions among various scientific findings sometimes result in an administrator's saying that one might as well trust common sense because behavioral science findings cannot be trusted anyway. Comments of this kind fail to take into account the fact that scientific studies utilizing established methods and instruments can take extensive data into account and disclose relationships which are beyond the means of casual or direct observation.

The scientific method does not eliminate all subjectivity, but it tries to limit it through the use of scientific procedures, that is, through specified techniques, precise measurements, and validation by consensus. A scientific finding is one which various people can agree upon through repeating the same procedures or experimental tryouts. Scientific findings in the area of the behavioral sciences will doubtless continue to be subject to many revisions in the future, but it is safe to say that generally they are based on less error than the "common sense" perceptions of most individuals. No individual should be asked to ignore intuitive judgments, but by the same token, no professional individual can afford to dismiss lightly modern scientific findings.

If administrators are to be in touch with reality, they need to develop ways of checking the accuracy of their perceptions. The best way for administrators to grow in interpersonal relationships is to communicate at a deeper level with the people close to them. By asking others for feedback in interpersonal relationships ("How did you read me when I took exception to your proposal?") and by responding typically in a nonpunitive way, the administrator can encourage further sharing of perceptions. Conferences and group meetings in which there is openness rather than a highly judgmental or contentious atmosphere promote the validation of perceptions through consensual testing.

To be in touch with reality, an administrator needs also to consider both his or her own and others' motivations, for only as motives are known can human behavior be understood. If consideration of motives leads to suspicion, it can have deleterious effects upon interpersonal relationships. However, if an administrator can consider motives and still maintain a reasonable sense of trust, remaining tentative in his judgments concerning motivations, he will have a useful device for achieving a better understanding of why people behave as they do.

5. *The goal of effective human relationships is continual improvement in the functioning of individual persons and groups. To achieve this goal, attention must center both on the processes of functioning and on the completion of important work tasks.*[14] Human relationships which are effective are those which enhance individual personality through time. The goal is not to create a pleasant situation at a particular time or to win approval of staff members and citizens. The goal is rather to help the various persons learn, grow, and develop. This goal requires both hard work and play, administrative decisions which sometimes are pleasing and sometimes are not, and leadership which makes the administrator part of the group but which also contributes to his or her separateness.

As we have already seen, the development of self is central to the

[14] While some persons would conceptualize the desired changes in individuals and groups as representing "maturation" or "better mental health," I believe that these change phenomena are more accurately and usefully conceptualized as improvement in functioning.

improvement of human relationships. It is thus a means to a desired end. Yet the development of self, the enhancement of individual personality, is also an end in itself. It is important that each individual be enabled to develop his or her own potentialities to the greatest possible extent.

Improvement in group functioning is closely related to improvement in individual functioning. Like an individual, a classroom group or a school faculty has a personality of its own. Furthermore, the individuals in a group—through their actions, their relationships with other group members, and their responses to forces outside the group—determine the group's functional level at any specific point in time. By the same token, the group's functioning affects the development of each individual group member. It is important that groups mature in order to enhance individual personality and to provide effective ways of achieving work goals.

Growth and improved functioning on the part of the administrator are a necessary condition for improvement in functioning on the part of the individuals and groups in an organization. Research evidence indicates,[15] and personal experience confirms, that an administrator's personality—for good or bad, for chaos or order—is felt throughout an organization. An administrator who is improving in functioning is helping those who associate with him or her to function more effectively, and these individuals in turn affect their associates. When there is evidence of poor functioning within an organization, the administrator had better consider what he is contributing to it. When he has come to terms with his own functioning, better functioning of the individuals and groups in the organization has been promoted. An administrator holds a crucial position, and cannot expect any more in the way of personality development on the part of the persons in the organization than he can achieve himself.

If human relationships are to contribute to continual improvement in individual and group functioning, an administrator's goals in the resolution of a problem in human relationships must include both the solution of the immediate problem and the long-range development of constructive relationships. The latter goal—the development of constructive relationships—could be compared to the goal in a game. The purpose of a wise competitor in a game is not only to win the game but also to strengthen his opponent, for it is only as both sides become stronger that the game is improved.

Similarly, in human relationships the need is for efforts which lead to greater strength and better functioning on the part of all. In re-

[15] See Chapters 8 and 10.

lating to other persons, an administrator may find the need to fight back. The other person may be overaggressive, rude, selfish, or dishonest. Yet often there are different ways in which an administrator can fight back. Instead of trying to hurt the other, an administrator may aim for a course of action which protects his or her own interests and, at the same time, helps the other to learn. It is this approach that is the goal when individual personality is valued, for it leads in the direction of human relationships which serve the best interests of everyone.

6. *Human relationships can best be understood through the utilization of systems theory.* The need for an administrator to understand human behavior in order to be able to work more effectively with people has been evident for some time. Organizational and other phenomena, however, have often been too complex to be accounted for by the behavioral science theories which were considered valid at a particular time. In addition, research findings have brought a growing realization of the complexities of human behavior.

Gradually systems theory has developed. Rather than refute previously held theories, it tends to subsume them and provide for their utilization either as concepts or as devices for changing behavior. Systems theory is useful to an administrator because it makes possible the conceptualization of many complex phenomena.

Although systems theory is implicit throughout this book, it is fundamental to the theoretical moorings of the book and is therefore considered specifically in the next chapter.

SUGGESTED READINGS

Dreikurs, **Rudolf** with **Vicki Soltz,** *Children: The Challenge.* New York: Hawthorn Books, Inc., 1964.

Glasser, **William,** *Schools Without Failure.* New York: Harper Colophon Books, Harper & Row, Publishers, 1969.

Hamachek, **Don E.,** ed., *The Self in Growth, Teaching, and Learning. Selected Readings.* Englewood Cliffs, N.J.: Prentice-Hall, Inc., 1965.

Maslow, **Abraham H.,** *Motivation and Personality,* 2nd ed. New York: Harper & Row, Publishers, 1970.

McGregor, **Douglas,** *The Human Side of Enterprise.* New York: McGraw-Hill Book Company, 1960.

Missildine, **Hugh,** *Your Inner Child of the Past.* New York: Simon & Schuster, 1963.

Montague, Ashley, *On Being Human,* new and rev. ed. New York: Hawthorn Books, Inc., 1966.

Rogers, Carl R., *On Becoming a Person.* Boston: Houghton Mifflin Company, 1961.

Saxe, Richard W., ed., *Perspectives on the Changing Role of the Principal.* Springfield, Ill.: Charles C Thomas, Publisher, 1968.

Zaleznik, Abraham and David Moment, *The Dynamics of Interpersonal Behavior,* Part 2, "Interpersonal Dynamics." New York: John Wiley & Sons, Inc., 1964.

THE SCHOOL AS A SYSTEM   3

Recent years have witnessed the development of systems theory, and it seems to be increasingly clear that a knowledge of systems theory is helpful in understanding human behavior in any organization. Unfortunately, much of the literature on human behavior has been written without reference to systems concepts. Another problem is that within the general field of systems theory, ideas are changing rapidly. In a ten-year period the ideas of a single writer may change considerably. In addition, new concepts from other fields, such as the concept of feeling systems,[1] may not be consistent with generally accepted formulations and may necessitate the revision of relatively well-established conceptualizations. Finally, there is the problem of language; the language that is most useful for analytical purposes is not always the most useful for a practitioner.

The school may be looked at as a system in two quite different ways: first, in terms of actual interacting persons; and second, in terms of analytical abstractions. The first approach is considered essential in the present discussion, both because a school consists of real people and can be understood only in terms of people, and because new findings such as those relative to feeling systems may violate current social systems theory and may necessitate revisions

[1] Explained in Chapter 8.

in present analytical models. The second way in which to view system — in terms of analytical abstractions — is rather well established through acceptance by research sociologists. This approach has often been distorted in the field of school administration. Both means of viewing systems have their uses, and hence both will be briefly considered in this chapter.

GENERAL SYSTEMS THEORY

General systems theory represents an attempt to resynthesize knowledge. As science and the accompanying technology have developed, human endeavor has become increasingly specialized. Not only have individuals become specialists, but knowledge itself has been highly fragmented. Research also has become more and more highly specialized, studying with increasing precision problems ever narrower in scope. The outpouring of recorded information in the form of books and other materials has become so great that vast libraries and sophisticated systems of information retrieval have been constructed.

The problem posed by the development of specialization is that important relationships between one specialty and another may be neglected. Furthermore, with the seemingly endless tendency to narrow scope, problems studied out of context frequently result in erroneous findings. In the field of education, for example, research has sometimes been so limited in scope as to investigate learning in subject-matter achievement only, rather than growth in the child's person as a whole. In such instances, teaching procedures which have utilized grades, frequent tests, and other means of compelling children to study have been assessed positively because they resulted in an improvement in subject-matter achievement during the period of the research study. Such studies have often led to fallacious conclusions because the limitation in scope eliminated from consideration matters such as children's motivations, whether they were learning to like or dislike intellectual activities, whether they were learning to live zestfully, whether they continued after the research study to acquire more subject matter, and even whether or not they remembered for any appreciable time the subject matter allegedly acquired. Thus, the specialization of knowledge has its vices as well as its virtues. General systems theory is a movement toward the discovery of all kinds of meaningful relationships as the following excerpt aptly describes.[2]

[2] Anatol Rapoport, "General Systems Theory," *International Encyclopedia of the Social Sciences*, 15, 452–58.

General systems theory is best described not as a theory in the sense that this word is used in science, but rather as a program or a direction in the contemporary philosophy of science. The outlook represented by this direction stems from various sources, and its adherents emphasize different aspects of the program. However, all the variants and interpretations have a common aim: the integration of diverse content areas by means of a unified methodology of conceptualization or of research.

Although general systems theory looks in the direction of integration, there are two divergent conceptualizations with their corresponding methodologies for bringing about such integration. On the one hand, many social scientists adhere to a point of view known as *reductionism*, which holds that all phenomena can be reduced to their parts or components, and that these can be studied as one would study chemistry or physics. On the other hand, there are the *vitalists*, who maintain that life is a special type of phenomenon which can be studied meaningfully only if one uses procedures which recognize the special qualities involved in consciousness and the development of self in a human being. As Rapoport points out, "The main theme of general systems theory is . . . the explicit fusion of the mathematical approach with the organismic."[3] I believe that this trend is useful if research scientists do indeed take account of the wholeness of each person, utilizing mathematical and other devices to express interrelationships. If such a fusion of various approaches can contribute to precision without the loss of attention to the uniqueness and dynamic aspects of human personality, it can prove to be fruitful. On the other hand, if the proposed fusion in concepts and methodologies results in downgrading or neglecting consideration of the unique elements in the human condition, it may be expected to make the social sciences less viable as fields of study.

Before proceeding further, we should define the word "system." This word has been explained by Rapoport as including "(1) something consisting of a set (finite or infinite) of entities (2) among which a set of relations is specified, so that (3) deductions are possible from some relations to others or from the relations among the entities to the behavior or history of the system."[4]

A more explicit statement concerning the principal properties of empirical systems is made by Parsons and Shils as follows.[5]

---

[3] *Ibid.*, p. 457. For an excellent discussion of this matter see *Ibid.*, pp. 452-58.
[4] *Ibid.*, p. 453.
[5] Talcott Parsons and Edward A. Shils, "Categories of the Orientation and Organization of Action," in *Toward a General Theory of Action*, eds. Talcott Parsons and Edward A. Shils (Cambridge, Mass.: Harvard University Press, 1962), p. 107.

The most general and fundamental property of a system is the interdependence of parts or variables. Interdependence consists in the existence of determinate relationships among the parts or variables as contrasted with randomness of variability. In other words, interdependence is *order* in the relationship among the components which enter into a system. This order must have a tendency to self-maintenance, which is very generally expressed in the concept of equilibrium. (That is, if the system is to be permanent enough to be worth study, there must be a tendency to maintenance of order except under exceptional circumstances.) It need not, however, be a static self-maintenance or a stable equilibrium. It may be an ordered process of change — a process following a determinate pattern rather than random variability relative to the starting point. This is called a moving equilibrium and is well exemplified by growth. . . .

A system is thus a group of interacting parts or bodies forming a unified whole. If one part of the system changes, the other parts will either change or force the deviant to conform to the existing system. Because a system is characterized by interrelationships, its parts can be understood only in relation to each other and to the whole, and the whole can be understood only in relation to its component and integral parts.

THE SCHOOL AS A SOCIAL SYSTEM

As indicated earlier in this chapter, the school may be viewed as a social system in two different ways: 1) in terms of actual interacting persons; and 2) in terms of analytical abstractions. The following two models illustrate these two ways.

Getzels-Guba-Thelen Model

A framework for the study of educational administration, formulated in terms of actual interacting persons, was developed by Getzels,[6] with later contributions made by Guba[7] and Thelen.[8]

---

[6] For an early statement of Getzels' ideas see J. W. Getzels, "A Psycho-Sociological Framework for the Study of Educational Administration," *Harvard Educational Review*, 22 (Fall 1952), 235-46.

[7] J. W. Getzels and E. G. Guba, "Social Behavior and the Administrative Process," *The School Review*, 65 (Winter 1957), 423-41. See also Egon Guba, "Research in Internal Administration — What do We Know?" in *Administrative Theory as a Guide to Action*, eds. Roald F. Campbell and James M. Lipham (Chicago: Midwest Administration Center, The University of Chicago, 1960), pp. 113-30. See also Jacob W. Getzels, "Administration as a Social Process," in *Administrative Theory in Education*, ed. Andrew W. Halpin (New York: The Macmillan Company, 1958), pp. 150-65.

[8] Jacob W. Getzels and Herbert A. Thelen, "The Classroom Group as a Unique Social System," in *The Dynamics of Instructional Groups. Sociopsychological Aspects of Teaching and Learning*, ed. Nelson B. Henry, Fifty-ninth Yearbook of the Society for the Study of Education, Part 2 (1960), p. 80.

In commenting on the development of theory, Getzels indicated a belief that the reformulation of theory and practice "might well be along the lines of the educational situation as a social system."[9] The major elements in the Getzels-Guba-Thelen model are portrayed as follows.[10]

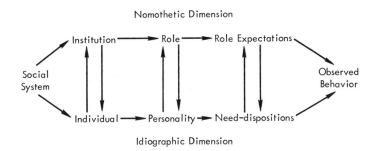

In explaining the diagram, Getzels makes the following comments.[11]

We may think of a social system (whether a single classroom, an entire school, or a community) as involving two classes of phenomena. There are first the institutions with certain roles and expectations that will fulfill the goals of the system. And there are second the individuals with certain personalities and need-dispositions inhabiting the system, whose observed interactions comprise what we call social behavior. We shall assert that this behavior can be understood as a function of these major elements: institution, role, and expectation, which together refer to what we shall call the *nomothetic* or normative dimension of activity in a social system; and individual, personality, and need-disposition, which together refer to what we shall call the *idiographic* or personal dimension of activity in a social system. . . .

A more complete version of the Getzels-Guba-Thelen model follows.[12] This model is applicable to an organization even though it was developed to represent the classroom. Although the model includes a *group* dimension, it does not detract from the emphasis given to the *institution* and to the *individual* in the Getzels-Guba-Thelen conceptualization.

The more complete model developed by Getzels, Guba, and

[9] Jacob W. Getzels, "Theory and Practice in Educational Administration: An Old Question Revisited," in *Administrative Theory*, eds. Campbell and Lipham, p. 53.

[10] J. W. Getzels and E. G. Guba, "Social Behavior and the Administrative Process," *The School Review*, 65 (Winter 1957), 429. Copyright 1957 by The University of Chicago.

[11] Getzels, "Theory and Practice," p. 54.

[12] Getzels and Thelen, "The Classroom Group," p. 80.

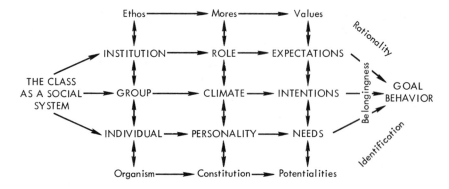

Thelen describes the school as a social system in terms of five dimensions, their parts, and the interrelationships among these parts as they all contribute to Goal Behavior. The social system includes the following three major dimensions: 1) the Individual, with Personality and Needs; 2) the Group, with its Climate and Intentions; and 3) the Institution, with its Roles and Expectations. Closely related to the Individual dimension is the dimension including Organism, Constitution, and Potentialities; and closely related to the Institution is the dimension including Ethos, Mores, and Values.

This concept of a social system, based upon the concrete realities of Individual, Group, and Institution, is one of the most useful and suggestive for the purposes of school administration yet developed.

The Parsons Model

In contrast to the previous model, Parsons and his associates developed a model in terms of analytical abstractions. Unfortunately, Parsons' conception of a social system is often loosely referred to as if it were based upon concrete elements such as those in the model just described when actually his model is quite different.

Parsons comments on his concept of social systems as follows.[13]

We are treating social systems, including societies, not as the concrete aggregate of interacting and otherwise behaving human beings, but as an analytically defined subsystem of the totality of human social action, abstracted with reference to the interaction processes and the structures assumed by the relationships among actors. . . .

Those aspects of behavior which directly concern "cultural-level" systems, "as distinguished from the metabolic physiology," Parsons

[13] Talcott Parsons, "An Overview," in *American Sociology: Perspectives, Problems, Methods,* ed. Talcott Parsons (New York: Basic Books, Inc., 1968), p. 322.

calls *action*, which in this technical sense includes four generic types of subsystems: 1) the organism; 2) the social system; 3) the cultural system; and 4) the personality.[14] These subsystems are described as follows.[15]

The first is simply the organism, which, though quite properly treated as a concrete entity in one set of terms, becomes, on a more generalized level, a set of abstract components (i.e., a subsystem) in the culturally organized system of action.

A second subsystem is the social system, which is generated by the process of interaction among individual units. Its distinctive properties are consequences and conditions of the specific modes of interrelationship obtaining among the living organisms which constitute its units.

Third is the cultural system, which is the aspect of action organized about the specific characteristics of symbols and the exigencies of forming stable systems of them. It is structured in terms of patterning of meaning which, when stable, imply in turn generalized complexes of constitutive symbolisms that give the action system its primary "sense of direction," and which must be treated as independent of any particular system of social interaction. . . .

Fourth, the analytical distinction between social and cultural systems has a correlative relation to the distinction between the organism and those other aspects of the individual actor which we generally call the personality. . . . Personality, then, is the aspect of the living individual, as "actor," which *must* be understood in terms of the cultural and social content of the learned patternings that make up his behavioral system. . . .

In the Parsons formulation, roles are of crucial significance in a social system. The social system is a system of interaction among persons, and the role constitutes and defines the participation of a person in an interactive process. "The abstraction of an actor's role from the total system of his personality makes it possible to analyze the articulation of personality with the organizations of social systems."[16]

It is to be noted that the actions which make up a large proportion of social roles are not minutely prescribed, and hence that "a certain range of variability is regarded as legitimate."[17] "Roles vary in the degree of their institutionalization." If the role expectations and sanction patterns are integrated with commonly held values, conformity to role expectations will be rewarded and deviance will be punished.[18]

[14] Talcott Parsons, "Social Systems," *International Encyclopedia of the Social Sciences*, 15, 459.

[15] *Ibid.*

[16] Talcott Parsons and others, "A General Statement," in *Toward a General Theory*, eds. Parsons and Shils, p. 23.

[17] *Ibid.*, p. 24.

[18] Talcott Parsons and Edward A. Shils, "The Social System," in *Toward a General Theory*, eds. Parsons and Shils, p. 191.

In the Parsons formulation, social systems function in relation to three types of environment: 1) the organic-physical environment; 2) the cultural environment; and 3) the psychological environment. While these environments can be differentiated, they are interrelated with one another and are in continuous interrelationship, interaction, and interpenetration with the social system.[19]

In concluding this brief explanation it should be noted that in terms of the Parsons conceptualization, the school is not only a social system, but includes the other three types of systems as well: the organism, the cultural system, and the personality. These components of the Parsons model are dealt with in this book on the basis of a different conceptual framework.

The Thrust of Social Systems Theory

A significant element common to social systems theories is the emphasis upon *system*, that is, upon human interrelatedness. The two formulations of social systems theory by Getzels, Guba, and Thelen, and by Parsons, point out many interrelationships. According to Getzels, Guba, and Thelen, there are interrelationships among all fifteen aspects of the five dimensions of their model. In a similar vein, Parsons believes that the role choices of individuals are not random but rather are "cumulative and balanced" and result from selections which are "stabilized and reinforced by the institutionalization of value patterns."[20] Parsons also calls attention to the interrelatedness, interaction, and interpenetration of social systems and the different types of environment.

Systems theory thus suggests that human behavior can be understood only when viewed within the context of the situation in which it occurs, and particularly within the context of its human system.

For example, a small suburban school typically experienced the firing or resignation of one faculty member each year. Viewing these occurrences as individual phenomena, one would infer that the school included a number of weak individuals who for one reason or another were fired or decided to resign. The utilization of systems theory, however, suggests a different conclusion. Closer observation of the group as a whole revealed a feeling of administrative repression on the part of a number of faculty members. The individuals whose employment was terminated served as scapegoats against whom the feelings of frustration could be safely directed. In a sense, these individuals "volunteered" to be the scapegoats by violating the mores

[19] Parsons, "Social Systems," pp. 466-70.
[20] Parsons and others, "A General Statement," p. 25.

of the group in various ways, possibly because they felt themselves to be low in status and hence felt the need to prove their worth by standing up against the group.

In another situation a university class at the graduate level was having an apathetic discussion when a bitter argument broke out between two of the class members. At this point the rest of the class became quiet and the "fight" went on for some time. Viewing the argument between the two as individual phenomena, one would infer either that both individuals felt deeply about the issue, or that they strongly disliked one another. The utilization of systems theory, however, led to a different line of thinking. Investigation revealed that the apathetic nature of the discussion resulted from the class members' resentment over some assignments which had just been made. The frustration felt by the entire class put the two adversaries in a fighting mood. In a sense, the two "volunteered" to perform a function which the whole class wanted performed. If the class had not wanted the "fight," it could have stopped it. Thus, the bitter argument was not simply an occurrence between two individuals, but was in reality a function of the entire social system.

The concept of social system means that the behavior of an individual is not an isolated phenomenon but rather occurs as part of a system and is intertwined with the behavior of others. When behavior is considered as an individual phenomenon, symptomatic behaviors are often mistakenly identified as being causal. When behavior is viewed as a system phenomenon, however, individual behavior can be perceived as being symptomatic of the system, and causal elements can more readily be identified.

SYSTEMS THEORY AND THE ADMINISTRATOR

If one accepts the proposition that a school is a system made up of a number of subsystems, and that the school is itself a subsystem within larger systems such as the school system and the community (which in turn are subsystems within still larger systems), then systems theory has important implications for the administrator. Although the emphasis here is upon the school as a social system, as an organization it may also "be considered as being a *data-processing system* and *decision network* . . . a system of funds flows . . . an economic system" or some other type of system.[21] In all these cases,

---

[21] Seymour Tilles, "The Manager's Job — A Systems Approach," *Harvard Business Review* (January-February 1963). Reprinted in *Organizational Development Series*, Part 1. Reprints from *Harvard Business Review*. Publication no. 21140, pp. 153-61.

the concept of system emphasizes the interdependence of parts and variables.

The concept of systems stresses the interrelationships among the behaviors of individuals. While people sometimes behave as separate individuals, individual behavior is often, at least in part, symptomatic of what is happening in a group or an organization. If a single individual in a school expresses strong feelings such as satisfaction, dissatisfaction, resentment, or appreciation, it is probable that others in the school feel much the same way. If a staff member resists doing a fair share of the work, this resistance may be symptomatic of the interpersonal relationships which the individual is experiencing in the staff. If there is a lack of creativity, individual staff members may simply be behaving in accordance with group norms.

Systems concepts suggest that the effects of all actions are more far-reaching than is generally realized. Not only are the behaviors of individuals interrelated in a small group, but the behaviors of individuals and groups in a large organization are interrelated. An action taken by a department in one part of a school may, through student and faculty reactions, have a ripple effect throughout the entire school, or it may enhance or damage relationships with an important segment of the community, thereby affecting the regard in which the school is held by the community.

Administrators can usually anticipate the short-range consequences of their own and others' actions in the organization, but they need to devote greater attention to the far-reaching consequences of administrative and organizational actions. For example, when a school superintendent's recommendation of a plan of staff reorganization was approved by the board of education, the superintendent thought that the board's approval ended any substantial conflict over the matter. However, the organizational chart for the school system was subsequently redrawn and copies were sent out to the schools. Several groups of staff members saw that their program directors now appeared at a lower level on the chart than had previously been the case. These staff members went to the parents expressing bitter feelings of resentment over having been "demoted." The parents in turn attacked the school superintendent and board of education. Controversy over the reorganization plan extended to the school budget. Attack directed against the school superintendent broadened and intensified. Finally the school superintendent resigned under pressure, in part at least, because of the attacks upon him subsequent to his recommendation of the reorganization plan.

Systems theory implies that stress is a function of the system rather than of a single interpersonal relationship. Stress is not confined to the interpersonal relationship where it originated, but may be transmitted and multiplied within an organization. The stress which began in one relationship is reflected and duplicated in other organizational relationships. Direct observation suggests not only that stress is a function of the system, but also that individuals involved in stressful relationships in organizations are seldom aware of the systems nature of these problems. Problems of stress may come from the larger social system, from social systems which interlock with the school system or school through overlapping memberships, or from within the school system or school itself.

An assistant principal in a high school, who was involved in a stressful relationship with the principal, selected and fired several personal secretaries in a period of only a few months. In this instance, the stress between the school principal and the assistant principal moved on to the relationship between the assistant principal and his secretary. The determination to fire the secretary had little to do with her competency. Instead, it was primarily a result of the stress experienced by the assistant principal in his relationship with the principal. The following diagram illustrates this type of chain effect.

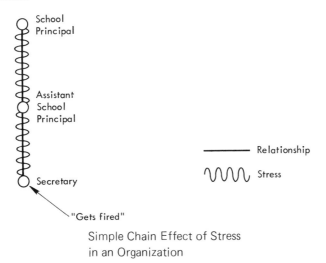

Simple Chain Effect of Stress
in an Organization

In this relationship, the origin of the stress was the interpersonal relationship between the principal and the assistant principal. However, the stress was not confined to that relationship but moved to the relationship between the assistant principal and the secretary, who ultimately was fired. A more complicated example follows.

In the diagram shown below, stress develops in the relationship between the principal and one of the department heads. Because this department head is thoroughly upset, stress develops between

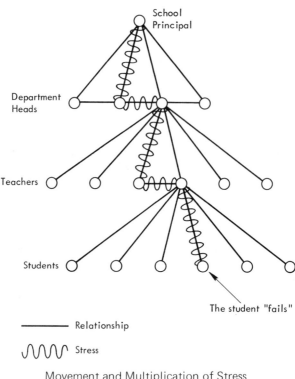

- ———— Relationship
- ᴠᴠᴠᴠ Stress

Movement and Multiplication of Stress
Within an Organization

the department head and another department head. The second department head becomes so upset that stress develops between him and one of the teachers, who in turn becomes involved in an imbroglio with another teacher. Feeling the stress keenly, this teacher gives a failing mark for the year to a student. Thus, the student and his parents discover that the student "has failed."

The concept of human systems underscores the far-ranging effects of administrative actions. An administrator's relationships with individuals and groups help to set the tone for an organization. They may serve as a model which others follow or may provoke negative reactions.

Systems theory suggests that an important task of an administrator is to provide leadership in the integration of the system, both internally and with external and superordinate systems. Such integration implies the need for differentiating the function of each system and subsystem, and then providing for the development of relationships between and among them. The traditional approach has been to provide for specialization on the part of the individual and the organizational unit, with the result that in most instances the organization has tended to become fractionated. The advantages of thinking in terms of systems and subsystems is that administrators can focus attention upon the interrelatedness of the objectives, activities, and resources represented by the various individuals and units in the organization.

Because of the interrelationships in a system, change in a school organization needs to be viewed in terms of the organization as a whole. Change on the part of individual faculty members is most likely to occur if the whole faculty is involved in change. If a single faculty member experiments independently with a new plan, the rest of the faculty may resist adopting the new plan regardless of the success of the experiment. On the other hand, if an individual is authorized by a faculty to conduct an experiment on behalf of the faculty as a whole, the faculty will almost surely have a greater sense of identification with the experiment and a greater willingness to look objectively at the results. Change in any one part of an organization has implications for the rest of the organization, and these implications need to be taken into account when projected change is initiated.

One of the most effective ways of promoting change in an organization is seeing new relationships among various parts of the organization. These new relationships can enable the organization to utilize its resources more creatively. Since new relationships can contribute to staff growth, provision for the development of new relationships within an organization can lead to an increase in human resources and hence to better educational programs.

In an institution such as the school, in which education is the supreme mission, an increase in human resources is crucial. This point can be illustrated by considering the programs now offered in most universities, especially in the applied fields such as education, law, medicine, psychiatry, clinical psychology, social work, and nursing. On most university campuses, these different fields have been established as separate colleges or schools (except for clinical psychology, which is often part of the department of psychology, and psychiatry, which is ordinarily part of the school of medicine) and within each such school, separate departments have been created. As scientific knowledge has developed, however, it has become increasingly clear that many interrelationships exist among the knowledge and competencies of different departments within a college or school in the university, and among these various schools. Present organizational structures tend not only to ignore these interrelationships but even to obscure them. These interrelationships need attention if university programs are to meet needs more creatively. New systems which cut across the conventional departmental and school lines are being established in a number of universities, and further developments of this type which strengthen the human resources are needed.

Similarly, in elementary and secondary schools, organizational subsystems which cut across traditional lines such as those of departmental or grade-level units are also needed. While no single blueprint for effecting such changes can be offered, a task force or special administrative team, including members drawn from throughout the organization, can be useful in achieving organizational change.

From a systems point of view, the school or the school system should be defined in much broader terms than is often true. Schools are ordinarily thought of as including pupils, staff, administrators, and possibly board of education members. At times, however, it is useful to think of a school as being part of a system which includes other individuals and groups such as parents, social agencies, governmental agencies (local, state, and federal), profit and nonprofit enterprise, the mass media, and indeed all citizens. The task of the administrator is to be aware of the significance of the existing and potential relationships among these various groups and the schools, and to realize that at times school problems can be dealt with realistically only when the interrelationships among various groups and agencies are taken into account.

An administrator who thinks in terms of systems recognizes the importance of the current social scene for the goals and procedures used in the schools and helps to relate the school program to the everchanging needs of the society within which it operates. Warning signals in the society indicate clearly that unless the schools become more sensitive to contemporary problems, they face the real possibility of being replaced by more viable systems of education. The development of an inter-organizational structure, in which local school systems, the state department of education, and institutions of higher education work cooperatively on common concerns, is an example of the kind of cooperative action which can result when the importance of statewide inter-institutional relationships is recognized.

CONCLUSION

Two conceptualizations of the school as a social system have been presented: one, in terms of actual persons, and the other, in terms of analytical abstractions. To the extent that these conceptualizations mirror reality, they are useful in helping one to see the school as it really is, an integral system (encompassing subsystems, and as part of superordinate systems) functioning through continuous interactional relationships.

An administrator who views the school as a system will function quite differently from one who views the school as consisting of many separate and discrete parts. In the former case, the administrator will be concerned with the functioning of the whole system and will consider the implications of a specific action for the whole system. Moreover, in diagnosing problems, an administrator with a "systems" view of the school will look to causal elements which are reflected in the functioning of the *system* rather than solely to individual behavior.

Listed below are some administrative questions suggested by systems theory:

1. How can communication be utilized in such manner as to unify a school organization?
2. How can organizational structure accommodate the many interrelationships called to attention by systems theory?
3. What are the implications of systems theory for an understanding of administrative roles in education?
4. How does systems theory relate to the development of an enabling climate in a school?
5. How can school-community relationships be improved through systems concepts?
6. How can analysis of situational elements in a system contribute to effective leadership?

The foregoing questions are among those explored in subsequent chapters.

SUGGESTED READINGS

Ackoff, Russell L., *Redesigning the Future. A Systems Approach to Societal Problems*, chaps. 1-5. New York: John Wiley & Sons, 1974.

Allport, Floyd H., *Theories of Perception and the Concept of Structure. A Review and Critical Analysis with an Introduction to a Dynamic-Structural Theory of Behavior*, chap. 18, "The System Viewpoint — Cybernetics: Its Psychological Implications and Contribution to Perceptual Theory." New York: John Wiley & Sons, Inc., 1955.

Baker, Frank, ed., *Organizational Systems: General Systems Approaches to Complex Organizations*. Homewood, Ill.: Richard D. Irwin, 1973.

Berrien, F. Kenneth, *General and Social Systems*. New Brunswick, N.J.: Rutgers University Press, 1968.

Boulding, Kenneth E., "General Systems Theory: The Skeleton of Science," *Management Science* (April 1956), pp. 197-208.

Buckley, Walter, ed., *Modern Systems Research for the Behavioral Scientist. A Sourcebook.* Chicago: Aldine Publishing Co., 1968.

Churchman, C. West, *The Systems Approach.* New York: Dell Publishing Co., 1968.

Deutsch, Karl W., *The Nerves of Government: Models of Political Communication and Control.* New York: The Free Press, 1966.

Emery, F. E., ed., *Systems Thinking.* Baltimore: Penguin Books, 1969.

General Systems: Yearbook of the Society for General Systems Research. New York: Society for General Systems Research.

Katz, Daniel and Robert L. Kahn, *The Social Psychology of Organizations.* New York: John Wiley & Sons, Inc., 1966.

Laszlo, Ervin, *The Systems View of the World: The Natural Philosophy of the New Developments in the Sciences.* New York: George Braziller, 1972.

Miller, E. J. and A. K. Rice, *Systems of Organization.* London: Tavistock Publications, 1967.

Thompson, James D., *Organizations in Action: Social Science Bases of Administrative Theory.* New York: McGraw-Hill Book Company, 1967.

Vickers, Sir Geoffrey, *The Art of Judgment: A Study of Policy Making.* London: Chapman & Hall, 1965.

von Bertalanffy, Ludwig, *General System Theory: Foundations, Development, Applications.* New York: George Braziller, 1968.

Wiener, Norbert, *The Human Use of Human Beings. Cybernetics and Society.* Garden City, N.Y.: Doubleday Anchor Books, 1954.

COMMUNICATION 4

Communication is the *sine qua non* of human relationships. Without communication, meaningful relationships would not be possible; and without relationships among people, communication would not be needed. Because human relationships are of major importance in the life of an organization, the communications process is a matter of primary concern in effective administration.

Communication permeates all human relationships, and in a sense this whole book deals with communication. Yet unless specific attention is paid to the actual communications transactions which take place between people, an important aspect of human relationships is neglected.

Consideration of interpersonal dynamics in administrative communication has suffered from neglect in the literature of the field. For the most part, the emphasis has been upon communications devices and techniques including books, pamphlets, newsletters, speeches, charts, graphs, diagrams, pictures, audio and video tapes, films, records, and others. The use of these devices has been discussed in books and other publications, in speeches, and in university courses such as English, speech, journalism, supervision, and public relations. Competence in utilizing the various communications devices is essential if communication is to be effective, but is not considered here because our concern is with the more basic relationships which these devices are designed to serve.

In this chapter consideration will be given to the nature and types of communication, the interplay between personality and communication, communications processes in organizations, and suggested administrative competencies.

COMMUNICATION DEFINED AND CLARIFIED

Communication has traditionally been defined as the transfer of thoughts and feelings from one person to another. Webster's Dictionary defines communication as[1] "a process by which information is exchanged between individuals through a common system of symbols, signs, or behavior." Consideration of the complexities involved suggests that communication includes "all the procedures by which one mind may affect another."[2] These definitions imply that communication does not necessarily occur when one person speaks or writes to someone else. Communication occurs only to the extent that the message sent is received. An administrator who is talking or writing is not necessarily communicating, for the message sent may not be received. No message is ever received without an element of loss or distortion. Sometimes the message is lost completely; at other times a message may be received so completely and accurately that it would be difficult to support the idea that there has been a loss of meaning in the communication transaction, yet some loss inevitably occurs. In a sense, therefore, "communication" is a relative term, for only the essence of a message can be received since the reception can never be perfect in completeness or accuracy.[3]

[1] By permission. From Webster's New Collegiate Dictionary © 1976 by G. & C. Merriam Co., publishers of the Merriam-Webster dictionaries.
[2] Wilbur Schramm, "The Nature of Communication Between Humans," in *The Process and Effects of Mass Communication*, rev. ed., eds. Wilbur Schramm and Donald F. Roberts (Urbana, Ill.: University of Illinois Press, 1971), p. 12.
[3] A number of communications models have been developed. For example, see Claude E. Shannon, "The Mathematical Theory of Communication," in *The Mathematical Theory of Communication*, Claude E. Shannon and Warren Weaver (Urbana, Ill.: University of Illinois Press, 1949), p. 5. For a modification of the Shannon-Weaver model and an explanation of the model in human terms see Wilbur Schramm, "The Nature of Communication," pp. 22–34. See also Carl I. Hovland, "Social Communication," *Proceedings of the American Philosophical Society*, 92 (1948), 371. Richard Braddock, "An Extension of the Lasswell Formula," *Journal of Communication*, 8 (Summer 1958), 88–93. C. E. Osgood, "A Vocabulary for Talking About Communication," in *The Process and Effects*, p. 24. D. K. Berlo, *The Process of Communication* (New York: Holt, Rinehart & Winston, 1960), p. 72. For additional communications models see James C. McCroskey, *An Introduction to Rhetorical Communication* (Englewood Cliffs, N.J.: Prentice-Hall, Inc., 1968), p. 25.

TYPES OF COMMUNICATION

Communication takes place in a number of different ways. These different ways provide the potentiality for infinitely rich and varied means of communication in an organization.

Verbal Communication

Verbal communication is a distinctive characteristic of the human species. While there is no doubt that other creatures such as animals and birds communicate through the use of sounds, we have reason to believe that no other species can convey the many distinctive meanings which words make possible. Words can be manipulated to express explicitly a vast array of meanings, and hence they have greatly improved the capacity of human beings for communication. They enable individuals to express complex ideas comprehensively and with a degree of precision. Words make it possible to send ideas through the airwaves to many people. Words permit the expression of thoughts and feelings which may be read a few minutes or many centuries later. It is important to note also that an individual can be held responsible only for explicit verbal statements and cannot be held responsible for ambiguous nonverbal messages.

The capacity to utilize verbal communication effectively is essential for an administrator. Verbal communication makes possible the identification of purposes, the development of strategies and behaviors for achieving purposes, and the processes of complex and precise thinking and learning. One person may say something to someone else or to a group of people. Perhaps he or she speaks on radio or television, or addresses a large audience, or writes a letter, a notice, a newsletter, a statement of procedure, or a directive. Perhaps there is a group discussion or a large deliberative assembly. These means of communication, all based upon the use of words, are important because they make it possible for individuals consciously wanting to communicate to make fine distinctions in order to convey subtle meanings.

One area of communications with which all administrators should be concerned is that of meanings (hence, semantics). Because each individual experiences life in a unique way, words mean different things to different people, and phrases, sentences, paragraphs, and books have different meanings for different people even though the words and syntax may be precise from the viewpoint of the communicator.

A word contains no validity in and of itself. It is simply an abstraction which has been adopted through usage to refer to a concrete object or to a concept. This point is made in a telling way by Stuart Chase, who wrote as follows:[4]

Dictionary definitions are useful, but the semanticists make no obeisances to verbal absolutes. David Guralnik, who supervised a recent drastic revision of Webster, reported that his friends were shocked at his temerity.* He was shattering their faith in the infallibility of "the dictionary," and probably, by extension, of the Scriptures and other sacred writs.

"The view that meanings belong to words in their own right," says Richards, "is a branch of sorcery, a relic of the magical theory of names."[5]

A word simply calls into awareness the thoughts and feelings which it suggests to the individual, and a communicator has no control over what these thoughts and feelings will be. He can sometimes anticipate them and can phrase his communication accordingly, but he can never dictate what they will be.

Failure to take semantic problems into account can result in endless communication difficulties, as anyone who has thought about communications problems can testify. An administrator talking to a faculty group about the reporting system may be thinking about a comprehensive system that includes reports on various subjects to many different types of groups, whereas the teachers may be thinking about the report cards sent to parents. The "curriculum" may mean, to one person, the total school experiences of each child; to another, a series of publications in the form of curriculum guides or courses of study; and to another, the teaching of the three R's and a few "frills." Values clarification may mean, to a supervisor, the clarification and strengthening of values which a child already possesses; to a teacher, forthcoming textbooks with information concerning differing value systems; and to a parent, the intention of the school to replace traditional values such as honesty, hard work, and patriotism with Communistic beliefs.[6]

A school system which was under attack decided to publish a monthly brochure setting forth policies and facts concerning the

*Paper read before Rowfant Club, reprinted by World Publishing Co., 1953.

[4] Stuart Chase, *Power of Words* (New York: Harcourt Brace Jovanovich, Inc., 1954), pp. 128-29.

[5] Ivor Armstrong Richards, *The Philosophy of Rhetoric* (New York: Oxford University Press, 1936).

[6] For a discussion of this type of problem see C. K. Ogden and I. A. Richards, *The Meaning of Meaning. A Study of the Influence of Language Upon Thought and of the Science of Symbolism*, 8th ed. (New York: Harcourt, Brace and Co., 1956).

schools. Because the school system was trying to meet the challenges imposed on it by current problems and conditions, the decision was made to call the publication "Meeting the Challenge." When the first copy of the brochure was published, many citizens thought the title meant that the school administration was declaring that it was willing and eager to fight with its critics. In another instance, some of the citizens in a community strongly opposed a survey report which called for the construction of "secondary" schools, for they felt that their children were entitled to first-rate rather than "secondary" schools.

Because of the differences in meanings which different people attach to the same word, verbal communication can never be entirely accurate. Distortions of the meaning intended by the communicator are inevitable.

Furthermore, a communicator can never say all there is to say on any subject. When the word "pencil" is used to indicate an object, much has been left unsaid. How long is the pencil? What about its shape? For what special purposes is it designed? Who made it? Of what materials? Where did they come from? What is the pencil's history? Is it to be used for writing or for some other purpose? What about the pencil in relation to pens and other writing materials? What are some of the literary and musical masterpieces which pencils have recorded? Will pencils ever be replaced by dictating equipment?

The list of questions or topics about the pencil, or about any subject, is endless. Hence some semanticists suggest a liberal use of *et cetera* (etc.). Whether this solution is used or not (and it is controversial), the problem which it seeks to alleviate is real. Because a communicator can never fully discuss a subject, and because what is said will always be distorted to some extent by the person receiving the communication, the task of the communicator is to select those symbols which are most likely to convey to the communicatee the essence of the intended communication. In order to communicate effectively, an administrator needs to consider what the various words and expressions mean to the people with whom he or she is attempting to communicate, and then must attempt to eliminate any possible sources of misunderstanding. The reactions of other individuals to a tentative draft of a letter or document can be helpful in identifying possible sources of misinterpretation.

Some of the major contributions to the field of semantics, made originally by Korzybski, have been summarized by Stuart Chase as follows:[7]

[7] Chase, *Power of Words*, p. 182. See also pp. 145–48. Based on Alfred Korzybski, *Science and Sanity. An Introduction to Non-Aristotelian Systems and General Semantics* (New York: The International Non-Aristotelian Library Publishing Co., 1933).

No two events in nature are identical.
Nature is best understood in terms of structure, order, relationships, process.
Any event has unlimited characteristics. We abstract only what we need.
A word is not a thing: a map is not the territory.
Abstract qualities are in our heads, not in nature.
At the end of all verbal behavior are undefined terms.

Nonverbal Communication

In addition to communication by use of words, nonverbal messages are being sent continuously. Nonverbal communication may be easily recognized, or it may be so subtle that the cues are missed by the other completely. Messages are sent by a person's tone of voice, posture, crying, slamming a door, doodling, wiggling of feet, putting the head down on a desk, by clothing, automobile, place of residence, and indeed, by all aspects of behavior.

A school principal may call a faculty member into his office and say, "Mary Smith cannot take lunch duty on Wednesday. Will you do it for her?" The faculty member may answer: "Yes, I will be glad to." Yet an administrator who is sensitive to nonverbal communication may notice a blush which says in effect: "The boss is playing favorites again." Or a frown may mean: "I am so loaded down now; I don't know how I'll live through the week."

A chairman may ask the group members whether they think the discussion should continue and, seeing a nodding of heads, prolong the meeting. Yet a more sensitive administrator might receive a more accurate communication by noting nonverbal cues: sleepy eyes, mouths with corners turned down, heads propped on hands, legs swinging slightly, feet moving nervously, drooping posture, longing glances out the window.

From the sender's point of view, nonverbal communication is almost always a direct indication of motives and feelings, for most of us do not think much about our nonverbal communication, and even when we do, we have difficulty in controlling it. We are usually reacting in accordance with our feelings when we blush, stumble over words, clear our throat, speak slowly or rapidly or loudly or softly, exhibit nervous mannerisms, blink, frown, smile, maintain a particular posture, or assume a different facial expression.

Like verbal communication, nonverbal communication can be used to mislead another person. A gift may be a camouflaged bribe, or a child who has been throwing chalk may deliberately look angelic when the teacher enters the room.

Yet actions are honest in the sense that they always express an individual's motives and feelings, even though such expressions may sometimes be devious. The behavior of the child who looks angelic, if taken in its entirety (including the throwing of the chalk), is an honest expression of the child's motives and feelings. A burglar may say that he believes in property rights, but the real test is whether or not he continues to steal. A person may say that he respects others, but the real test is in how he relates to them.

Although actions are essentially honest communications, as non-verbal messages they are subject to gross errors of interpretation. No one person can fully understand anyone else. Our judgments are based on limited observation of a small segment of the other person's behavior. As a result, the dangers of misinterpretation are great indeed.

A student went to a professor's office to ask a few rather simple questions. Unfortunately, the professor's facial expression, in fact his whole manner, became so dour that the student felt that he had offended the professor. Later that day, the student went back to the professor and said: "I could tell from your expression this morning that something I said offended you. I am sorry, and I am wondering what I said or did that offended you." The professor thought a moment and then replied: "You didn't offend me. As we were talking, my thoughts turned to my father, who is critically ill." The professor's behavior had sent an honest communication — that he was troubled — but this communication had been misinterpreted by the student.

The dangers in nonverbal communication are that it may be mis-interpreted or ignored. The advantages of nonverbal communication are that it is often powerful, is essentially honest, and adds a whole new dimension to the communications process.

Behavior as Communication

Thus all behavior is potential communication, and much behavior results in actual communication. Behavior is always meaningful as an expression of individual personality, for it is directed by a person's motivations and represents the individual's attempts to cope with the environment. If behavior can be understood from the viewpoint of the behaver, it becomes direct and meaningful communication.

Some administrators have little or no understanding of human behavior and thus are unable to learn from the vast amount of potential communication which surrounds them all of the time. Others who have some understanding of human behavior fail to see the implications of this knowledge for improving communica-tion. If administrators with a reasonably good understanding of human behavior will ask themselves what messages lie in the be-havior which they observe, they will be able to tap a rich source of communication.

When a faculty member fails to attend faculty meetings, many administrators apply pressure to require attendance. While the application of administrative sanctions (actual or threatened rewards or penalties) may solve the immediate problem and may indeed be appropriate, such use of sanctions may endanger important potential communication. If a faculty member is absent from meetings because he feels that his work is not valued, the administrative sanctions may eliminate this manifestation of discontent only to find that the discontent reappears in other forms such as poor teaching, late or inaccurate reports, gossip, or personality conflicts; and a battle of wits may develop, with the administrator applying one pressure after another. In this type of game, the administrator always loses, and the staff member always loses also.

When an administrator can grasp the communication implicit in another's behavior, he or she may or may not decide to act in light of the communication, but in any event the administrator has additional information upon which to base decisions.

Of course behavior constitutes potential communication for staff members and others as well as for the administrator, and an administrator's actions are often interpreted by others as being an important source of information. The interpretations may or may not be reasonably accurate. Staff members may find clues in an administrator's actions regarding the extent to which their work is valued by the administrator: whether their work assignments seem to carry prestige; whether the physical facilities made available are desirable; whether their requests for funds for special purposes are granted; whether they have ready access to the administrator; whether the administrator develops an in-group (professional or social) from which some staff members are excluded; whether their work is recognized in many other ways.

If administrators are to communicate effectively with words, there needs to be reasonable congruence between their behavior and verbal expressions. Lack of such congruence results in conflicting communications.

As all behavior is potential communication, so all administrative behavior is potential communication. The behavior may be misinterpreted; the communication may be distorted or lost. But implicit in all administrative action is potential communication of a powerful order.

Policies and Procedures as Communication

Like administrative behavior, the policies and procedures of an organization implicitly provide potential communication. In a sense, organizational policies and procedures are nothing more nor less than the organization's stated norms of behavior, and inferences are drawn by some individuals concerning the meaning of this behavior. The organizational policies and procedures provide implicit communication which goes beyond the immediate purposes of the written statements and indicate important value judgments.

The whole area of personnel policies is especially meaningful in this respect to most staff members. Matters such as salary, sick leave, seniority rights, retirement plans, and working conditions are of course important in and of themselves, and policies indicate the kinds of administrative action which can be expected on these matters in the organization. Beyond indicating a line of administrative action, the policies and procedures suggest to many individuals whether their work is valued by the administrator, the school system, the board of education, and society; they indicate the kinds of activities which those with power deem to be important; they imply the purposes which the organization intends to pursue; they provide a glimpse of the value system upon which organizational decisions are based.

It is not in any sense to oppose adequate salaries to point out that the concern which teachers have for salaries goes beyond a consideration of dollars. To many teachers, salaries not only represent a standard of living, but also indicate the value placed upon teachers and their work by society. Teachers grumble about the unfairness of a system in which physicians, lawyers, dentists, and others are paid so much more, and yet the amount which the other professions are paid has relatively little to do with a teacher's standard of living. High payments to other groups may affect prices, but most teachers are concerned over comparative salaries because they sense that the relationship of their salaries to those of others communicates something important about their own status in the community, about their perceived importance as contributors to the community welfare, and often about their significance as individuals. A salary schedule thus indicates not only material benefits, but also the extent to which a staff can expect to receive intangible rewards, which are often more important to staff members than those which are tangible.

The communications to staff through administrative behavior and through verbal messages can never be separated from the totality of the policies and procedures of an organization.

Discovery as Communication

If communication is conceptualized as including all the procedures by which one mind may affect another, then communication takes place when one person is able to affect another by providing experiences which enable the other to discover information or meanings independently. Such communication is indirect but may make a strong impression because the individual is learning through experience. While indirect communication of this type can be subverted as a means of manipulating another, it can also serve the highest and noblest purposes. Numerous examples of this type of communication come to mind. In one instance, a consultant who was aware of problems created by faculty rank (instructor, assistant professor, associate professor, professor) suggested that a faculty group strongly favoring rank study the effects on salaries of the limitations which allowed only a certain percentage of the faculty members at the institution to be in the upper ranks at any one time. When the faculty group discovered that many competent individuals on the faculty could never achieve the upper ranks and the corresponding salaries under the existing percentage limitations, the faculty voted overwhlemingly to abolish rank. In another instance, a conference planning group which was to disseminate ideas developed during the conference decided that the best means of idea dissemination would be to hold a series of similar conferences at which the participants could develop ideas for themselves. Communication through discovery is utilized by all effective teachers.

If provision is made for experiences that allow people to learn for themselves, there is no assurance that the ideas arrived at will be those which the planners originally hoped to communicate. On the other hand, one may be sure that the ideas will be somewhat changed as a result of different needs, interests, and perceptions. They may even be improved. This indirect approach to communication, though both time-consuming and open to abuse by those who would manipulate others, can be effective in helping individuals, groups, and organizations to understand and embrace ideas toward which they had originally been defensive. Ideas acquired in this way have a validity for the persons involved which is possible only when they have been gained through individual and group discovery. Opportunities for individuals, groups, and organizations to learn through their own experience are a necessary adjunct to the ordinary processes of communication if some of the problems relating to defensiveness in communication are to be resolved.

PERSONALITY AND COMMUNICATION

As was suggested in the previous chapter, each person is a system, and each functions as part of a social system. The relationship of one social system to another affects the perceptions of individuals in these systems and hence the relationships of individuals in the various systems. Thus, even though elementary and secondary school teachers may feel loyal and trusting toward one another when the teachers are about to strike for better pay, the same teachers may become highly distrustful of each other if blame is being assessed for poor skill development on the part of students. In the latter instance, the elementary teachers may blame the high school teachers for student deficiencies, and vice versa.

In addition, the perceptions of individuals are affected by the personal interrelationships within a social system, especially when these interrelationships are deeply significant to the individual, that is, are emotionally intensive. Individuals who feel that they are valued and are performing well in an important group will have a different outlook on life from those who feel they are continually made scapegoats and are performing poorly.

The relationships which an individual experiences in a social system affect not only the person's current functioning but leave their mark on the individual. A personality develops as a result of meanings attached to the experiences of a lifetime, and a concept of self develops out of the meanings inferred from interpersonal relationships. Feelings about self give rise to needs and goals, and an individual's perceptions are selective in relation to these goals.

Thus, each person perceives uniquely as a result of the interplay between individual personality and the social systems which he or she is currently experiencing. An individual experiences life in a unique way and perceives messages in a unique way. When an administrator talks to two hundred people, there are two hundred and one messages — the message which the administrator is sending, and the two hundred somewhat different messages being received. Unless there is two-way communication to provide opportunities for clarification, an administrator can be sure that the two hundred messages being received will be varying distortions of the message being sent.

The effect of perception upon communication is illustrated by the following instance.

A school superintendent had a good friend who strongly recommended a particular candidate for a specific opening in the school system. The superintendent, much impressed by a recommendation coming from someone in whom he had great confidence, forwarded the recommendation to a selection committee which had been appointed to fill the position. When the selection committee recommended someone else for the position, the superintendent inquired about the candidate recommended by his friend. The selection committee members voiced their opinion ("He doesn't have the competencies we need"), but the superintendent went ahead and employed the man anyway. The superintendent had become so interested in the candidate that he had been unable to "hear" what the staff members were saying or to follow the usual selection procedures.

Every seasoned administrator who is sensitive to communications problems has experienced this phenomenon of perceptual blocks and distortions in communication. The most explicit directions, even in writing, may be misconstrued. Administrators may explain the purposes of a particular program carefully only to find that the program is nevertheless misunderstood and has become the basis for groundless fears of one kind or another. They may set up safeguards against potential dangers in a program only to have their motives distorted by others. They may take the leadership in providing a well-rounded program for all the children of the community only to be attacked by some segment of the community for indifference to its particular needs and interests. In every instance, differences in perception are creating problems in communication.

When individuals perceive danger, whether physical or psychological, they naturally want to protect themselves. If they feel attacked or threatened, they either flee, seek protection from someone else, or muster their resources in self-defense. Just as physical blows can hurt and can be destructive, so psychological blows can hurt and be destructive, and it is only natural for a person to try to protect against such blows. One of the problems is that although a person is conscious of physically harming another person, he or she may be unaware of the hurt resulting from actions which are perceived by another as constituting a psychological attack.

The need to be defensive, experienced by every person from time to time, creates innumerable problems in the area of communication. An example of the effects of defensiveness upon communication is shown on pg. 57.

In this illustration, communication which began as an analysis of the board meeting breaks down quickly. Each of the two persons feels attacked, and each in trying to defend himself poses a threat to the other. Unless the communication can be straightened out and the two can resolve the misunderstandings which are beginning to develop, the exchange between them will have a deleterious effect not only on the immediate situation but on future attempts to communicate.

An administrator has a right to expect others to be open in their communications only to the extent that he or she is willing to be open. For several reasons, many administrators do not function openly. Aside from the problems imposed by personality limitations, administrators who have tried to be open have sometimes been badly hurt. Moreover, in addition to the hazards encountered by all people in their everyday living, administrators have been plagued by a strong autocratic heritage. Even today, administrators are often thought of as being a special kind of person. An administrator is supposed to work the hardest, be the most responsible, and know the most. The myth

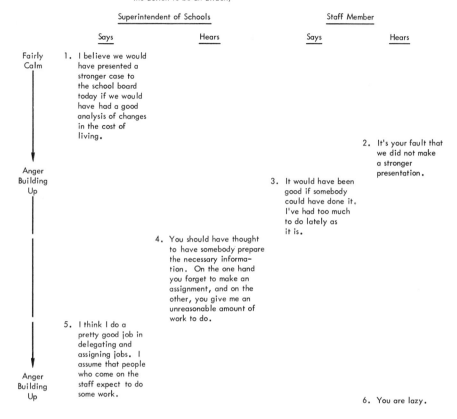

Example--Defensive Superintendent and Staff Member
(Each intends only to defend, but the other perceives
the action to be an attack)

Superintendent of Schools		Staff Member	
Says	Hears	Says	Hears

Fairly Calm

1. I believe we would have presented a stronger case to the school board today if we would have had a good analysis of changes in the cost of living.

2. It's your fault that we did not make a stronger presentation.

Anger Building Up

3. It would have been good if somebody could have done it. I've had too much to do lately as it is.

4. You should have thought to have somebody prepare the necessary information. On the one hand you forget to make an assignment, and on the other, you give me an unreasonable amount of work to do.

5. I think I do a pretty good job in delegating and assigning jobs. I assume that people who come on the staff expect to do some work.

Anger Building Up

6. You are lazy.

that a school administrator is a superman who should have few if any weaknesses dies slowly. And too often administrators have tried to give the appearance of living up to these expectations.

If an administrator is viewed as a superman, then anyone who falls short of being a superman has reason to feel guilty and inadequate and to hide failings. Administrators need to be seen and to see themselves as human beings who have weaknesses and make mistakes like anyone else. Administrators who can accept themselves on these terms are more capable of being open and of encouraging open communication on the part of others.

To emphasize the problems which are inherent in communication does not mean in any sense that communication is hopeless. On the other hand, communication can be used effectively to maintain meaningful contact among individuals and to enable an organization to accomplish its purposes. The basic problem in devising communications processes and messages is how to utilize the understandings of personality and communications processes which are presently available. The various problems inherent in communication can be turned to advantage by a thoughtful administrator as a basis for improving communications processes.

FEEDBACK

If communication is to be effective in improving individual and organizational performance, an administrator needs a continuous flow of information to indicate both the effectiveness of the actions taken and the extent to which accurate and complete communication is taking place. The process of getting such information is called "feedback."

Feedback refers to the collection of data from the surrounding environment by an individual, a group, or an organization, for utilization in the evaluation of behavior or performance. The concept of feedback originated in relation to mechanical types of operations. As an example, a thermostat is set at a particular level. The thermostat gets data from the surrounding atmosphere and, if the temperature falls below the desired level, takes action (sends a message to the furnace control) to turn on the furnace. When the temperature reaches the desired level, the thermostat acts to have the furnace turned off.

Feedback is used similarly in an organization. An organization has certain standards or expectations of achievement, often refined through planning. The executive obtains data concerning the organization's performance in relation to these expectations and utilizes the data as a basis for executive action. If the organization and its communication systems are functioning well, deviations from effective functioning are picked up and corrective action is taken. If the communications systems are not functioning well, however, deviation from organizational expectations may go undetected.[8]

Every system which provides information that indicates the effectiveness of actions taken in an organization is a type of feedback. The accounting system provides feedback on the extent to which appropriations are being expended for designated purposes.

---

[8] For a model and further discussion of this point see Kenneth E. Boulding, *The Organizational Revolution. A Study in the Ethics of Economic Organization* (New York: Harper & Brothers, 1953), pp. xxvii–xxxiv, 66–72. See also Charles E. Redfield, *Communication in Management. The Theory and Practice of Administrative Communication*, rev. ed. (Chicago: The University of Chicago Press, 1958), p. 153.

Test scores and other types of information provide feedback on pupil progress. Reports on staff vacancies and filled positions provide feedback concerning staff recruitment and selection.

Though school systems have devised many forms of feedback, feedback relative to various aspects of human behavior is often neglected. Feedback is useful not only for an organization as a whole, but in considering the communications of an individual or a group.[9] As administrators relate to other people, they may obtain many clues concerning their own effectiveness. If an administrator is talking to a group and is reasonably sensitive to reactions, he or she can tell how the talk is being received. If individual members of the audience look tired or sleepy, appear to be daydreaming, or cough frequently, the administrator may decide to adjust to these audience reactions by summarizing or attempting some humor, and then continue to observe the audience to obtain feedback on the effectiveness of the action.

In practically every situation, data exist which can be utilized for purposes of feedback if an individual or group is reasonably sensitive. One individual talking to another individual or to a group can observe verbal and nonverbal clues. A group can observe the behavior of persons affected by its actions. An individual who uses mass media may receive letters or telephone responses. Through feedback, the perceptions of other persons can be utilized as a means of arriving at a more objective appraisal of one's own behavior. This calls to mind Robert Burns' well-known line: "Oh that we could see ourselves as ithers see us!"

The fact that an administrator is aware of the opinions of others does not mean that he should accept their judgment in place of his own, but rather that the judgments of others may be useful in helping him to be more objective. Many of the great research discoveries would never have been made if the researcher had waited for approval before going ahead with the research. Innovations are often possible only when an innovator trusts his or her own judgment. Likewise in school administration, an administrator needs to have personal convictions. However, the importance of individual convictions does not detract from the value of feedback for, in many instances, the reactions of others are useful in assessing the effects of one's own behavior.

---

[9] For a report on some experiments with feedback see Harold J. Leavitt and Ronald A. H. Mueller, "Some Effects of Feedback on Communication," in *Small Groups: Studies in Social Interaction*, rev. ed., eds. A. Paul Hare, Edgar F. Borgatta, and Robert F. Bales (New York: Alfred A. Knopf, Inc., 1965), pp. 434-43.

Requests for feedback relative to one's behavior will often result in unfavorable as well as favorable comments, and administrators who first experience intensive feedback may need to develop a toughness which they did not have previously. Feedback is useful if it enables an individual or a group to be more objective about behavior; it is not useful if it results in greater defensiveness on the part of the individual or group.

To enable a person to become more objective rather than more defensive, feedback is usually more useful when it is requested rather than imposed, is kept confidential, expresses one's own feelings rather than evaluates the other, utilizes objective data when evaluations are necessary, is specific rather than general, and respects a person's right to individual perceptions, feelings, and opinions.

Administrators need both to utilize feedback as a means of improving their own behavior and to provide for feedback to others. If a new program is being developed, goals can be formulated as criteria indicating the information needed to provide suitable feedback. Some groups for many years have provided for a brief evaluation — oral, written or both — at the end of each meeting. Some school faculties provide for feedback from students to faculty members through the use of questionnaires answered anonymously, collected and placed in a sealed envelope by a student, and forwarded through the school office to the teacher. In other instances, there have been peer evaluations of teachers by their colleagues.

In all instances of evaluative feedback, it is important that the intent of the feedback be clear, and that procedures be consistent with the intent. It is an unfortunate fact that systems of feedback adopted ostensibly for the purpose of professional growth have sometimes failed to serve that purpose because they have become a tool for administrative assessment of an individual's competence.

An administrator who is alert to the need for feedback relative to the organization's performance and his or her own behavior can find many means for its acquisition.

COMMUNICATION IN ORGANIZATIONS

Because one of the functions of organizational structure is to facilitate communication, organizational structure and communication are interrelated. These interrelationships need to be understood if administrative communication is to be effective. Accordingly, some of the implications of organizational structure for communication will now be considered.

Directional Flow of Communication

To be effective, any organization needs to utilize three kinds of communication within the administrative hierarchy: downward, upward, and horizontal.

Information is transmitted in a *downward* direction in the administrative hierarchy to provide for coordination of effort directed toward achieving the organization's mission. Such coordination is promoted through statements setting forth and explaining policies, procedures, and administrative decisions governing the entire operation, and through a flow of information to all parts of the organization. The exercise of administrative power necessitates the downward flow of communication in an organization, and the use of power is essential if an organization is to be effective.

The downward flow of communication is the most consistently utilized and, on the whole in most organizations, the most effective of the three directional types. An individual who wields administrative authority need only issue an order to send a message on its way. The downward directional type is thus easy to utilize, though whether the message is received and understood is another matter.

Five types of downward communication have been identified by Katz and Kahn as follows:[10]

1. Specific task directives: *job instructions.*
2. Information designed to produce understanding of the task and its relation to other organizational tasks: *job rationale.*
3. Information about organizational *procedures and practices.*
4. *Feedback* to the subordinate about his performance.
5. Information of an ideological character to inculcate a sense of mission: *indoctrination of goals.*

Of the five types of communication, those which administrators use most frequently in relating to professional personnel in school systems are probably those concerning job rationale, procedures and practices, and indoctrination of goals. The most neglected type with reference to professional personnel is feedback, primarily because of the mistaken notion that feedback is an appraisal which can be given to an individual only by an immediate superior in the organization. With reference to nonprofessional personnel, the neglected types of downward communication include organizational goals, job rationale, and feedback, with the result that there is often unnecessary friction in the organization, people are unsure of their relation-

---

[10] Daniel Katz and Robert L. Kahn, *The Social Psychology of Organizations* (New York: John Wiley & Sons, Inc., 1966. Reprinted by permission of John Wiley & Sons, Inc.), p. 239.

ship with the administration, and personnel who are important to the enterprise lack a sense of mission.[11]

Some typical forms or media for issuing instructions have been listed by Redfield as shown below.[12]

Visual	*Audio-Visual*
Written	Sound Films and Film Strips
Individual Messages	Television
Circulars	Demonstrations
Manuals	Video Tapes*
Handbooks	*Audial*
Bulletin-Board Notices	*Face-to-Face*
and Announcements	Conversations
Newsletters	Interviews
Pamphlets	Meetings
Signs	Conferences
Employee Publications	*Intermediate Contact*
Standard Forms	Telephone
Pictorial	Radio
Pictures	Intercom
Photographs	Public Address System
Diagrams	*Symbolic*
Maps	Buzzers
Pictographs	Bells
Written-Pictorial	Other Signals
Posters	
Silent Films	
Film Strips	
Charts	
Cartoons	
Symbolic	
Insignia	
Flags	
Lights	
Other Signals	

*Added by author.

[11] This paragraph is based upon *Ibid.*, pp. 239–42.
[12] Redfield, *Communication in Management*, p. 72.

Because administrative officials issue both orders and suggestions, a fine sense of discrimination in the wording of such statements is necessary to prevent confusion between orders and suggestions. The matter of these distinctions is discussed by Redfield as follows.[13]

The necessary distinction between mandatory and discretionary orders is partly a matter of clarity and partly one of adaptability. Expressions such as *must, shall, will,* and *is to* are alike in the way they order action, while expressions such as *may, wherever practical,* and *it is recommended* do not clearly order anything. The word *should* is on the border line. Whether one uses mandatory or discretionary terminology depends on the problem being dealt with, the competence of the personnel and their identification with the organization, and the meaning that words seem to have within a particular organization.

The downward flow of communications is complicated by the reactions which people have toward a person in authority. Downward communications from someone in authority tend to assume the nature of directives whether or not they were so intended. Some people will tend to acquiesce too readily to suggestions, and others will tend to be suspicious and want to fight back. This difficult problem must be taken into account constantly in downward communication. It suggests that precise wording is a minimal requirement for successful downward communication.

Administrators generally make the faulty assumption that when a message is sent, it will be accurately received by the people for whom it is intended. In general, the chance for misunderstandings will increase as the organization space for which a communication is intended increases. A message is interpreted by the members of each organizational unit in terms of perceptions developed from a particular vantage point in the organization, and the farther a message goes from one part of an organization to another, the greater the differences in perception are likely to be. If a message is sent throughout a large school system, provision needs to be made for interpretation of what the message means to each particular unit and for feedback to determine whether or not the message is getting through. Individual school and departmental meetings constitute a device which can serve these purposes admirably on matters important enough to warrant such an investment of time.

The *upward* flow of communication in a school or school system is necessary if resources are to be adequately utilized, necessary information is to be available in the making of decisions, and the

[13] *Ibid.,* p. 57.

effectiveness of the organization is to be continuously evaluated. The importance of an upward flow of communication is indicated by some research done by Janowitz and Delaney,[14] who in a study of three agencies (including the Detroit Public School System) found that "the higher the bureaucratic position, the less well informed the bureaucrat would be about agency clients' perspectives";[15] in other words, the higher the administrative position in a school system, the less well informed the administrator will be about student perspectives.

In most organizations, the upward flow of communication is second in effectiveness of the three directional types of communication.

Upward communication provides for the transmittal of reports; opinions, ideas, and suggestions; and complaints, grievances, gripes, and rumors.[16] It includes "what the person says (1) about himself, his performance, and his problems, (2) about others and their problems, (3) about organizational practices and policies, and (4) about what needs to be done and how it can be done."[17]

Despite its importance, upward communication is beset by many problems. Most individuals have some fear of administrators, who have power which can be used to affect them, and whether or not these fears are justified by the actions of the administrators in a specific organization, they often prevent the initiation of upward communication. The pressures for conformity in schools and school systems (as in any organization) are strong and sometimes subtle, and are often promoted even by administrators who believe that they are respecting individuality and encouraging creativity. The most important obstacle to the initiation of upward communication is usually the feeling system in the organization, or in parts of it, which may cause an individual to say what he or she thinks the administrator wants to hear or to hesitate to initiate a message, or it may even paralyze the individual's capacity for critical analysis.

Furthermore, messages are normally transmitted through established communications channels, and a message can therefore be stopped at any point. People who are at strategic points in the communications system (e.g., a line official or the superintendent's secretary) have a powerful effect upon upward communication because they can decide what messages and what people get through to the higher levels of the hierarchy. Yet typically some of them are

---

[14] M. Janowitz and W. Delaney, "The Bureaucrat and the Public: A Study of Informational Perspectives," *Administrative Science Quarterly*, 2 (1957), 141–62.
[15] *Ibid.*, p. 150.
[16] Redfield, *Communication in Management*, p. 23.
[17] Katz and Kahn, *The Social Psychology*, p. 245.

not professionals, and they may not even have been instructed by the administration.

Much of the information which reaches an executive is the result of inferences drawn by others and thus may or may not be factual. Firsthand evidence concerning the behavior of an individual or a problem in a school or school system is not ordinarily available to the administrator; instead he or she usually must rely on reports from various persons in the organization. Even when reports purport to be objective descriptions of situations or of specific behaviors, they are usually heavily loaded with inferences based upon the observer's perceptions. Because inferences are often substituted for firsthand evidence, an individual who confidently makes assertions can often get an administrator or group to accept them as a basis for action. Unless administrators take account of the bias of the person making a report or an assertion, or can check the accuracy of the reports given to them, they will often act on the basis of inaccurate information.[18]

Distortion in upward communication is inevitable. All of the information which goes up the line has been colored by the individual perceptions of the people doing the communicating; most of the information has been condensed and summarized; and much of it consists of inferences rather than fact.

Even if an accurate message reaches an administrator, there may be problems. The administrator may not want the information and may discount its usefulness and value. He or she may interpret the information as being a personal attack, and feel angry and defensive; may prefer to do nothing rather than take the action called for; may dismiss the communication on the grounds that the communicator lacked sufficient facts or failed to recognize some of the practical problems involved in carrying out a suggestion. The administrator may sense that a suggestion is not consistent with his or her own value system.

Because upward communication is beset by many difficulties, an administrator needs deliberately to take steps to encourage it. First of all, he or she should make clear to others in the organization — both by words and actions — that upward communication is desired. For example, a typical school principal will from time to time respond to a directive from the central office and prepare requested information or accede to some other demand despite the fact that he believes the requested report to be a waste of time or

---

[18] See James C. March and Herbert A. Simon, *Organizations* (New York: John Wiley & Sons, Inc., 1958), pp. 161-69.

the directive to be unnecessary or even undesirable. A superintendent can encourage people to voice their objections in such instances without encouraging chaos.

Second, an administrator should indicate the types of information which are needed. Staff members may otherwise fail to provide the desired information simply because they do not know what is wanted. Many school principals and superintendents want to know in advance about trouble spots or possible "explosions" which may occur in school-community relationships, yet unless staff members are told, some of them will think it better not to worry the administrator with such information.

Third, an administrator needs to act upon the upward communication which is received. Such action begins with simple courtesy in acknowledging receipt of a message. It means that suggestions which have come up the line will be given thoughtful consideration, and that each person who made a suggestion will be informed of the action taken so that he knows that it was carefully reviewed, whether or not it was adopted. It includes recognition of the fact that petty grievances are often indicative of more general dissatisfaction and implies that sincere attempts will be made in considering grievances to discover and remedy the underlying sources of dissatisfaction.

Upward communication is possible only if a wholesome emotional climate is developed and appropriate communications devices are instituted. Some specific devices for promoting upward communication include modification of line-and-staff organization, tapping communication in the informal organization, suggestion boxes, opinion polls, awards for new plans or ideas, individual conferences, grievance committees, and standing and *ad hoc* committees.

Horizontal communication within a school or school system is necessary to provide for consistency in the organization's actions. Coordination of work efforts among peers is essential, and unless the administration is dictatorial, is possible only through horizontal communication. Horizontal communication also fills in gaps which occur in downward communication. If necessary information is not received from above in the organizational hierarchy, a staff member typically consults a peer to obtain the information or to decide upon a course of action. Finally, horizontal communication helps to meet many social and emotional needs.

Horizontal communication implies discussion among peers not only within organizational units but among the various working units of the organization as well. There is a natural tendency toward horizontal communication, for people tend to communicate more readily with their peers than with persons above or below them in status. Thus, a study in a large hospital found that doctors tend to associate with doctors, nurses with nurses, and employees of lower status with other personnel of similar status.[19] If a person in one unit in an organization wants to communicate with someone in another unit, he or she does not typically send a message up the line to the top of the organization and then down again to the person in the other unit, but instead communicates directly with that person. This type of communication has the disadvantage that the school principal or superintendent may not be informed, but has the advantage of directness and of increasing the amount of communication.

Of the three directional types, horizontal communication is used the least effectively in most organizations. Large school systems are invariably plagued by a lack of adequate horizontal communication, with the result that a child moving from one school to another may experience a sharp change in teaching methods and indeed may experience such differences within an individual school. In a school system these differences in program may result from differences in teacher or administrator personalities, differences in beliefs as to what is effective teaching of a particular subject or class group, differences in levels of professional competence, differences in the children in the class and the school, differences in parental and community values and mores, or differences in the resources available. Clearly some of these differences are valuable and should be cherished. In a democracy, personality differences, freedom of belief, and variety in community mores are to be nurtured. On the other hand, communication in an organization needs to be utilized to provide cohesion and consistency. A central problem of communication is how to provide needed consistency while at the same time encouraging the diversity which characterizes democratic societies.

Horizontal communication tends to be the most neglected type because the need for such communication often goes unrecognized. Administrators and others in any organization ordinarily think of organizational communication as being vertical in nature, either downward or upward, and tend to forget that much important organizational communication is horizontal in direction. The result is that in many organizations one part of the organization is competing with and sometimes trying to thwart another.

One of the best ways of providing for horizontal communication is the creation of policy-forming and decision-making groups which cut across the structural boundaries of a formal organization by in-

[19] Albert F. Wessen, "Hospital Ideology and Communication Between Ward Personnel," in *Patients, Physicians, and Illness*, ed. Jaco E. Gartly (Glencoe, Ill.: The Free Press, 1958), pp. 453-58.

cluding representatives of various organizational units in their membership. In a school system, there may be a systemwide representative group which may be granted authority to make policies internal to the school system, that is, to adopt directives and guidelines which provide direction for the school system consistent with board policies but which do not require board action. In addition, the group may prepare policy recommendations for transmittal to the board by the superintendent. Such a group may include elected faculty representatives from each of the various schools, elected student representatives, and administrators who are ex officio members. Comparable groups may be organized for individual schools and other units within the school system.

Other devices for horizontal communication include team teaching, interdisciplinary courses and programs, committees, study groups, house organs, bulletin boards, closed circuit TV and other mass media, study councils, and consortia.[20]

Organization implies that communication will be utilized in the interest of organizational objectives, that not everyone in an organization will be communicating with everybody else, that communications channels will not be used indiscriminately to transmit any kind of information. Organization is thus inherently faced with a dilemma: on the one hand, organization is possible only through the use of specific communications channels; and on the other, regardless of communications channels, information must be able to flow freely within an organization in order that resources may be utilized fully in meeting objectives. One of the major problems for an executive is to promote the use of specific channels to achieve organizational purposes without discouraging the initiation of new communications channels as need arises.

Communications Overload

The communications channels in an organization are selected for use by students, staff, and members of the community, in terms of the appropriateness of the channel for serving a particular need or task. As conditions change, there is corresponding change in the extent to which the various channels are used. Thus, at times some communications channels are used less while others become overloaded. More information may be sent than a channel is able to pro-

[20] For specific suggestions of internal communications devices and procedures used in some school systems, see *Communicating With Staff: Some Guidelines for Internal Communications* (Washington, D.C.: Administrative Leadership Service, Educational Service Bureau, Inc., 1967).

cess. Staff members may find that they are becoming so inundated with communications and reports that in attempting to cope with so many messages, they are losing some or much of their effectiveness.[21]

Some of the ways in which overload can be constructively handled are through selective response, that is, through responding only to those matters deemed to be of greatest importance to the organization; through delayed response, that is, through responding immediately to matters of highest priority and responding to other matters when more time is available; and through diverting some of the messages into other communications channels, that is, redirecting messages to other persons or units in the organization.[22]

School systems sometimes put so much emphasis on the free flow of information that communication overload is inadvertently created. Memoranda, questionnaires, and requests for various types of information all take time which might be used in more creative ways. Administrative action to reduce the volume of communication may be necessary.

Formal and Informal Organization

In addition to the formal organization, there is an informal organization that also is involved in communication. People talk together over coffee, at lunch, in the faculty room, in offices, and in the corridor. A grapevine develops through which information and rumor pass from one person to another. Administrators learn to depend on various individuals for information. Individuals who may not even be shown on an organization chart are consulted and wield substantial power.

The communication which occurs through the informal organization is desirable, and whether the administrator wants such communication or not, it is inevitable. The informal communication enables people to make friends, to express grievances, to pass information back and forth to one another, to explore ideas which may later be introduced into the formal organization, and to obtain suggestions for solving specific problems. These functions are important and can never be performed adequately by the formal organization alone.

Administrators need to be aware of the communication in the informal organization. They cannot control it, but they can work with it. If they desire, they can dip into the informal organization and receive valuable communication by eating lunch occasionally with individuals and groups or by meeting them informally elsewhere. At

[21] For an analysis of both coping and defensive reactions to information overload, see Katz and Kahn, *The Social Psychology*, pp. 231-35.

[22] Based upon *Ibid.*

such meetings, staff members often feel free to explore incipient ideas or to express petty grievances which they hesitate to discuss within the confines of the formal organization. If an administrator meets with informal groups too often, however, his or her presence will tend to restrict free and open discussion. In such a situation the staff is likely to sense that their informal group is being used by the administrator for formal organization purposes, and the informal organization will then find expression through other groups which the administrator is not privileged to attend. An administrator's problem is to keep in touch with the informal communications system without damaging it and without playing favorites among the members of the staff.

Rumor

Rumor is a form of communication which occurs in every organization. Because of the importance of communication, rumor can have a powerful impact upon a school system's effectiveness. Especially when rumor runs rampant and feelings are strong, rumor must be understood and dealt with or an organization's functional level will deteriorate. Furthermore, it has been found that when tensions mount, violence occurs only if the way has been prepared by rumor.[23]

The conditions which create rumor have been clearly identified.[24] Rumor occurs whenever the demand for news exceeds the supply available. Thus, when there is need for a sharp increase in the news available, or when there is censorship or indifference on the part of authorities to the need for news, people rely upon one another for information and create rumors to take the place of unavailable authoritative information. The yearning for news may arise not only from organization conditions but also from repressed impulses. Thus, Jung found that "a rumor, in a girls' school, of sex relations between a teacher and one of the students . . . became disseminated only because of the active participation of a number of students; the girls had similar erotic interests, and the portrayal tapped something that was 'already in the air.'"[25]

According to Allport and Postman, rumors affect the news in three ways. Because of *leveling*, a rumor "tends to grow shorter,

[23] Gordon W. Allport, *The Nature of Prejudice*, 1954, Addison-Wesley, Reading, Mass., pp. 63-65.
[24] In the remainder of this section I have drawn freely from Tamotsu Shibutani, "Rumor," *International Encyclopedia of the Social Sciences*, 13, 576-80.
[25] *Ibid.*, p. 578.

more concise, more easily grasped and told."[26] *Sharpening* is "the selective perception, retention, and reporting of a limited number of details from a larger context."[27] *Assimilation* is the tendency of reports to become more consistent with the interests, expectations, class or racial memberships, or personal prejudices of the reporter.[28]

The conclusions of Allport and Postman have been challenged by a number of other investigators. Thus it was found that among American soldiers in the South Pacific in World War II, many reports became more accurate as they spread. Because their lives were at stake, the soldiers tried to check on the accuracy of unverified reports.[29] Furthermore, it was found that individuals whose reports in the past had proved to be inaccurate tended to be eliminated from the communications networks which spread the rumors. The finding that rumors go through a *leveling* or shortening process has also been challenged,[30] for some rumors apparently embroider and enlarge upon the report.

The differences of opinion about what happens seem to indicate that different situations affect the content of rumors in different ways. "Rumor is something that is composed in social interaction. Persons deprived of authoritative news speculate about what is happening. They piece together what information they have . . . and the definition that eventually prevails is the one that appears most plausible."[31] The rumor which is formulated and which prevails is one which "allows relief from tension, justifies emotions that are unacceptable, or makes the world more intelligible."[32]

A reasonable amount of rumor mongering is perfectly normal. However, excessive circulation of rumor, either in the number of rumors or in the extent of the inaccuracies, is indicative of conditions which are not wholesome.

A number of means of dealing with rumor are available to a school administrator. First, it is important that adequate information be made available to the students, staff, and general public from author-

[26] Gordon W. Allport and Leo Postman, *The Psychology of Rumor* (New York: Russell & Russell, Inc., 1947, 1965), p. 75.

[27] *Ibid.*, p. 86.

[28] *Ibid.*, pp. 100-115.

[29] Theodore Caplow, "Rumors in War," *Social Forces*, 25 (1947), 298-302. As cited in Shibutani, "Rumor."

[30] Leon Festinger and others, "A Study of Rumor: Its Origin and Spread," *Human Relations*, 1, 464-85. Warren Peterson and Noel P. Gist, "Rumor and Public Opinion," *American Journal of Sociology*, 57, 159-67. As cited in Shibutani, "Rumor."

[31] Shibutani, "Rumor."

[32] *Ibid.*, summarizing findings in Allport and Postman, *The Psychology of Rumor.*

itative sources. When change is occurring rapidly or tensions are mounting, people need additional information and, if such information is not made available by the authorities, will create it. Secondly, sources from which authoritative information can be obtained need to be specified. In periods of stress, some school systems and communities have advertised a *rumor center* with a telephone number which can be called twenty-four hours a day to ascertain the validity of a report. Thirdly, if a particular source consistently spreads rumor, this fact can sometimes be made known and the source thus discredited. For example, a school system may bring in a speaker to describe in objective terms how a powerful antischool organization operates, or PTA groups may discuss attacks on schools and the source of the attacks. It is to be noted that suppression tends to foment rather than stop rumors.

Crossing System Boundaries

If a school or school system is to be effective, two-way communication between the formal school organization and the people outside the organization is essential: on the one hand, information needs to go from the school organization to parents and other citizens; and on the other, from individuals, groups, and organizations in the community to the school. Education is a joint venture in which both the school system and the parents and other citizens have a vital stake. Moreover, the school cannot carry out its mission effectively without information from the community at large.

The whole matter of school-community relationships is crucial to the work of the schools. A school is significantly affected by the thinking in the community, for the attitude of citizens not only conditions the thinking and learning of the children but serves in varying degrees to facilitate or impede progress, to help attract or repel potential staff members, and to provide or deny adequate financial and psychological support.

Administrative Competencies

Because a school organization can function successfully only if there is effective communication, an administrator is responsible for helping to facilitate communication. Meeting this responsibility adequately is possible only through a high level of administrative competence in a wide range of processes, procedures, and skills which effective administrators utilize in day-to-day work on various kinds of problems.

In addition to the other competencies, highly developed communications skills can enable an administrator to be more effective in all aspects of administration. Furthermore, if the administrator can demonstrate a capacity to utilize communication in ways which help to promote and achieve organizational purposes, he or she can serve as a model encouraging and enabling others in the organization to develop their own communications skills.

Most administrators are reasonably competent in communicating with others when the problems are intellectual in nature and the other persons involved are logical. When the other persons are emotional and illogical, however, many administrators are perplexed because they lack the necessary skills.

Because the development of communications skills is a field which goes far beyond the scope of this book, only a few skills are mentioned here. Those selected for inclusion are among the ones generally lacking and most urgently needed. They relate primarily to the emotional aspects of communication. Utilization of these skills can enable an administrator to be more humane in communicating with others and can help to resolve problems with people whose feelings are so strong that the problems can be resolved only if attention is given to the accompanying feelings.

Obviously, the reading of a few paragraphs will not be sufficient to enable an administrator to change his or her whole communications style. It is hoped, however, that this brief description of a few skills will encourage readers to seek growth opportunities in this important area. A weekend workshop often helps.

The competencies which follow are useful in facilitating the expression of feelings.

1. Analyze the Situation.

An administrator needs first to analyze the situation. Though such an analysis will typically be informal and may often take place simultaneously with the communications act itself, analysis is an essential aspect of effective communication. The better an administrator understands the human behavior in a specific situation, the better he or she will be able to relate to it.

An administrator should decide first of all whether the surface problem is the real problem, or whether the real problem concerns feelings related to the surface or "intellectual" problem. The failure of an individual to complete a task on time may indicate incompetence; however, it may be that the individual is competent, and that the real problem involves feelings of resentment directed against the administrator or the organization and expressed in neglect of the task. A problem between two individuals may be symbolic of more basic differences between them, or it may be merely a surface manifestation of the conflicting interests of two different groups with which the two individuals feel identified. The skills necessary for communicating with a person with a "feeling" type of problem are quite different from those needed for a person with an "intellectual" problem.

In addition, the analysis should include consideration of the administrator's and others' counterfeelings in the situation. What kinds of feelings on the part of the administrator have been provoked by the actions of others? What kinds of feelings does he or she expect will be provoked? By analyzing counterfeelings, an administrator can monitor his own behavior, and by identifying the counterfeelings which he would expect to have in a future situation, may be able to keep the situation in better perspective. Some people who know that they become very angry when attacked can predict their future counterfeelings and can steel themselves for the attack so that when it comes, they remain cool and in command of themselves.

Lastly, an administrator needs to consider the present counterfeelings of others and the counterfeelings which his or her actions are likely to engender. What is contributing to the counterfeelings of others? If certain actions are taken, what are the likely consequences in terms of others' counterfeelings? What actions can the administrator responsibly undertake which will result in desired counterfeelings?

2. Clarify Own Intent in the Situation.

Administrators can function with integrity only if they understand their motivations. Specifically, an administrator needs to know whether he or she really wants to relate to another person in terms of the other's needs, or seeks to control the other person's actions, to avenge some real or imagined wrong, to gain prestige, to maintain the status quo, or to satisfy some other personal intent.

The pressures from the culture and indeed from the profession are such that it is sometimes difficult for administrators to face up to their real intent in a situation. In the culture as a whole, there is strong emphasis on the idea that a person *ought* to be "good," to do what is right, to be unselfish, to be willing to help others. Ideas such as these are expressed in a family by the parents and tend to be internalized by the children. In the field of educational administration, there is a similar emphasis. An autocratic administrator is generally considered to be "bad," whereas a democratic administrator is "good." An administrator is supposed to work within the group to develop goals and to facilitate group process, is not supposed to pursue selfish ends. An administrator is supposed to have consideration for the feelings of others, not to experience strong feelings.

These emphases have tended to cause many administrators to hide their motivations from themselves. No one is completely aware of his or her own motivations. However, to the extent that an administrator can be aware of and can accept his own motivations, he is in a position to act with integrity. Actions can be purposeful in relation to intent, and there can be consistency between the actions and words of an administrator.

On the other hand, administrators who are unaware of their intent in a situation are unable to exercise conscious control over their behavior. If an administrator thinks that he wants to relate to another's needs when he actually wants to control the other, his intent will usually become apparent. Rather than relating to the other's needs, he will succeed only in adding to the other's resentments over the attempts to control.

3. Utilize Appropriate Skills.

After analyzing a situation and clarifying his or her own intent, the administrator is in a position to utilize appropriate skills in resolving the problems. An adequate resolution of problems may take many weeks or months or may never be possible. A school administrator cannot expect to solve all interpersonal problems for all time, but can develop competence in working with them. Following is a brief description of some of the skills which may be useful. Such skills should be used discriminatingly rather than in every situation.

a. *Lean into the relationship.* Although leaning toward another person physically may help to dramatize one's desire to build a relationship with the other, one's psychological posture is more significant. If you will really listen to another person and can develop a conception of what the other is trying to say about how he or she feels, your counterfeelings of caring will usually arise, and you will respond with warmth and concern. One of the wonderful aspects of being human is that almost all of us respond sympathetically to other people when we really understand how they feel.

As a conference begins, an administrator can quickly put aside the materials on his desk, thus saying nonverbally that for the duration of the conference, he is pushing aside his other concerns in order to pay full attention to the other person; or he may move from behind his desk in order to demonstrate that he does not want a status barrier to interfere with the communication.

b. *Recognize feelings.* If one person is to communicate in relation to another's feelings, he or she must be able not only to recognize strong feelings but to identify the nature of these feelings. It is necessary to have some sense of whether the other person is angry, jealous, resentful, satisfied, or is experiencing other strong feelings. Although no one person can fully understand another, an individual needs reasonably accurate perceptions of the other's feelings in order to facilitate communication of feelings. This skill involves two phases: 1) recognizing that the other person has strong feelings; and 2) identifying the *specific* feelings of the other. Sometimes the specific feelings become apparent at the outset of a conference or an encounter, but often they become recognizable only as communication proceeds.

c. *Verbalize feelings.* The person in the helping role needs to put the other's feelings into words to demonstrate that the feelings have been "heard." We are so used to hearing and communicating in relation to intellectual problems only that we all have reason to assume that our feelings have not been recognized unless the other person explicitly indicates awareness of them. If a parent demands angrily that a child be moved to another class section, a school principal might respond by verbalizing the parent's feelings: "It's important to you that your child be with a good teacher." Or (to a mother): "I realize that a situation such as we are discussing can be upsetting to a parent who really cares about her child." When a conscientious secretary who has been heavily overloaded with work, hands copies of the budget to the superintendent with the comment "At last it's finished," the superintendent may respond to her intellectual or to her feeling-level message. He may use the former type of response and say: "Yes. Now it goes to the board for their consideration." But a superintendent who has heard the secretary's feeling-level message may say: "Yes. The budget has been a big job. You must be tired." Or if a teacher says: "I'm really discouraged. I've tried every device I can think of, and the children still are not learning arithmetic," the principal may respond to the intellectual message by saying: "Have you used enough drill with them?" If he is sensitive to the feeling-level message, however, he may say: "Teaching is frustrating at times, isn't it? Especially when one cares whether or not the children learn."

In each of these illustrations of a feeling-level response, very little time is required for the comment, but in each such instance the administrator is demonstrating awareness of the other's feelings, showing respect for the other's feelings as being natural in the situation, and indicating through a question (explicit or implied) that the other is invited to correct or affirm the administrator's perceptions of the other's feelings.

In other cases more time may be required if communication at a feeling level is to be used effectively. In these instances, the administrator will need to decide whether the problems as he or she understands them warrant a further investment of time.

When a person's feelings are expressed nonjudgmentally by another, he or she is often encouraged to say more about them. Unfortunately, administrators sometimes say: "I know how you feel." Such a statement is too general to be useful, and is unconvincing. More specific comments can be of greater help.

d. *Check the accuracy of our perceptions with the other person.* Only one person can know how someone feels, and that is the individual himself. No one else can ever be sure. We often fool ourselves about our own feelings because the culture labels negative feelings as being unworthy of a mature person. While an individual may not know what his or her real feelings are, certainly nobody else can know for sure. Because one person's perceptions of another's feelings may be inaccurate, an administrator invariably needs to check his perceptions with the other. This checking may be done explicitly: "You don't like it, do you?" It may be done by voice inflection so that the verbalizing of feelings takes the form of a question: "You resent it?" It may be done by a pause after a statement: "You're concerned about your son . . ." Whatever the method, there should be a standing invitation to the other to correct misperceptions of his or her feelings.

e. *Ventilate feelings.* The other person can be encouraged to air his or her feelings freely. This skill is especially useful in talking with someone who is angry. A person with a feeling-level problem can communicate feelings only if allowed by the administrator to do most of the talking.

f. *Identify common purposes.* When common purposes have been identified, people can usually do a better job of tolerating disagreements. For example, when parents can be helped to realize that what they really want is whatever is best for their child, and that the teacher or administrator wants whatever is best for the child (when this is so), a basis has been laid for a fruitful exploration of mutual problems.

The foregoing description of skills is rudimentary. It is hoped that readers who have not already developed a high level of competence in the use of such skills will be prompted to do so. As communications skills are developed, individuals often find that they are looking at interpersonal problems in new ways and that more open communication provides useful data on many problems. Problems which seemed incapable of resolution can frequently be resolved when communications competence is improved.

CONCLUSION

In this chapter the nature and types of communication have been considered, and some of the ways in which individual personality affects communication have been pointed out. The importance of communication in organization has been emphasized, and the different kinds of organizational communication have been described. Finally, attention has been directed to some communications competencies needed by an administrator.

Although this chapter has presented some basic considerations relative to communication in school organizations, a number of problems and issues relative to communication remain to be explored. For example:

1. How can communication be facilitated in small groups?
2. What kind of organization best facilitates communication?
3. How is communication affected by different types of administrative roles?
4. How can a school organization develop a climate which promotes more open communication?
5. How can two-way communication between the school and the community be encouraged?
6. How is communication related to effective leadership?

These matters are among those which will subsequently be addressed.

SUGGESTED READINGS

Cathcart, Robert S. and Larry A. Samovar, *Small Group Communication: A Reader*, 2nd ed. Dubuque, Iowa: Wm. C. Brown Company Publishers, 1974.

Ginott, Haim G., *Between Parent and Child*, chap. 1, "Conversing with Children." New York: Avon Books, 1965.

Goldhaber, Gerald M., *Organizational Communication*. Dubuque, Iowa: Wm. C. Brown Company Publishers, 1974.

Gordon, Thomas, *T.E.T. Teacher Effectiveness Training*. New York: Peter H. Wyden, 1974.

Hall, Edward T., *The Silent Language*. New York: A Premier Book, Fawcett World Library, 1959.

Hollister, William G., "The Specific Skills of the Supportive Relationship," *Journal of the Tennessee State Dental Association* (October 1951).

Johnson, Wendell, *Your Most Enchanted Listener.* New York: Harper & Row, Publishers, 1956.

Lane, Willard R., Ronald G. Corwin, and William G. Monahan, *Foundations of Educational Administration. A Behavioral Analysis*, chap. 3, "The Communication Process." New York: The Macmillan Company, 1967.

McMurry, Robert H., "Clear Communications for Chief Executives," *Harvard Business Review*, 43, no. 2 (March–April 1965), 131-47.

Newell, Clarence A., "Human Relationships in Administration," *Journal of the American Physical Therapy Association*, 49, no. 11 (November 1969), 1215-23.

Rogers, Everett M. and Rekha Agarwala-Rogers, *Communication in Organizations.* New York: The Free Press, 1976.

Sanford, Aubrey C., Gary T. Hunt, and Hyler J. Bracey, *Communication Behavior in Organizations.* Columbus, Ohio: Charles E. Merrill Publishing Company, 1976.

Schneider, Arnold E., William C. Donaghy, and Pamela Jane Newman, *Organizational Communication.* New York: McGraw-Hill Book Company, 1975.

Schramm, Wilbur and Donald F. Roberts, eds., *The Process and Effects of Mass Communication*, rev. ed. Urbana, Ill.: University of Illinois Press, 1971.

Simon, Herbert A., *Administrative Behavior. A Study of Decision-Making Processes in Administrative Organization*, 3rd ed., chap. 8, "Communication." New York: The Free Press, 1976.

Steele, Fritz, *The Open Organization. The Impact of Secrecy and Disclosure on People and Organizations.* Reading, Mass.: Addison-Wesley Publishing Company, 1975.

Steinberg, Danny D. and Leon A. Jakobovits, *Semantics. An Interdisciplinary Reader in Philosophy, Linguistics and Psychology.* Cambridge, England: Cambridge University Press, 1971.

Tubbs, Stewart L. and Sylvia Moss, *Human Communication. An Interpersonal Perspective.* New York: Random House, 1974.

Wiener, Norbert, *The Human Use of Human Beings. Cybernetics and Society.* Garden City, N.Y.: Doubleday Anchor Books, 1954.

SMALL 5
GROUP
RELATIONSHIPS

Like so many aspects of human relationships, group relationships are inevitable. School administrators will be involved in group relationships whether they want to be or not, whether they are skillful in working in groups or not. Educational administrators are involved in meeting with groups that include teachers, students, parents, fellow administrators, agency and community representatives, and other citizens. These groups may be formally organized and meet at specified times, or they may be organized informally as delegations, temporary committees, or persons meeting for some other specific purpose. They vary all the way from groups organized by the school administrator to those organized in opposition to administrative actions or to the administrator.

Groups are inevitable because they satisfy basic human needs. Each person needs to relate to others. Groups can help to meet a person's needs to care about others and to be valued, to feel safe, to feel significant, and to belong. In addition to meeting basic personality needs, groups are necessary as a means for achieving social and organizational purposes. Groups are necessary to provide for adequate organizational communication, effective decision making, and opportunities for professional growth.

The importance of groups to organizational productivity has been well documented. In general, the more loyal nonsupervisory workers are toward their work group, and the more pride they have in its ability to produce, the more productive the work group. However, high peer group loyalty does not guarantee high production. Instead, it can result in agreement to limit production or to thwart the goals of the organization. Productivity tends to be high when work groups develop high peer group loyalty and also accept organizational goals. Research evidence indicates that the development of these characteristics of work groups is related to the type of administration and supervision provided.[1] An educational administrator has many opportunities for working with groups. These opportunities can be used to advantage if the administrator has an understanding of group processes.

In this chapter the nature of groups is clarified, and the development of theory and research concerning groups is noted. The goals and needs served by groups and the types of communications patterns which develop are then discussed. Special consideration is given to Bion's theory of groups. Finally, attention is directed toward means for facilitating effective group functioning.

SOME DEFINITIONS AND CLARIFICATIONS

The word "group" has been defined in various ways. When applied to human relationships, it is used to describe relationships not only in a physical sense but in a sociological and psychological sense as well.

A simple definition is that of Olmsted:[2] "A group, then, may be defined as a plurality of individuals who are in contact with one another, who take one another into account, and who are aware of some significant commonality." The concept of system is captured in the definition by Stogdill:[3] "A group may be regarded as an open interaction system in which actions determine the structure of the system and successive interactions exert coequal effects upon the identity of the system. . . . In a group consisting of more than two members, it is possible for subgroups to be formed. A subgroup is an interaction system within a larger interaction system."

---

[1] Rensis Likert, *New Patterns of Management* (New York: McGraw-Hill Book Company, 1961), pp. 26–43.
[2] Michael S. Olmsted, *The Small Group* (New York: Random House, 1959), p. 21.
[3] Ralph M. Stogdill, *Individual Behavior and Group Achievement* (New York: Oxford University Press, 1959), pp. 18–20.

The concept of "group" has been differentiated from "logical class" by C. A. Mace in the following:[4]

It was the Cambridge philosopher McTaggart who liked to illustrate the concept of a logical class by reference to "red-haired archdeacons." The class of red-haired archdeacons is just the plurality of individuals who both are red-haired and exercise archdeaconal functions. They do not form a social group, face-to-face or otherwise. They do not interact with each other in any context more than they interact with bald headed arch-deacons or red-haired archbishops. So, too, with "the Smiths." The Smiths constitute a logical class the members of which have little or no fellow feeling for each other and do not interact with each other more than they interact with the Browns. But we must be careful. This is more doubtfully the case with the Campbells, the McDonalds, and the McGregors. And what about "the pedestrians"? Are they a mere logical class or a social group? If they are not a class conscious social group they may at any moment become one if motorists provoke them beyond the limits of their endurance. And if anyone thinks the question is of "merely academic interest" he should take the cases of "the People," "the Workers," "the Proletariat," "the Bourgeoisie," and "the Capitalists." It is a bone of con-tention whether the capitalists are as innocent a plurality as the red-haired archdeacons or a genuine social entity interacting and cooperating in overt or clandestine ways to achieve some common purpose. So, too, are "the workers" a self-conscious integrated group cooperating in the pursuit of worker-goals, or are they a simple logical class wishfully thought of by reformers as a genuine social group, or are they perhaps a logical class in process of becoming a real social group?

Thus, a logical class should not be confused with a group, for people can be members of a logical class but have little if any aware-ness of one another. In all groups, people are aware of and interact with one another, and in formal organizational groups, people inter-act with one another to clarify and achieve common goals in a face-to-face setting. Some of the goals in a group may be divergent, but some goals are held in common.

Primary and Secondary Groups

Sociologists recognize two types of groups: primary and second-ary.[5] Primary groups are typically warm and intimate and fulfill social and emotional needs, the best example of a primary group being the family. On a school staff, primary groups may appear in

[4] C. A. Mace, "Editorial Foreword," in *Human Groups*, W. J. H. Sprott (Baltimore: Penguin Books, 1958, 1966), pp. 7-8.
[5] For the original statement of the primary group concept by its orginator see C. H. Cooley, *Social Organization* (New York: Charles Scribner's Sons, 1915), chaps. 3, 4 and 5.

the form of friendship groups, lunch or coffee groups, or cliques. Secondary groups represent a different type of interpersonal relationships. Such groups are not an end in themselves but are created to serve particular purposes. Examples of secondary groups on a school faculty are those groups formed to serve organizational purposes and include departmental faculty groups, grade-level faculty groups, committees, the administrative team, and the faculty as a whole. Recreational groups such as bridge clubs or bowling teams which often begin as secondary groups may develop many of the characteristics of primary groups as well.

Forces Affecting Groups and Individuals

According to an interesting theoretical proposition propounded by Schutz,[6] a group follows the same psychological laws as a person, and *vice versa*, a person follows the same psychological laws as a group. Schutz's theory suggests that whatever is known about individual psychology is true also of group psychology and that whatever is known of group psychology is applicable to individual psychology. The theory implies, for example, that since it is known that each person perceives situations and events in an individualistic and unique way, so each group perceives in a unique way, and on the other hand, that since various stages of emotional maturation in the life of a group have been discovered, these same stages are also characteristic of individuals.

Schutz claims that he is not simply trying to establish an analogy, but that the same laws actually hold for both individuals and groups. Whether or not the Schutz formulation is valid as theory, it has practical utility because it automatically doubles one's working knowledge of individuals and groups. It suggests that an administrator who understands individual psychology has comparable knowledge of group psychology, and that what an administrator knows about groups can be applied also to individuals.

DEVELOPMENT OF THEORY AND RESEARCH

An extensive body of theory and research pertaining to small groups has developed during the past half century. While this development is still in its infancy, enough has been discovered to provide

[6] William C. Schutz, "The Ego, FIRO Theory and the Leader as Completer," in *Leadership and Interpersonal Behavior*, eds. Luigi Petrullo and Bernard M. Bass (New York: Holt, Rinehart & Winston, Inc., 1961), pp. 48–65.

a basis for the practitioner who seeks to understand the forces operating in small groups and who wants to develop competence as a small-group participant and leader.

Studies of small groups have been conducted with reference to leadership, supervision, and communication; school, club, industrial, and military groups; families, neighborhoods, villages, and crowds; groups, interaction, and leadership in organizations; and many other subjects.[7] While many of these studies are not directly relevant to administration, they warrant the attention of anyone who wants to develop an understanding of groups in some depth.

Possibly the two best known research devices for the study of small groups are the technique of sociometric assessment devised by J. L. Moreno,[8] and the Interaction Process Analysis developed by Robert F. Bales.[9] Moreno's sociometric technique discloses feelings which group members have toward each other, and thus makes possible the unearthing of the preference structure of a group at a given time. In the Bales system, the observer in a group records who says what to whom in relation to twelve observational categories. A tally mark is made every few seconds to record each interaction unit. The categories include both social-emotional areas related to personal needs and task areas related to accomplishing the work of the group. The categories and their relationships to one another are shown in the following figure.

Perhaps the best known device for the study of interaction in classroom groups is the Flanders Interaction Analysis.[10] This instrument, though not unlike the Bales, is specifically adapted to the classroom situation and enables the observer to differentiate between "teacher talk, student talk, and silence or confusion."

---

[7] For an introductory overview, see Olmsted, *The Small Group* and Sprott, *Human Groups*. For some research studies see Dorwin Cartwright and Alvin Zander, eds., *Group Dynamics: Research and Theory*, 3rd ed. (New York: Harper & Row, Publishers, 1968). A. Paul Hare, Edgar F. Borgatta, and Robert F. Bales, eds., *Small Groups: Studies in Social Interaction*, rev. ed. (New York: Alfred A. Knopf, 1965). Joseph E. McGrath and Irwin Altman, *Small Group Research: A Synthesis and Critique of the Field* (New York: Holt, Rinehart & Winston, Inc., 1966).

[8] J. L. Moreno, *Who Shall Survive*, rev. ed. (Beacon, N.Y.: Beacon House, 1953).

[9] Robert Freed Bales, *Personality and Interpersonal Behavior* (New York: Holt, Rinehart & Winston, Inc., 1970). *Interaction Process Analysis* (Cambridge, Mass.: Addison-Wesley Publishing Co., 1950).

[10] Edmund Amidon and Ned A. Flanders, *The Role of the Teacher in the Classroom: A Manual for Understanding and Improving Teachers' Classroom Behavior* (Minneapolis, Minn.: Paul S. Amidon and Associates, 1967). See also Ned A. Flanders, "Teacher Influence, Pupil Attitudes, and Achievement." U.S. Office of Education, Department of Health, Education and Welfare, University of Michigan, dittoed, 1962. Ned A. Flanders, *Analyzing Teacher Behavior* (Reading, Mass.: Addison-Wesley, 1970), p. 34.

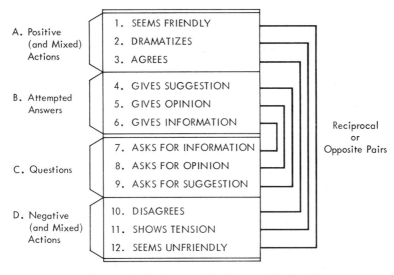

Categories for Interaction Process Analysis*

*From *Personality and Interpersonal Behavior* by Robert Freed Bales. Copyright © 1970 by Holt, Rinehart and Winston, Inc., Reprinted by permission of Holt, Rinehart and Winston, p. 92.

GOALS AND NEEDS

While it may seem obvious that a faculty's effectiveness is greatly influenced by the extent to which individual faculty members are committed to common goals, the fact remains that faculty deliberation is often impeded by confusion over goals. Sometimes faculty members are so idealistic that they set unrealistic goals for themselves with resulting disillusionment and confusion. Sometimes groups get caught up in their own enthusiasm and launch projects without adequately defining the purposes of the activity. Sometimes individual faculty members use a group to serve selfish purposes. Sometimes faculty groups are unclear as to purposes because they have been assigned projects to serve an administrator's personal goals. For example, an administrator may want the faculty to make a good showing on a particular project in order that the administrator may obtain a promotion.

Confusion over goals is also likely to arise when different groups are brought together to work on a common problem. For example, in a large county school system, the County Council of the Parent-Teacher Association and the League of Women Voters entered into a joint study of the basic school needs of the county. Although the study proceeded well for a number of months, it gradually became apparent that the Parent-Teacher group expected the study to eventuate in a program of action for school improvement whereas the members of the League of Women Voters thought that the study was to be limited to providing information on the findings to the public.

A goal is a condition which is pursued to satisfy a need. Group goals include both long-range or superordinate goals and proximate or more immediate goals. The superordinate goals represent the conditions which the group believes to be the ultimate in desirability whereas the proximate goals are those which may be achievable in the foreseeable future.

Agreement on at least some goals is necessary as a basis for determining how a group is to proceed. Goals are needed first to provide direction for a group's work. They help a group to know what problems are within the scope of its work and what procedures are appropriate. Secondly, goals help group members to utilize conflict constructively and thus contribute to group cohesion. They encourage openmindedness in work on the group task and tend to foster a sense of belonging and of trust in the group members. Thirdly, common goals provide a basis for evaluation of a group's work, for the important consideration in any evaluation is the extent to which goals are being achieved.

Explicit consideration of goals should be undertaken at a time when a group is ready to consider goals. Otherwise, discussion of goals will turn out to be a futile exercise. An administrator can often sense the time when goal clarification is necessary. For example, when an administrator finds that group members are often frustrated, involved in petty disagreements, and quibbling over how to proceed, he or she would do well to determine whether goals are held in common by the various group members and whether attention should be explicitly directed toward consideration of group goals.

Types of Goals

Several types of goals come into play in any organizational group. These goals affect group functioning in various ways.

1. Common group member goals may be agreed upon either explicitly or implicitly. In addition to goals which are openly expressed, a group may also develop hidden goals or agenda.

2. Agency and organizational goals come into play. Group members often reflect the goals of their organizations. On the other hand, faculty groups sometimes find their efforts frustrated because they are working at cross purposes with the goals of the organization.

3. Individual goals held by the various group members may or may

not be expressed explicitly to the group as a whole. These include personal motivations as well as group-oriented goals. Many of these goals will and should continue to be an individual's private affair.

4. Administrative-team or administrative-cabinet goals often come into play. These goals can be designed to help provide consistency in the actions of the various members of the administrative team. Team members may arrive at agreements concerning their roles in the group, expectations for group achievement, and ways in which to proceed. Often agreements of this type are not communicated adequately to the staff as a whole.

5. Individual goals are invariably held by the administrator or other status leader in a group. The leader may have in mind some specific expectations for group accomplishment, limitations concerning acceptable solutions or actions which the group may agree upon, and processes it will use. The leader may also see the group as a device through which his or her own ideas and ambitions can be furthered.

Hidden Agenda

A group is always working on agenda at two levels — the explicit or stated agenda and the hidden agenda. In addition to its stated agenda, a group may try to find ways of establishing its own prestige as being higher than that of another group, may try to make life difficult for the administrator, may try to use other groups or individuals as scapegoats on which it can vent its hostilities and resentments, or may try to find some way to terminate a meeting.

A subgroup may continue to argue a point after it realizes that it is wrong as it searches for a way to save face. It may yield quickly in an argument as a means of placating the administration. Or it may be rude as its members talk and laugh as a means of expressing hostility to an individual or to the group as a whole.

Individuals in the group may present ideas or argue for certain points of view as a means of ingratiating themselves with the administration, in order to obtain adoption of an action plan which would embarrass other group members, or as a means of attaining status in the group. Or they may withdraw from active participation as a means of expressing negative feelings toward the group and its members.

Group deliberations are often hindered by the implicit assumption that goals which serve selfish purposes are unworthy and should therefore be kept hidden. When a group and its members pretend to be working on certain goals but are actually working on others, the group deliberations are likely to become circuitous and time-consuming. If faculty members want changes in policies governing course programs required of students in order to help assure enrollments of a certain size in their classes but feel that they must present their case under the guise of increasing the number of course offerings, time will be wasted and a satisfactory solution to the real problem will become more difficult. Individuals may want to protect their status, to teach an advanced section which someone else wants to teach, to lighten their teaching loads, to obtain positions with higher salaries, to receive recognition from the administration or the community, or to enjoy additional perquisites. Goals of this type, though essentially selfish in nature, are legitimate and should be so recognized unless they become an obsession that interferes with the goals of education.

Hidden agenda exist whenever hidden purposes come into play. Everyone possesses hidden motives and feelings which are brought along to any meeting. Many of these hidden motives are latent at any given time. It is when they become active in a group situation that they have important effects upon group functioning.

Often it helps to bring the hidden agenda into the open. If the hidden agenda are blocking group progress, the group may be unable to move ahead until it can discover and deal with the hidden agenda. On the other hand, hidden agenda which cannot be tolerated or dealt with by the group may be disruptive if brought into the open. The greater problem is usually, however, to recognize and reveal hidden agenda so that the group may deal with these matters deliberately.

Cohesiveness

Groups vary widely from one to another in the extent of their cohesiveness, that is, their attractiveness or drawing power for the members of the group. The cohesiveness of a group is determined by the degree to which the group appears to each group member to be the best means available for meeting the individual's needs. An individual may value membership in a group because of group and group-related activities, because of attraction to the group members, or because of the high prestige conferred by group membership, either by high rank in the group or by the high prestige attached to membership in a particular group. The cohesion of any group is always subject to the attractiveness of other groups which promise to satisfy needs more effectively.

Cohesiveness is important because it affects the power of a group. Groups develop norms or standards of behavior, and it has been found that "the more cohesive the group, the more effectively it can influence its members."[11] The norms of the group may put pressure on individual workers to turn out neither too little nor too much work, as was found to be the case in the Western Electric studies,[12] or they may set high or low performance goals. In addition, a review of pertinent research studies leads to the conclusion that "cohesiveness in work groups has a clear positive effect on absenteeism, turnover, and tardiness. . . ."[13] It can also be inferred from research findings that a more cohesive work group not only is more powerful in affecting its members, but it can more readily withstand outside pressures and be productive in clarifying and working toward its own goals. The cohesiveness of work groups is thus significant to the productivity of any organization.

Conformity and Nonconformity

All groups develop norms or standards of behavior for group members, and these norms consist of shared expectations as to what constitutes acceptable behavior in a particular situation. Some norms are adopted by individuals because the norms are consistent with their existing attitudes and behavioral tendencies. On the other hand, individuals conform to some norms because of group pressures.

Although a group need not become an instrument for conformity, most groups and organizations in our culture create powerful pressures for enforcing conformity in the actions and even the thoughts of their members. This finding is supported by many research studies, some of which are now classics. A famous experiment by Sherif[14] demonstrated that group norms do affect individual perceptions. Another famous study, conducted by Asch,[15] led the experimenter to the similar conclusion that when people perceive the same situation, there is a strong tendency on the part of numerous individuals to alter their own perceptions to fit those of the majority. In another well-known study,[16] it was found that persons who deviate from

[11] Leon Festinger, Stanley Schacter, and Kurt Back, "Operation of Group Standards," *Social Pressures in Informal Groups* (Stanford, Calif.: Stanford University Press, 1950, 1963), p. 100.

[12] F. J. Roethlisberger and William J. Dickson, *Management and the Worker* (Cambridge, Mass.: Harvard University Press, 1939, 1970), p. 522.

[13] Orlando Behling and Chester Schriesheim, *Organizational Behavior. Theory, Research, and Application* (Boston: Allyn and Bacon, Inc., 1976), p. 124.

[14] Muzafer Sherif, *The Psychology of Social Norms* (New York: Harper & Brothers, 1936), pp. 104-5.

[15] S. E. Asch, "Effects of Group Pressure Upon the Modification and Distortion of Judgments," in *Groups, Leadership, and Men,* ed. Harold Guetzkow (Pittsburgh: Carnegie Press, 1951), pp. 183-84.

[16] Stanley Schacter, "Deviation, Rejection, and Communication," *Journal of Abnormal and Social Psychology,* 46 (April 1951), 190-207.

group norms are more readily rejected by other group members than are those who conform. Furthermore, the more cohesive the group, the more power it has in enforcing its norms.

Even administrators who are skillful in talking about group process and who are convinced that they encourage freedom and creativity often foster strong pressures for staff conformity. This phenomenon occurs because feelings have so much to do with the way a person behaves. An administrator may learn many ideas about how to work with groups and may become adept at speaking or writing about them. When relating to other people, however, an administrator tends to behave in ways consistent with his or her feelings. Thus, administrators sometimes verbally encourage faculty decision making but then cultivate close social relationships with a few favored faculty members who can be trusted to promote the ideas of the administration and to block any decision which would deviate very much from that viewpoint.

Every group enforces a code of conformity through its emotional acceptance or nonacceptance of the individual members and subgroups. If an individual departs significantly from the group norm, the individual loses prestige, has less power in the group, and in extreme cases is expelled psychologically or physically from the group. It is not unusual for faculty members to complain bitterly about the regimentation in the schools where they work and yet in faculty meetings or in conferences with the administrator to indicate agreement with the procedures which they find so objectionable.

One of the ways to enable a group to deal with the problem of conformity is, through both word and deed, to encourage it to adopt *acceptance of nonconformity* as a norm. Such as norm does not mean that group members may ignore policies and regulations. Instead it means that group members may behave in nonconformist ways, provided such behavior does not adversely affect the other group members or the group as a whole. In addition, it means that new or different ideas will receive a fair hearing and that the individuals expressing them will not be ostracized or lose status in the group. If a group believes in *acceptance of nonconformity* as a norm, the tendency of the group to require conformity to its norms can actually support nonconformity.

COMMUNICATION PATTERNS IN TASK-ORIENTED GROUPS

Various types of communication patterns in groups have been identified, and research studies indicate that differences in these patterns have important effects upon group communications.[17] Some of the different types of patterns which may exist are illustrated by the following figures.

In the All-Channel pattern, any person may communicate with anyone else. In the Circle pattern, each person may communicate with only two people, one on either side, without relaying a message through someone else, and with all persons in the group with not more than one relay. In the Chain, each person communicates directly only with the one or two adjoining persons, and communications to all members of the group require from one to three relays. In the Wheel and Arrow patterns, all communications center in a key individual, and each person may communicate with all the others through a single relay or, in the case of the key person, directly. The Wheel and Arrow may portray identical patterns of communication; however, if the vertical position of the dots is used to represent vertical or power relationships in the administrative hierarchy, then the Arrow pattern is different from the Wheel because it includes another hierarchical level.

In a practical working situation, the All-Channel pattern exists when each person feels free to communicate with other persons in the group. The Circle and Chain are most likely to occur in a group in which free expression is not permissible. The Wheel is the typical group in which most communications pass between the administrator or chairman, who has considerable prestige, and the individual group members. The Arrow pattern may represent vertical or line relationships, including relationships such as those shown in the Wheel pattern plus another level in the administrative hierarchy.

[17] Alex Bavelas, "Communication Patterns in Task-Oriented Groups," in *Group Dynamics*, 3rd Edition, edited by Dorwin Cartwright and Alvin Zander (Harper & Row, 1968), pp. 503-11. Harold Guetzkow, Figure 1 "Open Channels used in three nets" and summary of figure, in *Group Dynamics*, eds. Cartwright and Zander, pp. 512-26. See also Marvin E. Shaw, "Communication Networks," in *Advances in Experimental Social Psychology*, Volume I (New York: Academic Press, 1964), pp. 111-47. Murray Glanzer and Robert Glaser, "Techniques for the Study of Group Structure and Behavior: Empirical Studies of the Effects of Structure in Small Groups," in *Small Groups*, eds. Hare, Borgatta and Bales, pp. 400-426.

Communication Patterns
and Group Structure

Although research evidence on the various communications patterns is limited, it seems safe to make certain generalizations. Free communication among all members of a group (All-Channel) is the most efficient way of enabling a group to draw upon the thinking of all the group members and allowing free interaction among them in the identification and solution of group problems. Such communication thus maximizes the capability of a group to be creative. In this type of communication pattern, communication may also be the most accurate because it can be direct and need not be relayed from one person to another. Morale is generally highest with the All-Channel pattern. A plan in which all share in communications opportunities and in responsibility for the group requires a high level of understanding and responsibility on the part of the individual group members. In such a group, the structuring of interpersonal relationships may be expected to change from time to time in relationship to the group's task. While adaptations of the group's structure to the task at hand can facilitate a group's work by providing a dynamic organization which continues to be functional as conditions change, this lack of continuing structure provides less security. An individual in a group with an indefinite or unstable structure may not know what to count on, whom to ask for directions, or who will provide protection from the aggression of other group members. Without clearly defined structure, individuals must rely more on their own resources, and greater maturity on the part of group members is required.

Communication in a group may be affected through the structuring of the interpersonal relationships (the patterns other than All-Channel). Clear-cut structure makes it possible to fix responsibility on specific individuals, with the result that one individual or small group of individuals may be able to develop superior competence through time. Structure makes control possible, enabling a group to solve simple problems quickly. Structure can also help to provide continuity in a group's actions even though the individuals who comprise the group may change. In addition, structure provides an element of security for the group members because it helps them to know what they can count on. On the other hand, structure may tend to limit communication within a group, for individuals no longer relate as freely to everyone else and, if they were to do so, might find that the ideas of some are backed by authority (the Wheel and the Arrow) whereas others are not. Groups with highly structured relationships are generally less able to tap the resources of

all members in the group in the solution of problems and are therefore less creative. To the extent that structure is rigid, it is less
adaptable to the needs of the group and hence is less functional.

Although the type of structure needed depends upon the conditions relating to a specific group, it is probably true that most school
groups today adopt too much structure and that it is too rigid. The
alternative of too little structure, tending toward chaos and confusion, is not acceptable either. Research evidence indicates clearly
that some structure with one or more positions of centrality is
necessary for a group to be effective and efficient.[18] However, a
study of communications networks together with first-hand observation of school systems suggests that the typical group and organizational structures in education are designed to assure control and
security at the expense of creativity and personal growth.

Relationships with Others

A group always functions in relationship to other groups and
organizations, individuals outside the group, and society in general.
Groups are affected by these relationships in ways which are similar
to those experienced by individuals in relationships with others. A
group which feels that it is valued, that it is making an important
contribution, and that it is growing and becoming stronger in the
process, tends to be a productive group. On the other hand, if a
group meets failure and frustration time after time, it tends to become discouraged and to desist in its work. The behavior of a group
is conditioned by its emotional system and can be explained only to
the extent that the feeling aspects are understood. At times a group
may function logically with a minimum of emotion, but at other
times group actions may be strongly influenced by the need for
recognition, rivalry with another group, frustration in obtaining
necessary administrative action, or hostility toward authority in
general.

BION AND RELATED THEORY

Bion's Theory of Groups

One of the most important theoretical contributions to an understanding of groups has been made by Bion,[19] who has paid particular

---

[18] For example see G. B. Cohen, *The Task-Tuned Organization of Groups*
(Amsterdam: Swetz and Zeitlinger, 1969), pp. 32–37.

[19] Adapted from *Experiences in Groups* by W. R. Bion © Tavistock Publications (1959) Limited, 1961, Basic Books, Inc., Publishers, New York. For a

attention not only to the rational but to the nonrational aspects of group life. In his explanation of the word "group," Bion includes relationships which some writers would include under the term "organization"; that is, Bion considers a group to be in existence if the people have a sense of common purpose or interrelatedness whether or not they are in the same physical location. Bion's formulations are especially helpful in enabling one to understand the emotional life of groups and organizations.

Bion's formulations have special relevance to administration. Since Bion emphasizes the relationships of group members to persons in positions of authority, the relationships between group members and leaders as described by Bion often apply to relationships between faculty members and school administrators.

Bion points out that in every group there are two basic aspects. One of these is the work group, which concerns the rational activities of the group as these are designed to accomplish the group's task. The work group refers to the life of the group when it tends to be in touch with reality in working constructively on group tasks such as the definition of common goals, the development of appropriate procedures for accomplishing the goals, the delegation of tasks in accordance with the competencies of the members, and the development of the human resources within the group. "Any group of individuals met together for work shows work-group activity, that is, mental functioning designed to further the task in hand. Investigation shows that these aims are sometimes hindered, occasionally furthered, by emotional drives of obscure origin."[20]

The other aspect of group life concerns the nonrational activities of the group which develop in response to the anxieties in the group. It is almost as if ten people in a group actually constituted two groups of ten people each, with one group functioning rationally in dealing with the group's tasks and problems, and the other group functioning nonrationally. The two styles alternate from time to time in the group of ten persons and frequently intrude upon one another. From the activities of the group, one who is sensitive to mental and emotional group life may deduce whether the group at any given time is functioning as a rational work group, a nonrational group, or a combination of the two. The goal in a mature work group is to combine the two aspects of group life in such a way as to utilize the nonrational tendencies constructively to further the task accomplishment of the group.

relatively brief and simplified version of Bion's theory, see Margaret J. Rioch, "The Work of Wilfred Bion on Groups," *Psychiatry*, 33, no. 1 (February 1970), 56-66. Copyright © 1970 by the William Alanson White Psychiatric Foundation, Inc. In this explanation the author has drawn upon both the above sources.

[20] Bion, *Experiences in Groups*, p. 188.

The Basic Assumptions

Three basic assumptions have been identified by Bion. These assumptions typically are not explicitly formulated by members of a group, and in fact, the group members are usually unaware of them. However, group members at times act as if they had agreed upon certain basic assumptions. For example, if a person continually infringes upon the rights of others, it may be deduced that this person has little respect for individual rights, or in other words, the person acts as if the basic assumption is that the rights of others are unimportant. It is in this sense that Bion uses the term "basic assumption," that is, that at times group members act as if they held in common a certain basic assumption about relationships among group members, among group members and the leader, and among the group and persons, groups, or objects outside the group. Bion has identified three major basic assumptions: dependency, fight-flight, and pairing.

Dependency. When a group functions with *dependency* as the basic assumption, the group members seek security through alliance with an omnipotent, omniscient leader. The group members act as if the leader knows everything and they know nothing. The leader is expected to protect the group members by knowing what to do in every situation. The members act as if the leader is much wiser than they, as if they are mere bystanders in the group processes, as if the leader does not even need information from them in order to make wise decisions. If the leader is aware of the importance of promoting task performance, he or she will realize that the expectations of the group are unrealistic and, in attempting to direct the energies of the group back to more realistic work on the task, will arouse hostilities and resentments. When discrepancies develop between the group's desire to be taken care of and the leader's ability or willingness to serve the dependency needs, the group begins to look for a new leader, and the more ambitious members of the group assert themselves in attempts to take over the leader's position. If such a person succeeds in ousting the leader, he or she will usually succumb to the same fate as the original leader because the claim to leadership is based upon the unrealistic basic assumption of the group. As soon as the group moves to another basic assumption or becomes a work group, the new leader is no longer able to meet its basic needs. When a group is functioning under basic-assumption dependency, the group members seem to be helpless and to rely on the leader to solve problems and to take care of them.

Fight-Flight. When *fight-flight* is the basic assumption, a group operates as if its central goal is self-preservation, and as if the only means of preserving itself is to attack or to run away from someone or something. In such a group, a strong leader is needed to provide for the desired action. If the leader does not meet real or imagined demands upon the group which afford opportunities for aggression or flight, the leader is ignored. The "successful" leader is somewhat paranoid and therefore quick to recognize danger and enemies and to mobilize the group to attack or withdraw. Because the group is so concerned with its own preservation, it is unable to be concerned with the preservation of the individual, and individuals are sacrificed. The group is unable to feel much concern for individuals because of its obsession with real or fancied dangers to the group itself.

Bion believes that panic, flight, and uncontrolled attack are essentially the same emotional phenomenon. When rage or fear develops into frustration without an appropriate outlet, fight or flight provides for an immediate expression of the emotion. It is to be noted that, like the other basic-assumption groups, fight and flight are usually alternatives to a constructive approach to a problem — that is, fight-flight is a basic assumption which often stands in the way of constructive action by the work group.

Pairing. When a group is functioning with *pairing* as the basic assumption, it acts as if its central purpose is reproduction. This reproduction may take the form of the birth of a messiah, an idea, or an organization. One or more pairs may form on behalf of the group to provide for the reproduction. Because the group is expecting a new birth which will solve all its problems and relieve its feelings of hatred, destructiveness, and despair, as well as protect it from such feelings on the part of others, there is an air of expectancy and hopefulness in the group. The hopefulness continues unless a new leader or idea is actually born, in which case the new savior is typically rejected. If a new leader or idea acceptable to the group is actually found or created, the group will soon lose its feelings of hopefulness, for it will discover that the new leader has not been able to solve all its problems. In such a situation, feelings of destructiveness, anger, and hatred soon return.

Relationships Among Basic Assumptions. In order to explain the readiness with which individuals enter into association with others in basic-assumption activity, Bion has created the concept of valency, a term "borrowed from the physicists to express a capacity for instantaneous involuntary combination of one individual with another for sharing and acting on a basic assumption."[21] In using the term "valency," Bion is expressing the idea that all individuals have a tendency to enter into group life, including the nonrational and

[21] *Ibid.*, p. 153.

unconscious aspects of group life. A person may have high or low valency, but all persons are drawn toward group life in greater or lesser degree.

All basic-assumption groups involve the existence of a leader, although in the pairing group the leader is unborn. The leader need not be a person but may be an idea or an inanimate object. A record of a group's meetings may become a "bible" to which appeal is made for various types of decisions. "The group resorts to bible-making when threatened with an idea the acceptance of which would entail development on the part of the individuals comprising the group." Whenever a basic-assumption group is operative, whether the assumption be *dependency, fight-flight,* or *pairing,* "a struggle takes place to suppress the new idea because it is felt that the emergence of the new idea threatens the *status quo.*"[22]

Effective Group Functioning

For effective group functioning, both the *work* group and the *basic-assumption* group are necessary. For a group to be effective, however, "the basic assumptions must be subservient to and used in the service of the work task. They make good servants and poor masters."[23] Thus, a union of the rational life of a group with its non-rational or emotional life is necessary if the group is to be effective.

Bion's formulations, which have been outlined here, provide a means for conceptualizing in depth the various processes and procedures which take place in groups. Bion's theory is especially helpful in explaining covert group processes and warrants thorough study by any person who is interested in relationships between members of groups or organizations and individuals in positions of authority.[24]

Group Maturation

The conceptualizations set forth by Bion,[25] Thelen and Dickerman,[26] and others,[27] have been combined, changed, and restated by

[22] *Ibid.,* pp. 154–55.

[23] Rioch, "The Work of Wilfred Bion," p. 64.

[24] A model which enables participants to experience the phenomena described by Bion was developed largely through the work of A. K. Rice of the Tavistock Institute of Human Relations in London. Each year a number of group relations conferences based on this model are held at various locations throughout the United States. See A. K. Rice, *Learning for Leadership* (London: Tavistock Publications, 1965).

[25] Bion, *Experiences in Groups.*

[26] Herbert A. Thelen and Watson Dickerman, "Stereotypes and the Growth of Groups," *Educational Leadership,* 6 (1949), 309.

[27] Robert F. Bales and Fred L. Strodtbeck, "Phases in Group Problem-Solving," in *Group Dynamics,* eds. Cartwright and Zander, pp. 389–98.

Hollister[28] to formulate a theory of group maturation. Although Hollister has drawn heavily upon Bion, he is not always consistent with Bion, and the two conceptualizations should not be confused with each other. In some instances, Hollister uses Bion's terms to describe phenomena different from those described by Bion. Hollister's statement is thus not simply a restatement of Bion, but is to some extent a change in conceptualization.

In the Hollister formulation, there are five stages of group maturation. Even before a group meets, emotional forces begin to affect it, leading to misperceptions concerning the group and its purposes, members, and leaders. When group members meet, the first stage is *dependency*. A faculty group in this stage wants a leader who will provide both answers to their individual problems and a plan of work for the group. The second stage is *counter dependency*. In this stage, group members are in revolt against the leader. They are just as dependent as before, but now, rather than needing the leader to follow, they need the leader to fight against. The third stage is *independence*. If communications channels have been opened up and opportunities for full-fledged participation made available, the mounting anxiety causes most members of the group to seek relief through changes in the group's modes of operation, and attempts are made to relieve tension by minimizing or eliminating conflict and substituting hard work on the group's or individual assignments. The fourth stage is *pairing* or *co-dependency*. The phenomenon of pairing develops as the group members begin to sense a lack of direction in group efforts. A member who feels uneasy about the group's progress shares his or her concerns with another member, and gradually the whole group tends to break down into pairs or very small groups in which mutual concerns are discussed. The fifth and final stage is *interdependence*. In this stage, the group makes important decisions and develops plans and procedures to carry out its decisions. Group members work productively and, at the same time, are critical in evaluating the progress of the group. The leader facilitates group action and effectively carries appropriate leadership responsibilities based upon respect for strong individual selves. The anxiety level of group members at this stage drops to a fairly low level where it continues with relatively small fluctuations as the work of the group continues.

Although one stage of maturation may predominate in a group, the various group members at any given time may be in different stages of maturity. According to Hollister, most groups probably

[28] William G. Hollister, "The Risks of Freedom-Giving Group Leadership," *Mental Hygiene*, 41, no. 2 (April 1957), pp. 238–44.

function to some extent in all five stages at the same time. It is probably true also that most members in most groups spend a great deal of their time functioning in the first two stages of dependency and counter dependency. However, if the individual group members are sufficiently self-actualized and if the leadership is supportive, the group's operation will gradually become characteristic of the later stages of group maturation. Although it is perhaps too much to expect that all individuals in a group will function in ways consistent with the interdependence stage of group maturation, a group which has reached the later stages of maturation, especially the interdependence stage, can help its individual members to grow in functional competence.

Implications of the Bion and Hollister Theories for Administration

The Bion and Hollister formulations have important implications for administration. If an administrator realizes that it is natural for groups at times to function under the basic assumptions of dependency, fight-flight, or pairing, the administrator can be more accepting of a group and of his or her own leadership when a group is involved in such behavior and is avoiding its task.

One of the greatest advantages of knowledge of the Bion-Hollister theories is that it can free an administrator from the need to take criticism personally and hence to feel highly defensive. If an administrator realizes that the hostility which he or she senses in a group is inevitable in a participant-leader relationship and would develop regardless of who the leader might be, the administrator may be able to accept the hostility and thus be free to take more constructive action.

An additional advantage of the formulations is that by having a better understanding of the group's emotional needs at a particular time, the administrator can be more helpful in enabling the group again to become a more effective work group.

The Bion-Hollister formulations suggest that when a group first meets, purposes are likely to be twisted and confused, and clarification of purposes is therefore necessary. Since the group members already have pre-images of the leader, the leader may want to decide whether to present himself in a manner consistent with or at variance with these preconceptions.

Awareness that a group is in a stage of dependency provides a basis for knowing how the group will react to leadership. An administrator who responds to the desires of the group will receive the approval of the dependent group members but at the cost of perpetuating a dependency relationship. If an administrator insists that the group participate actively in making decisions concerning its own work, the group has the opportunity to develop, but a stage of growing hostility toward the leader may be expected.

During the stage of counter dependency, group members who were initially inclined to oppose the administrator are joined by those who were dependent and are now disappointed because the leader has not made decisions for them or has made decisions which they do not like. While the safer course at this stage is for the administrator to stifle dissent by using sanctions against individual members or by keeping the group so busy that expression of complaints at group meetings is difficult, a willingness by the administrator to take the risks involved in participative leadership will, after a period of confusion and growing hostility toward the leader, usually lead to a more productive group. During this period the leader will find it useful to help group members develop the capacity to relate what is being said to ideas which have already been expressed ("Tom, how does your idea relate to what Joe just said?").

As a group moves into the stages of independence and pairing, the identification of hidden agenda assumes major importance. Hidden conflicts may be brought into the open and resolved. Dissatisfactions may be identified and considered. Life at this stage will be more peaceful if the administrator cooperates in keeping hidden agenda under cover, but by bringing issues out into the open and encouraging discussion of them, an administrator can facilitate the development of a group.

When a group moves to a stage of interdependence and exhibits the characteristics of an effective work group, the group will tend to make realistic demands upon the leader, and administrative responses consistent with such claims will lead to positive feelings and increased satisfaction on the part of the group members.

FACILITATING EFFECTIVE GROUP FUNCTIONING

The participation of individual members in group discussion is a matter of major concern in the development of an effective group. The involvement of all group members in a discussion is generally assumed to indicate a successful meeting, whereas if very few enter into the discussion, it is often assumed that a meeting has been less successful.

Vocal participation in a group, however, is not a true index of member involvement. A faculty member who is quiet in a group may be actively involved and may be doing a good deal of thinking.

On the other hand, someone who is talking a great deal may be doing very little thinking and may be talking simply to gain prestige in the group, to please the administrator, to forestall any embarrassment which might arise from periods of silence in the group, or for a variety of reasons.

Techniques which stimulate group discussion are sometimes useful because discussion may lead to greater involvement of the group members. However, many group leaders expend great amounts of energy in trying to get all group members to share equally in discussion. Sometimes there is so much pressure upon faculty members to talk that they resist by not saying much or even by withdrawing from the group. Contributions which are prompted by the inner motivations of the individual are more likely to be helpful in group deliberations than contributions which result from external pressure.

Administrators who want genuine participation in group deliberations must be concerned with the psychological dynamics of a group. They need to be sensitive to subtle clues concerning the motivations of individuals, subgroups, and the group as a whole, and need to help provide the conditions in the group which lead to genuine involvement.

Fundamentally, the autonomy of each individual needs to be cherished and protected. Every group is a system, and intensive feeling systems always have profound effects upon their members. An effective group climate is one which promotes involvement and self-expression through respect for the motivations and feelings of each member. In such a group, conflict is inevitable; however, conflict based upon respect for the opinions of each individual can be constructive because it tends to open up communication in the group and lead toward the resolution of the group's real interpersonal and task-related problems. Almost all groups function under severe restraints imposed by the administrator or by the group itself, with the result that many group members inhibit expressions of their thoughts at meetings, hiding their inner thoughts or revealing them in private discussions later. The goal is to develop a climate in which ideas and feelings so often expressed in essentially useless ways can instead be utilized in working toward the resolution of problems in the group or organization.

Setting the Stage for Effective Group Thinking

When a group is involved in decision making, it needs at the outset to know as specifically as possible the limits of its authority. If some other group is to make the final decision, it is particularly important that a policy-forming group know its limitations. Nothing is more shattering to a group's morale than to be delegated decision-making authority only to have that authority subsequently withdrawn and placed elsewhere.

It is generally useful for a group to know initially of any practical considerations that might limit its decisions. An administrator may be willing to accept any plan which a group develops provided that its cost does not exceed the five thousand dollars included in the budget, or may be willing to approve any faculty-adopted plan for the scheduling of classes on a particular day, provided the plan does not shorten the school day or shorten the time periods for certain school subjects as required by state law. If the faculty is responsible, the administrator may forego the prerogative of the veto provided that any plan proposed is within the general framework of school board policies and state laws. Although there are times when an administrator will prefer not to set forth the limitations within which a group proposal must be developed if it is to receive his support (especially when he himself may not know the limitations), the advantages to a group in knowing the boundaries within which it must work are obvious.

To help enable group members to think together productively, an administrator or chairman needs to do whatever is possible to open up communication. Many group members will not be willing to communicate freely until their own experience in the group convinces them that they are respected and that their contributions to the thinking of the group are valued. Group members ascertain whether or not open communication is the norm, not only from statements made by the administrator and other group members, but also from their assessment of the group's emotional climate. If group members feel that a group is psychologically safe, they will be free to express ideas which might otherwise be withheld.

A teacher new in a school system in which teachers were rated for salary purposes, happened to be in a policy-forming group with the school superintendent to consider matters of teacher welfare. When teacher rating was discussed, the new teacher opposed rating for salary purposes and cited a number of arguments which she considered to be substantial. She was shocked when the superintendent replied that if she did not like the salary policies in this school system, she could look for employment elsewhere. From then on the teacher refrained from communicating any facts or opinions which she thought might be offensive to the school superintendent.

In an entirely different situation, a teacher who was new in a school system noticed in a policy-forming group that other teachers stayed on friendly terms with the administrator even though they had argued with him and sometimes voted contrary to the way he voted. This teacher increasingly became more open in expressing ideas and opinions.

All group members affect a group's emotional climate, but the status leader, especially if an administrator, usually has the greatest influence. Because the administrator wields sanctions which can be used to reward or to punish group members, a group will tend to get many cues from him, and his actions thus have a considerable effect upon the type of emotional climate created.

If administrators or group chairmen want to create an open climate, they can use both verbal and nonverbal communication at the outset to express this intent. Informal procedures which convey the idea that assigned status is relatively unimportant in the group and that each person is important and valuable as an individual are useful for this purpose. Devices which have been used include provision of a pleasant physical atmosphere, informal seating arrangements, use of name tags, use of first names and nicknames, a different seating place for the status leader at each meeting, rotation of the chairmanship and other leadership roles, and the right to speak without waiting for recognition by the chairman. Although devices of this type have been criticized as being superficial, they may be useful at times as a means of supporting an emotional tone of acceptance of all members. More basic than the devices in setting emotional tone, however, is the total configuration of group relationships, including the feelings and counter feelings and the actions and responses of the status leader and all group members. It is the total system of relationships and feelings which is important in the long run for freeing communication within a group.

Steps in Group Decision Making

Group decision making can be facilitated if appropriate procedures are followed. On the other hand, if some of the steps in group thinking are neglected, group agreement may be difficult or impossible.

The steps which groups take in problem-centered deliberations do not always follow neatly in sequence, but an understanding of them is useful in deliberations on many group problems.

1. Exploring the field and need for study.

A group explores the field of its concerns and identifies specific needs. Decisions are made concerning the sequence in which problems are to be attacked, based upon the group's estimate as to which problems are most urgent, which can be resolved by the group, and the extent of the resources required by each.

2. Defining the problem.

The specific group problem (or set of problems) is defined. If a group has been asked to work on a particular problem, the administrator and group may need to meet together in order for the administrator to give the group its specific charge.

3. Selecting the ways for solving the problem(s).

The group discusses alternative ways of solving the problem (or set of problems). The advantages and disadvantages of each are considered. The group selects one or more ways which, in its opinion, will help to provide solutions and which are consistent with the resources of the group.

4. Delegating responsibilities and setting standards of work.

Specific tasks are assigned and deadlines for accomplishment of these tasks are agreed upon. The group sets standards which the group members are expected to meet in carrying out their specific assignments, and which the group as a whole expects to meet. Time limits are set for the activities of the group as a whole, including planning, data gathering, treatment of data, interpretation of data, group deliberations, and completion of work.

5. Considering alternatives and selecting the preferred solution.

Data are collected, treated, and analyzed. Conclusions are inferred from the data, and various alternative solutions are discussed. The consequences of the various plans are considered. While recognizing that there are no perfect solutions, the group selects the plan which appears to be the most promising and works out the details of the plan. The plan is recorded, and methods for evaluating it are devised.

6. Implementing and evaluating the plan.

The plan is put into effect. Once the plan becomes operational, steps are taken to provide for its evaluation. In time, needed changes are identified and replanning for modification or complete change in the plan is initiated.

Types of Group Decisions

One of the important functions which a group can perform is that of coordinating the work of various individuals. By formulating and adopting policies, a group can provide a framework which specifies the limits for individual action without interfering with the legitimate freedom of the individual. Many groups try, sometimes unconsciously, to regulate specifically the professional behavior of the group members. A teacher may be required, regardless of the needs of the children, to follow slavishly a prescribed course of study or to use textbooks and instructional materials without having a part in selecting them. Or when changes are made to incorporate new instructional devices, a great deal of pressure may be applied to teachers to adopt the new procedures. Or if a system of rotating personnel from one position to another is considered desirable, staff members may be required to become a part of the system whether they want to or not.

A framework of policy is necessary to provide for consistent organizational action, but the more professional a staff, the more latitude can be provided within the general framework for individual professional action. Sometimes in a university, an adviser of doctoral candidates will discuss an advisee about whom he needs to make a decision with an appropriate committee even though the adviser reserves to himself the right of decision. The same principle was observed some years ago when Paul Mort administered a research fund at Teachers College, Columbia University. The stipulated policy was that a professor who had obtained a grant from the fund would report periodically to a research board that would evaluate progress on the project. In the case of a negative evaluation, the policy left to the individual professor the decision as to whether the project should be continued or terminated. The same idea underlies many advisory councils appointed by administrators and school boards with the explicit understanding that the council is to serve as a sounding board and to react to proposals without having the power of decision. Study committees which help to identify needs and to formulate proposals are in some respects similar.

Methods of Decision Making

Groups generally use the following six methods of arriving at decisions.

1. Leader decision.

The leader makes the decisions and may or may not explain reasons to the group members. The group members are slaves in the sense that they are subservient to someone else's purposes.

2. Leader proposal.

The leader formulates and presents a plan or policy statement which group members may then accept, reject, or modify. Group members enjoy the freedom to make decisions relative to administrative proposals but not the freedom to develop their own proposals.

3. Compromise.

Two or more parties present proposals and subsequently modify their positions to obtain approval of part but not all of their original proposals. Group members have the freedom to be creative and to help make decisions, but bargaining necessitates that ideas be judged by their source rather than on the sole basis of merit.

4. Consensus.

Policies and plans are formulated by a group, with communication being sufficiently open so that all members of the group accept the resulting policy. Group members can be creative and ideas can be judged on the basis of merit. Minority opinion is nonexistent or is hard to identify.

5. Majority rule.

Proposals are presented by individual members or by subgroups for consideration by the group as a whole. The majority may allow individuals to be creative and to express differences freely. The preferences of the majority on any point prevail, and the ideas of the minority are rejected unless and until they are approved by a majority.

6. Constitutional government.

A constitution or set of bylaws is adopted to help assure the use of acceptable decision-making processes and to protect the group and its members against unfair practices. Some or all of the previous types of decision making are utilized. The goal is to utilize the insights of all group members and to protect the rights of both the majority and the minority.

Because many school faculties attempt to use consensus as a means of making decisions, an understanding of the advantages and disadvantages of this method is important. Consensus includes both an intellectual and an emotional aspect. The intellectual aspect of consensus refers to the capacity of group members to build upon one another's ideas and upon the relationships among these ideas so that the group decision or plan is better than that which could have been arrived at by any individual. Since group members are never able to comprehend and utilize fully the ideas of the others in the group, intellectual consensus in a group is a goal that cannot be entirely achieved. The emotional aspect of consensus refers to the fact that group members may wholeheartedly accept a plan or policy adopted by a group, not so much because of their unqualified agreement with it as their loyalty to the group and their confidence in its decisions. Sometimes group members will accept the judgment of the group as being superior to their own, as being the best that the group could arrive at, given the individual group members with all their personal beliefs and perceptions. These reactions represent a kind of consensus in which loyalty to the group itself plays an important part.

Although consensus has the advantage of utilizing the ideas of all staff members and helping all members to feel that they belong, attempts to achieve consensus should stop short of urging a single group opinion at the expense of individual beliefs and convictions. If a group becomes overconcerned with achieving consensus, it will pressure its members to minimize disagreements. In such a situation, individuals often find that it is more comfortable to go along with the group than to hold to their convictions. A minority report which represents deeply held convictions is part of the democratic process and can be very useful; in the long run, minority opinions sometimes turn out to be right, and they are almost invariably stimulating.

Because consensus decision making has both advantages and disadvantages, many faculty groups now utilize both informal and parliamentary procedures, alternating the two as seems desirable. Some of the considerations which need to be taken into account in choosing between informal discussion methods and parliamentary procedures are as follows:

1. Informal methods are more appropriate for exploratory discussion and for policy formulation; there is often greater need for parliamentary procedures when decisions are to be formalized or policies are to be adopted.
2. Informal methods are more appropriate for a small group; parliamentary procedures become more necessary in larger groups.
3. Informal methods are more appropriate for decisions of temporary significance only; parliamentary procedures become more necessary if a record of action is needed and are essential if a legal record of the group's decisions is required.
4. Informal procedures are more appropriate for developing a greater understanding on the part of all group members; parliamentary procedures are more appropriate for making a group's decision explicit and unmistakable.
5. Informal procedures are more useful if group members have not made up their minds on the matter; parliamentary procedures are more useful if individual members have definitely made up their minds.
6. Informal procedures may be useful as a means of considering complex problems deliberately; voting enables a group to save time and to arrive at categorical decisions quickly.

7. Informal procedures are less likely to be abused if the individual group members know each other well and feel that they can count on one another to participate in group decision making fairly; parliamentary procedures provide a safeguard if there is a possibility that individual group members or subgroups will try to take unfair advantage.

Procedures for Achieving Group Agreement

A number of techniques or procedures have been found useful in helping groups to achieve agreement. In general, such procedures tend to be useful only to the extent that the individuals in the group have open minds on the subject, for if each person is inflexible in his thinking, no change resulting from new facts and insights is possible. Because the procedures used need to be appropriate in terms of the situation, no specific procedure or set of procedures can be prescribed in advance as a remedy for a group's difficulties. Procedures will generally work more successfully to the extent that they are based upon an analysis of the group's problems and upon an understanding of the needs, interests, motives, and feelings of individual group members. The following procedures have been found to be helpful.

1. Appropriate facts are obtained.

Facts are ascertained through the seeking of information rather than through arguments. Group members learn to differentiate fact from interpretation or opinion.

2. Points and areas of agreement are identified.

These points or areas of agreement may include purposes, points of view, facts, elements of the proposed plan, or group procedures (including methods of judgment and evaluation). Group thinking is tested from time to time through questions, attempted summaries, or votes, to discover the areas of agreement and disagreement.

3. Areas of confusion and disagreement are
identified, and resolution of such problems
is attempted.

Effort is exerted to avoid polarization of group members in order that important differences may be thoroughly talked through. Group members learn to assess each idea on its own merits rather than on the basis of the individual or subgroup from which it came. The group members are alert to semantic problems which may arise and attempt to resolve such problems. Individuals are not expected to compromise their own ethical convictions or basic principles. Personal integrity takes precedence over group agreement, and minority reports are sometimes issued. Differences which are not significant to the work of the group are sidetracked or ignored.

4. An experimental approach to group procedures and decisions is utilized.

A group decision is considered to be authorization for the testing of a plan rather than a final agreement on the best solution. The group members realize that a plan's success or failure can best be evaluated by actually trying it out. Procedures within the group are sometimes tried experimentally. The group's processes and procedures for arriving at decisions are evaluated, and in exceptional cases (especially those involving other groups), a problem may be referred for negotiation or arbitration to obtain a decision.

5. The timing of decision making is such that a group is enabled to make decisions when ready.

Decisions are made rather than postponed when a group has thought through a problem and is ready to take action. If a group has difficulty in arriving at a decision, the resolution of conflicts in the group may be postponed: a) while the group seeks first to agree on basic points of view, or seeks additional facts; b) until there can be informal discussion in coffee breaks, subgroups, or between meetings; or c) in order for the group to evaluate its own processes and procedures.

6. Summaries and tentative agreements are made from time to time.

These agreements are to aid group thinking and are therefore tentative and subject to change, including revision when the group approves its final policy statement or report.

7. Group members are helped to become more competent in communication.

Problems in communication are discussed explicitly and growth opportunities are provided to enable group members to become increasingly sensitive to communications problems and increasingly competent in communicating both ideas and feelings.

Group Evaluation

Evaluation is necessary with reference not only to the policies which groups adopt but also with reference to the group processes themselves. Such evaluation is most useful when all group members feel responsible for the group and can evaluate its work without being excessively defensive. In addition to the informal evaluations continually made by individuals, formal evaluations are necessary to help assure that the work of the group does not deteriorate.

The methods of evaluation should be designed both in relation to the purposes of the group and the purposes of the evaluation itself. In any specific situation, assessments utilizing objective data as well as opinions and feelings warrant consideration. An effective evaluation, through gauging the extent to which a group is achieving its purposes, points the way to improvement through building and improving upon past performances.

Once an evaluation has analyzed a group's functioning, the group can develop and carry out plans for further actions. As soon as the plans are put into effect, needs for re-evaluation arise. Thus, a group which wants to be maximally effective will be continually involved in evaluating, planning, carrying out plans, re-evaluating, re-planning, and re-directing its activities.

Evaluation holds great potentiality for improved group work, but the potentialities are difficult to realize. The conditions for their realization are free and open communication, a reasonable degree of objectivity, clearly perceived goals, and insight into the relationships between goals, task-related procedures, and the interpersonal relationships within a group.

CONCLUSION

If the present trend toward dehumanization is to be reversed, means must be found to provide for deeper levels of communication. Modern organizations consist largely of secondary, task-oriented groups, and even in families in modern society, communication often takes place on only a superficial level.

Groups in school organizations can provide opportunities for the expression of personal reactions and for discussion of individual problems which are task related. Feelings about the organization, both positive and negative, need to be freely expressed. It should be possible for individuals in groups to discuss their goals and interests in relation to the mission and the requirements of the organization.

Individuals should be able to voice their concerns with a group of co-workers in a setting which minimizes threat to all involved.

If organizations are to become more humane, the bureaucratic organizational model needs to be modified, and organizations which recognize and provide for the human qualities of people must be developed to take its place. A climate which supports individuality needs to be encouraged, and leadership which promotes individual and group growth is necessary. These matters receive attention in subsequent chapters.

SUGGESTED READINGS

Bion, W. R., *Experiences in Groups.* New York: Basic Books, Inc., 1959.

Blumer, Herbert, *Symbolic Interactionism. Perspective and Method.* Englewood Cliffs, N.J.: Prentice-Hall, Inc., 1969.

Cartwright, Dorwin and Alvin Zander, eds., *Group Dynamics: Research and Theory*, 3rd ed. New York: Harper & Row, Publishers, 1968.

Cathcart, Robert S. and Larry A. Samovar, *Small Group Communication: A Reader*, 2nd ed. Dubuque, Iowa: Wm. C. Brown Company Publishers, 1974.

Hinton, Bernard L. and H. Joseph Reitz, eds., *Groups and Organizations. Integrated Readings in the Analysis of Social Behavior.* Belmont, Calif.: Wadsworth Publishing Company, Inc., 1971.

Lewin, Kurt, *Resolving Social Conflicts. Selected Papers on Group Dynamics.* New York: Harper & Brothers, 1948.

Lifton, Walter M. and David G. Zimper, *Groups: Facilitating Individual Growth and Societal Change.* New York: John Wiley & Sons, Inc., 1972.

Likert, Rensis, "The Nature of Highly Effective Work Groups," in *Organizations and Human Behavior: Focus on Schools*, eds. Fred D. Carver and Thomas J. Sergiovanni. New York: McGraw-Hill Book Company, 1969, pp. 356–67.

Luft, Joseph, *Group Processes: An Introduction to Group Dynamics*, 2nd ed. Palo Alto, Calif.: National Press Books, 1970.

Ofshe, Richard J., ed., *Interpersonal Behavior in Small Groups.* Englewood Cliffs, N.J.: Prentice-Hall, Inc., 1973.

Phillips, Gerald M., *Communication and the Small Group*, 2nd ed. New York: Bobbs-Merrill Company, Inc., 1973.

Roberts, Joan I., *Scene of the Battle: Group Behavior in Classrooms.* Garden City, N.Y.: Doubleday & Company, Inc., 1970.

Schein, Edgar H., *Organizational Psychology*, chap. 5, "Groups and Intergroup Relationships." Englewood Cliffs, N.J.: Prentice-Hall, Inc., 1965.

Sherif, Muzafer, *In Common Predicament: Social Psychology of Intergroup Conflict and Cooperation.* Boston: Houghton Mifflin Company, 1966.

Thelen, Herbert A., *Classroom Grouping for Teachability.* New York: John Wiley & Sons, Inc., 1967.

Zaleznik, Abraham and David Moment, *The Dynamics of Interpersonal Behavior*, Part 1, "Group and Interpersonal Processes," Part 3, "Organizational Aspects of Group Behavior." New York: John Wiley & Sons, Inc., 1964.

ORGANIZATIONAL   **6**
RELATIONSHIPS

The organizational relationships which develop in a school or school system are expressions of value systems in relation to human systems, the organizational task, and the perceived situation. The interpersonal relationships within an organization tend to take the form of patterns or structures. One person is recognized as the "boss"; certain others are delegated authority of one kind or another; specific individuals talk more frequently with some persons in the organization than with others; characteristic ways of interacting develop; coffee and lunch groups are organized; grapevines of communication develop; and individuals learn where to go and whom to consult for help on a particular project. These and many other kinds of relationships constitute organizational structure. Some of these relationship patterns are established through official action and constitute the "formal" organization. Others are not official and constitute the "informal" organization. Both the formal and informal organizations are important to the success of an enterprise and to the well-being of the individuals who are involved.

This chapter calls attention to the importance of organization and then describes the nature of both formal and informal organization. Some traditional concepts about organizations are presented and critically examined, and the development of organizational theory, especially as it pertains to human behavior in organizations, is traced. Finally, attention is directed to improving organizational relationships, including consideration of such matters as motivation in organizations, goal setting, decision making, and competition and conflict.

IMPORTANCE OF ORGANIZATION

Ironically, the importance of organizational structure is generally recognized by autocratic administrators who see clearly that some kind of organization is necessary if they are to have their own way, but it may not be sufficiently recognized by administrators who want to show respect for others and hence are opposed to systems which emphasize status or hierarchical relationships. Organization, however, is inevitable. Even if organizational structure were to be abolished, complete anarchy could not last for long. Someone would soon take control, and thus a new structure would emerge. The important question is not whether there should be structure, but rather, what kind of structure there should be.[1]

Organization is important because the structuring of relationships profoundly affects the ways in which people interact with one another. The extent of authority which one person exercises in relation to another colors the behavior of both individuals, and the associations which are systematized through structure affect both the thinking and the emotional reactions of the individual. The importance of organizational structure is demonstrated whenever someone is placed in a new position and behaves differently in accordance with the demands of the new role. When an individual who has been a teacher becomes a school principal, it is not unusual for the individual's attitude to change. A teacher who seemed friendly may now become aloof, or a teacher who opposed authority may become highly authoritarian.

In a story called *The Five Hundred Hats of Bartholomew Cubbins*,[2] a king lived on a hill overlooking a village of peasants. The king's view of the village made him feel big and important. Down in the village lived Bartholomew Cubbins, who looked up each day toward

---

[1] For examples of the extensive evidence on the inevitability of structure see Arthur M. Cohen, Ernest L. Robinson, and Jack L. Edwards, "Experiments in Organization Embeddedness," *Administrative Science Quarterly*, 14, no. 2 (June 1969), 208–21. Ralph M. Stogdill, *Managers, Employees, Organizations* (Columbus, Ohio: Bureau of Business Research, Ohio State University, 1965).

[2] Dr. Seuss, *The Five Hundred Hats of Bartholomew Cubbins* (New York: The Vanguard Press, copyright © 1938, 1965).

the king's castle. Bartholomew saw the same view each day as the king did, but he saw it backwards. And it made him feel small and unimportant.

The story of Bartholomew Cubbins is an example of the importance of organizational relationships. Because the king lived in the castle on the hill and the people lived in the village below, the king was perceived as being big and important, and the villagers were perceived as being small and unimportant. Organizational structure can be a powerful conditioner of perceptions.

In one of the schools in a university, a dean issued orders and made all the important organizational decisions for many years. On the relatively few occasions when the dean talked with staff, he saw one staff member at a time, and sometimes did not even provide a chair for the staff member while he talked to him. Then a dramatic change occurred. A new university president, on recommendation of a faculty committee, initiated a faculty senate, which in time required that each college or school have a faculty assembly. Each individual school faculty and dean were required to develop a plan of organization to submit to the university senate for approval. The plan of organization for the college as ultimately approved by the university senate required the dean to meet with the total faculty group several times each year for the purpose of policy making and planning, and as a result, the staff and the dean sat down together for the first time.

This change in organizational structure resulted in some real changes in the ways in which people related to each other. Whereas the dean formerly made the decisions alone in his office, he now was required to discuss certain matters with the staff. The change in organizational structure did not result in a sharp change in staff-administrator relationships, for into the new structure, the administrator and the staff brought their own past experiences and patterns of behavior. They had all been used to giving and receiving orders, to dominating and being dominated. However, the new organizational structure did constitute a strong educational force, for gradually the faculty and the administrator began to learn how to work together. Furthermore, when the old dean finally retired and his successor was appointed, the structure was such as to encourage cooperative relationships rather than continuance of the old autocratic patterns.

A school system committed to democratic principles will seek to develop an organizational structure based upon personal equality and differentiation of function and to provide encouragement of professional growth. Although certain individuals may be designated as administrators, these designations are provided, not because the individuals so designated are necessarily more able than anyone else, but simply because certain administrative functions need to be performed by someone who has developed the necessary administrative competencies. The misconception often exists, on the part of both the administrators and the students and staff, that the lower an individual is on the hierarchy of an organization, the less worthy he or she is as a person. It is ironic that the students, for whom schools are created, are so often the least respected persons in a school organization.

SOME DEFINITIONS AND EXPLANATIONS

A number of terms are used frequently with reference to organizational relationships. Some of these are defined and clarified below.

Organization

The word "organization" is defined by Kahn and others,[3] as follows:

We define an . . . *organization* as an open, dynamic system; that is, it is characterized by a continuing process of input, transformation, and output. Organizational input characteristically includes people, materials, and energy; organizational output typically takes the form of products or services, although it may consist mainly of direct psychological return to members. The openness of the organization as a system means that it is eternally dependent upon its environment for the absorption of its products and services, and for providing the necessary input which reactivates the process of transformation and thereby maintains the organization in existence.
   . . . As an open social system, the organization is defined and its boundaries determined by the relationships and patterns of behavior which carry out the continuing cycles of input-transformation-output. . . .

Another useful conceptualization is provided by Gross, who says that[4] "a formal organization may be regarded as a group or cooperative system" in which there is:

1. An accepted pattern of purposes
2. A sense of identification and belonging
3. Continuity of interaction
4. Differentiation of function
5. Conscious integration

Gross states also that:

Organizations aim at (1) satisfying human interests, of both members and

---

[3] Robert L. Kahn and others, *Organizational Stress: Studies in Role Conflict and Ambiguity* (New York: John Wiley & Sons, Inc., 1964. Reprinted by permission of John Wiley & Sons, Inc.), pp. 12-13.
[4] Bertram M. Gross, *Organizations and Their Managing* (New York: The Free Press, 1968), p. 52.

nonmembers, by (2) producing services or goods with (3) an efficient use of scarce inputs, by (4) investing in their own viability, (5) mobilizing the resources needed as inputs, and doing all these things (6) in conformance with certain codes of behavior, and (7) in a rational manner.[5]

This proposition is explained thoroughly in the Gross book.[6]

The foregoing statements place emphasis upon joint action in the achievement of purposes, that is, in the production of goods and services; upon people, materials, and energy; input, transformation, and output; and upon interrelationships and interaction within the organization and between the organization and its environment.

Informal Organization

For several decades a number of authorities have recognized that in any organization there are both formal and informal structural relationships, that is, relationships which are designated formally and explicitly in the organizational structure, and relationships which are informal in the sense that they are not officially recognized. Without any designation in the formal organization, small groups of compatible persons form to discuss workrelated and nonwork related matters and to join in social and recreational activities. The proverbial grapevine conveys news and gossip. Specific individuals come to be recognized for their power even though they do not carry formally delegated authority. An informal organization develops to help satisfy the needs of individuals and groups.

The informal organization has many effects upon a formal organization; it can either support or undermine the organization's efforts to achieve recognized objectives. A school administrator may find that discussion in the various groups officially recognized in the school organization may be highly favorable to a plan of action, yet may be surprised later to discover strong staff opposition or, if the plan is put into effect, may be embarrassed to discover that the staff is working resourcefully to scuttle the plan. In such instances, the informal organization may be responsible for the opposition and resistance, and the school administrator's problem may be to learn to work with rather than against the informal organization.

Some dimensions of formal and informal subsystems of organization have been identified by Argyris. Argyris' model represents[7] "a series of dimensions each of which is a continuum. On one end is the

[5] *Ibid.*, p. 276.

[6] *Ibid.*, see especially pp. 263-553.

[7] From *Organizational Leadership* by Chris Argyris, in *Leadership and Interpersonal Behavior,* edited by Luigi Petrullo and Bernard M. Bass. Copyright © 1961 by Holt, Rinehart & Winston, Inc. (Reprinted by permission of Holt, Rinehart & Winston), p. 338.

subsystem whose focus is on individual needs (informal); on the other, the subsystem whose focus is on the attainment of the formal objective." Following is the Argyris model.[8]

Formal Organization	Informal Organization
1a. At the outset interpersonal relations are *prescribed*, and they reflect the *organization's* idea of the most effective structure within which to achieve the *organization's goals*.	1a. At the outset interpersonal relations *arise* from members' interaction and reflect the *need* of *members* to interact with each other in order to fulfill their needs.
1b. The *leadership* role is assigned to the person the *organization* feels can best perform *organizationally* defined duties.	1b. The leadership role is delegated to the individual the *members* believe will best fulfill their needs.
2a. The formal behavior in organization manifested by an individual is "caused" by the individual's acceptance of *organizationally* defined reward and penalty (sanctions).	2a. All behavior of individual members in the group is caused by the attempts of individual members to *fulfill their needs*.
2b. The dependency of members upon the leader is *accepted* by members because of the existing organizational sanctions.	2b. *Dependency* of members upon the leader is created and accepted by members because they believe it will fulfill their *needs*.

In the last chapter the suggestion was made that an administrator can work with the informal organization by keeping in touch with the informal communications network. The major test which staff members apply in deciding whether an administrator can be trusted to be privy to communications in the informal network is the perceived degree of openness which an administrator tolerates in the formal organization. If the climate in the formal organization is open, encouraging the free expression of ideas, a group has less need to hide messages and perceptions which are circulating in the informal organization.

When communication is open, an administrator can encourage further development of the informal organization. He can suggest that people consult one another across departmental lines, that groups of individuals from different parts of the organization meet informally to discuss the interrelationships between their individual needs and organizational purposes, that an individual take the lead in exploring an organizational problem with colleagues in other departments with a view toward the formation of a policy-recommending group in the formal organization, that social and recreational groups be formed. In various ways, an administrator can unobtrusively

[8] *Ibid.*, p. 339.

strengthen the informal organization and, at the same time, can lessen the sharp distinctions which so often exist between the formal and the informal organization.

TRADITIONAL CONCEPTS

Traditional concepts of organization have emphasized fixed principles. In general, thinking concerning organizations has moved from the promulgation of a few fixed principles or directives to a much more flexible approach through which organizational phenomena are studied and analyzed.

School systems generally have adopted a line-and-staff type of organization. This type of organization was taken from the military services and business, and has served the needs of traditional organizations. Although line-and-staff organization at one time seemed to be the answer, the limitations of this concept for purposes of educational organization have gradually become apparent, and as a result, many school systems and universities have introduced modifications in the structure to facilitate policy making while continuing to use the line-and-staff type of organization for other purposes.

In general also, school administrators and boards have agreed upon the desirability of unit executive control. An organization may be so structured as to have one chief executive or to have two or more chief executives coordinate in rank. Unit executive control exists when there is a single chief executive (or superintendent of schools); dual executive control, when there are two chief executives coordinate in rank; multiple executive control, when there are more than two chief executives coordinate in rank. Unit executive control has generally been endorsed for the following reasons: a) unless there is a single chief executive committed to education, the business and other service aspects of an organization tend to become an end in themselves rather than a means of furthering educational purposes; b) only when there is a single chief executive can responsibility for the general success of the educational enterprise definitely be fixed; and c) dual and mutiple executive control often result in a great deal of rivalry between the various executives and their followers within a school system. Unit executive control is now being modified in many educational organizations by the concept of the administrative team or cabinet. This approach suggests that although an organization employs a single chief executive, major executive decisions are made cooperatively by a small cabinet including the executive and several high-level administrators or by an executive committee including the administrator and a few elected representatives of the staff.

Spans of control have received considerable attention by the military, and based upon such experience, it has generally been agreed until recently that the span of executive control should be limited to six; that is to say, administration can be most effective when no more than six persons report directly to each administrator. More recently has come the realization that when highly professional individuals predominate in an organization, as in a school, close supervision is not only unnecessary but may tend to limit creativity and lessen a sense of personal responsibility.

As limitations in traditional concepts have become apparent, many school systems and universities have introduced modifications in structure while continuing to use the concepts for some purposes. Prescribed rules for action have generally been found to be less useful than the capacity to analyze the condition of an organization and to develop plans for action and structure based upon purposes and the existing situation. Although the traditional concepts are still useful in certain respects, modern organizational theory when utilized with administrative insight allows more flexibility and requires less reliance upon fixed and rigid patterns.

ORGANIZATIONAL THEORY

History

The many contributions which have been made over the centuries to our understanding of organization have resulted in more recent years in attempts to develop organizational theory. The history of these ideas is traced elsewhere,[9] and only a brief summary of these developments to place the present work in context is included here.

Administration was originally developed by practitioners and has only within the last century been studied scientifically. As administration developed, certain administrative practices were accepted by persons knowledgeable in the field. As these practices were utilized, however, people began to question whether they were actually the best available methods. Sometimes severe problems developed. Officers in the military began to wonder if there were better ways to

[9] For the history of organizational theory see Bertram M. Gross, *The Managing of Organizations. The Administrative Struggle* (New York: The Free Press of Glencoe, 1964), pp. 91–190. See also Albert Lepawsky, *Administration. The Art and Science of Organization and Management* (New York: Alfred A. Knopf, 1949), chap. 4. For the early development of administrative theory and practice in the federal government see Leonard D. White, *The Federalists. A Study in Administrative History* (New York: The Macmillan Company, 1948).

run the armed services. Businessmen began to consider whether there were methods of increasing production through better administration. Educators began to explore better ways to provide for education. Administrators in many fields began to search for better ways. Gradually, as it became clear that administrative practice always reflects a view of the nature of organizations, the field of organizational theory began to emerge.

A major effort to conceptualize organization was made by Max Weber around the turn of the century.[10] Weber believed that an organization can and should function as a single mechanism. This emphasis, which still permeates the thinking of most practitioners and some theorists in administration, tends to downgrade the importance of the human beings in an organization, thus leading to administrative practices which exploit rather than enhance the individual person. Weber also emphasized the importance of the form of organizational structure, and strongly advocated bureaucracy as the best form for expressing community decision in social action.

The major characteristics of bureaucracy were considered by Weber[11] to be:

1. Policies, rules, and regulations
2. Hierarchical authority
3. Files and records
4. Specialized training
5. Full working capacity commitment by officials
6. Specialized administrative competence

In 1911 Frederick W. Taylor published his pioneering work entitled *The Principles of Scientific Management.*[12] In this work Taylor effectively brought together for the first time two elements which had been developing largely separate from one another: 1) a *science* of industrial management; and 2) the *practice* of industrial management.[13] Taylor advocated that organizations should be operated scientifically. The best way to perform various tasks should be determined by management, and the workers should be trained scientifically. "Planning should be based on time studies and other data related to production, which are scientifically determined and systematically classified; it should be facilitated by standardization

---

[10] H. H. Gerth and C. Wright Mills, *From Max Weber: Essays in Sociology* (New York: Oxford University Press, 1946).

[11] *Ibid.*, pp. 196-204.

[12] Included along with other works in Frederick W. Taylor, *Scientific Management* (New York: Harper & Brothers, 1947).

[13] Raymond Villers, *Dynamic Management in Industry* (Englewood Cliffs, N.J.: Prentice-Hall, Inc., 1960), p. 13.

of tools, implements, and methods."[14] In this work the emphasis was upon the management of production, and the human dimension in administration was not understood.

Taylor's principles were subsequently applied to school administration by Bobbitt.[15] These principles helped to systematize school administration, but they also promoted its dehumanization.

Further contributions in the development of organizational theory were made by Henri Fayol, Luther Gulick, and Lyndall Urwick, who gave attention to the processes of administration. Their work culminated in a number of principles, including Gulick's well-known mnemonic device POSDCORB (*P*lanning, *O*rganizing, *S*taffing, *D*irecting, *C*oordinating, *R*eporting, *B*udgeting).

These early writings on the nature of organization and administration prepared the way for the work of Mary Parker Follett,[16] the first theorist with any real insight into human behavior in organization. Follett viewed organization as a dynamic system of human relationships in which *integration*, both between the individual and the organization, and among the various parts of an organization, is a prime requisite for a successful enterprise. The thrust of Follett's viewpoint is contained in the following quotation:[17]

> The chief function, the real service, of business [is] to give an opportunity for individual development through the better organization of human relationships. Several times lately I have seen business defined as production, the production of useful articles. . . . But the greatest usefulness of these articles consists in the fact that their manufacture makes possible those manifold, interweaving activities of men by which spiritual values are created. . . . The *process* of production is as important for the welfare of society as the *product* of production.

The work of Mary Parker Follett was supported empirically by the work of Elton Mayo and Fritz Roethlisberger, who studied conditions affecting production in the Hawthorne Plant of the Western Electric Company. This work showed that although wage incentives and working conditions played a part in affecting production, they

[14] *Ibid.*, p. 29.
[15] Franklin Bobbitt, "Some General Principles of Management Applied to the Problems of City School Systems," *The Supervision of City Schools.* Twelfth Yearbook of the National Society for the Study of Education, Part I (1913), pp. 7–96.
[16] Mary Parker Follett, *Creative Experience* (New York: Longmans, Green, 1924).
[17] Henry C. Metcalf and L. Urwick, eds., *Dynamic Administration: The Collected Papers of Mary Parker Follett* (New York: Harper & Brothers, Publishers, 1940), pp. 140–41. Reprinted by permission of Pitman Publishing Ltd., London.

were not as important to production as the mental attitude of the workers.[18] The working conditions were not as important as the reactions of the workers to the changes in working conditions. Mayo and Roethlisberger also called attention to the importance of groups and their effects upon individual behavior.

The writings of Mary Parker Follett and the empirical work of Mayo and Roethlisberger suggested that there are two dimensions in organization: the *task* dimension and the *human* dimension. These two dimensions have been recognized by many writers beginning with Follett and continuing up to the present. In a classic work entitled *The Functions of the Executive*, Barnard developed the concepts of effectiveness and efficiency. According to Barnard, effectiveness relates to the achievement of organizational goals, and efficiency relates to the satisfaction of individual motives.[19] Barnard emphasized also the importance of both the formal and informal organizations.

Writing about the same time as Barnard, Roethlisberger and Dickson provided a similar emphasis. Their viewpoint was that[20] "an industrial organization may be regarded as performing two major functions, that of producing a product and that of creating and distributing satisfactions among the individual members of the organization."

Thus human behavior has come to be recognized as a major dimension of organizations. If an organization emphasizes production without consideration of the human beings, both the organization and the people in it will suffer a loss.

Recent Theory, Concepts, and Models

More recent theorists have for the most part continued to elaborate on the two concepts introduced by Follett, Barnard, and Roethlisberger and Dickson; that is, modern theorists writing about organization have emphasized the importance of *both production and human considerations*. There is a consensus among a number of leading writers in the field that the production and the human considerations are the two major factors which need to be taken into account in any study of organization. While not all organizational

---

[18] Elton Mayo, *The Human Problems of an Industrial Civilization* (Boston: Graduate School of Business Administration, Harvard University, 1933), p. 70.

[19] Chester I. Barnard, *The Functions of the Executive* (Cambridge, Mass.: Harvard University Press, 1938), pp. 55–61.

[20] F. J. Roethlisberger and William J. Dickson, *Management and the Worker* (Cambridge, Mass.: Harvard University Press, 1939), p. 552.

theorists use these two concepts, many theories are an exposition or variation of the production and human dimensions. Thus the Getzels-Guba-Thelen model, though it has been elaborated to place organizations in their societal context, includes the nomothetic (or legislative) and the idiographic (or idea) dimensions.[21] The writings of Chris Argyris[22] evidence concern over the conflict between the purposes of the *organization* and those of the *individual.* Argyris holds[23] that the organizational emphasis upon rationality tends to suppress the individual's emotionality, "penalize openness, levelling, and experimentation on the interpersonal and emotional levels," and thus tends to "decrease interpersonal competence within the organization."

The Tavistock conceptualization of organization as a socio-technical system also emphasizes the production and human dimensions in organization. In addition, considerable emphasis is given to the concept of the primary task. In order to be successful, Rice argues, an organization must achieve its primary tasks and mission. The primary task is the task which an institution has been created and developed to perform. The term "primary task" was originally meant to be exclusive because it was thought that an institution could have only one primary task. Reconsideration led Rice to the conclusion that some organizations, such as teaching hospitals and prisons, may have more than one primary task. A plurality of primary tasks, however, may lead to confusion over priorities and hence to conflict within an organization. "The mission is the overall objective. It includes all the tasks that are essential for survival, however many, and whatever their priority."[24] Work is essential to any living organism. If an organization is effective, work will be a source of social and psychological satisfaction. The Tavistock conceptualization[25] suggests that any organization or unit within an organization constitutes a system combining technology (task requirements, physical facilities, and materials) and a social system (including the people with their motivations, needs, roles, and interpersonal relationships). The nature of an organization results from an interplay among all these factors.

[21] See Chapter 3.

[22] Chris Argyris, *Interpersonal Competence and Organizational Effectiveness* (Homewood, Ill.: The Dorsey Press, Inc., 1962). Chris Argyris, *Integrating the Individual and the Organization* (New York: John Wiley & Sons, Inc., 1964).

[23] Chris Argyris, "On Consulting," in *Interpersonal Dynamics, Essays and Readings on Human Interaction,* eds. Warren G. Bennis and others (Homewood, Ill.: The Dorsey Press, 1964), p. 701.

[24] A. K. Rice, *The Enterprise and Its Environment. A System Theory of Management Organization* (London: Tavistock Publications, 1963), pp. 185-86.

[25] E. L. Trist and others, *Organizational Choice* (London: Tavistock Publications, 1963), p. 5ff.

As another example, the Blake-Mouton Grid Ⓡ,[26] designed to assist in the understanding of executive behavior, takes account of these same major dimensions — production and people. The grid consists of a square, with the horizontal dimension representing concern for production and the vertical scale representing concern for people. The behavior of an executive can be characterized by appropriate placement on the grid. An executive with high concern for production but low concern for people would be 9,1 on the grid; low

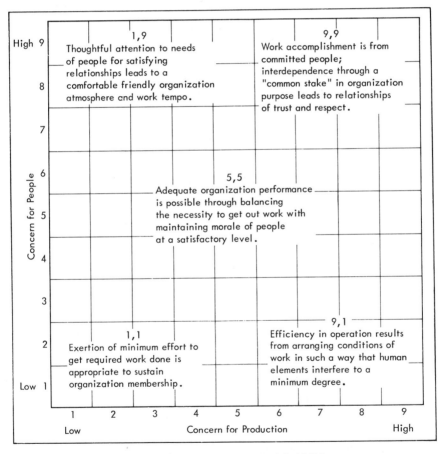

The Blake-Mouton Managerial Grid Ⓡ*

[26] The Managerial Grid figure from *The Managerial Grid*, by Robert R. Blake and Jane Srygley Mouton. (Houston: Gulf Publishing Company, copyright © 1964), page 10. Reproduced with permission.

concern for production and high concern for people would be 1,9; high concern for both production and people would be 9,9; and medium concern for both production and people would be 5,5.

With the recognition that human behavior is an important dimension in organization have come attempts at clarification of this dimension. A major contribution was made by McGregor, who identified two different sets of assumptions about human behavior which affect managerial decisions and actions, labelling them Theory X and Theory Y.[27] McGregor does not argue that these are the only possible assumptions which relate to organization, but rather that they are *"examples* of two among many managerial cosmologies."[28]

According to McGregor, Theory X represents "The Traditional View of Direction and Control," while Theory Y represents "The Integration of Individual and Organizational Goals." The assumptions which constitute Theory X, according to McGregor,[29] "are implicit in most of the literature of organization and in much current managerial policy and practice." Some of the more pervasive of these assumptions are identified below:

1. The average human being has an inherent dislike of work and will avoid it if he can.
2. Because of this human characteristic of dislike of work, most people must be coerced, controlled, directed, threatened with punishment to get them to put forth adequate effort toward the achievement of organizational objectives.
3. The average human being prefers to be directed, wishes to avoid responsibility, has relatively little ambition, wants security above all.

In contrast to Theory X, McGregor points out[30] that "the accumulation of knowledge about human behavior in many specialized fields has made possible the formulation of a number of generalizations which provide a modest beginning for new theory with respect to the management of human resources." These generalizations, which McGregor calls Theory Y, are as follows:

1. The expenditure of physical and mental effort in work is as natural as play or rest.
2. External control and the threat of punishment are not the only means for bringing about effort toward organizational objectives. Man will exer-

---

[27] Douglas McGregor, *The Human Side of Enterprise* (New York: McGraw-Hill Book Company, 1960).
[28] Douglas McGregor, *The Professional Manager*, eds. Caroline McGregor and Warren G. Bennis (New York: McGraw-Hill Book Company, 1967), p. 79.
[29] McGregor, *The Human Side*, pp. 33–34.
[30] *Ibid.*, pp. 47–48.

cise self-direction and self-control in the service of objectives to which he is committed.

3. Commitment to objectives is a function of the rewards associated with their achievement.

4. The average human being learns, under proper conditions, not only to accept but to seek responsibility.

5. The capacity to exercise a relatively high degree of imagination, ingenuity, and creativity in the solution of organizational problems is widely, not narrowly, distributed in the population.

6. Under the conditions of modern industrial life, the intellectual potentialities of the average human being are only partially utilized.

McGregor goes on to say that:[31]

The central principle which derives from Theory Y is that of integration: The creation of conditions such that the members of the organization can achieve their own goals *best* by directing their efforts toward the success of the enterprise. . . . The assumptions of Theory Y imply that unless integration is achieved *the organization will suffer.*

McGregor's Theory X and Theory Y can readily be applied to educational organizations. In fact, with the simple substitution of a few words, the statements are directly applicable to schools.[32]

Although the modern theorists who have been reviewed emphasize the dimensions of *production* and *people*, leading to more thorough consideration of each of these dimensions, the hallmark of modern organizational theory is its emphasis upon *system*, that is, upon the interrelatedness of the parts or subsystems of an organization, and its interrelatedness with subordinate systems. Recognition of this concept can be said to characterize current theory.

Of the various writers in the field, Likert is among those who have been particularly concerned with the concept of system. Although Likert is interested in practical problems rather than in theory *per se*, his emphasis upon system provides a theoretical orientation as illustrated in the following passage:[33]

The management system of an organization must have compatible component parts if it is to function effectively.

This conclusion has a very important implication: experiments in organizations must involve internally consistent changes. The traditional atomistic research design is not appropriate for experiments involving organizational

[31] *Ibid.*, pp. 49, 52.

[32] For details of a plan for business developed by Joseph Scanlon (the Scanlon Plan), consistent with the assumptions of Theory Y, see *Ibid.*, pp. 110-23.

[33] Rensis Likert, *The Human Organization: Its Management and Value* (New York: McGraw-Hill Book Company, 1967), p. 123.

theory or management systems. Every aspect of a managerial system is related to every other part and interacts with it. The results obtained by altering a single variable or procedure while keeping all others the same usually will yield quite different results from those obtained when the variable is changed along with simultaneous and compatible changes in all other aspects of the management system. The true influence of altering one aspect of the system cannot be determined by varying it and it alone. . . . *In experiments involving organizational theory and management systems, therefore, a systems approach must be used.* The organic integrity of each system must be maintained while experimental variations are being made.

Summary

Thus organizational theory has moved through three major stages. At first attention was paid only to the task, while the intricacies of human behavior were ignored. Next the human as well as the task dimension was recognized, and human behavior was explored as an important factor in organizations. Finally, the myriad interrelationships among people and tasks were acknowledged, and the systems viewpoint was increasingly accepted as a basis for organizational study and administrative practice.

IMPROVING ORGANIZATIONAL RELATIONSHIPS

Recognition of the human dimension in organization suggests that the problem of motivation with its concomitant problems is central to the life of an organization. If motivation is present, many other problems can be resolved. The assumption has generally been made in administration that people can be motivated from without — that it is possible for an administrator to motivate other people. This assumption has been refuted by scientific findings indicating that motivations come from within and cannot be imposed from without. If a staff is to be highly motivated, these scientific findings must be taken into account, and ways of helping individuals to identify and harness their motivations for organizational purposes must be utilized.

The human dimension suggests also that communication is essential to organizational effectiveness and that the procedures utilized in an organization should foster communication. If an organization can tap individual motivations, and if organizational procedures facilitate meaningful communication, an organization can meet many different situations effectively.

Motivation in Organizations

A considerable amount of research has been undertaken to identify those motivational factors which relate to job performance. Although the research results are controversial, they have practical implications that warrant attention.

Early studies by Herzberg found that satisfiers and dissatisfiers in organizations are not opposite ends of a continuum but rather are two separate and distinct groups of factors. Herzberg found[34] that "Five factors stand out as strong determiners of job satisfaction — *achievement, recognition, work itself, responsibility* and *advancement.*" On the other hand, "The major dissatisfiers were *company policy and administration, supervision, salary, interpersonal relations* and *working conditions.*" Herzberg pointed out that the satisfiers all seem to describe "man's relationship to what he does" whereas the dissatisfiers describe "the situation in which he does it."

Following Herzberg's lead, research was conducted by Sergiovanni[35] on "Factors Which Affect Satisfaction and Dissatisfaction of Teachers." In this study, three dominant factors were found to contribute to work satisfaction of teachers: achievement, recognition, and responsibility. The major factors contributing to dissatisfaction were: interpersonal relations with subordinates, interpersonal relations with peers, supervision-technical, school policy and administration, and personal life. Sergiovanni's findings were thus essentially consistent with Herzberg's, and the hypothesis that satisfiers and dissatisfiers tend to be a dichotomy was supported.[36] Similar findings for secondary school administrators were reported by Schmidt.[37]

Other research studies utilizing a variety of research methods failed to support the hypothesis that a satisfier-dissatisfier dichotomy exists.[38] In fact, Herzberg's own data, when reanalyzed, were found

[34] Frederick Herzberg, *Work and the Nature of Man* (New York: World Publishing Co., A Mentor Book, New American Library, 1966), pp. 92–94.

[35] Thomas J. Sergiovanni, "Factors Which Affect Satisfaction and Dissatisfaction of Teachers," in *Organizations and Human Behavior: Focus on Schools*, eds. Fred D. Carver and Thomas J. Sergiovanni (New York: McGraw-Hill Book Company, 1969), pp. 249–60.

[36] *Ibid.*, p. 257.

[37] Gene L. Schmidt, "Job Satisfaction Among Secondary School Administrators," *Educational Administration Quarterly*, 12, no. 2 (Spring 1976), 68–86.

[38] M. D. Dunnette, J. P. Campbell, and M. D. Hakel, "Factors Contributing to Job Satisfaction and Job Dissatisfaction in Six Occupational Groups," *Organizational Behavior and Human Performance*, 2, no. 2 (May 1967), 143–74. See also V. H. Vroom, "Some Observations Regarding Herzberg's Two-Factor Theory." Paper presented to American Psychological Association, Chicago, Ill., September 1–6, 1966.

not to support the hypothesis.[39] Yet Herzberg's conclusions seem to be consistent with other findings in the behavioral sciences which indicate the importance of intrinsic factors (those which come from work performance itself rather than those which are not inherent in the work) in effective personality functioning. Because Herzberg's conclusions appear to be supported indirectly by a large body of related evidence, they cannot be lightly dismissed.

Extending the previous line of research, studies of "need deficiency" of teachers and administrators were conducted by Sergiovanni and his associates.[40] The list of needs selected for study was the Lyman Porter modification of the Maslow needs hierarchy and included the following: Security, Social, Esteem, Autonomy, and Self-actualization. Some of the findings of these studies are: 1) individual teachers vary as to their unsatisfied needs; 2) in general, older teachers experience lower deficiency in need satisfaction, apparently because they are resigned to existing conditions and hence expect less; 3) the Security and Social needs of teachers are reasonably well met, but there is less satisfaction of the needs for Esteem, Autonomy, and Self-actualization; and 4) "the most pressing need of teachers is in the esteem area." Thus, "most of today's teachers will work harder for rewards at the esteem level than for other rewards."[41]

While most teachers' motivations are intrinsic to the work itself, there are some teachers whose motivations relate to the dissatisfiers. These people have been called "hygiene seekers" because they are strongly motivated to seek conditions which lead to preservation of health. Such teachers have been classified into three groups: 1) those who have potential for task motivation but are frustrated by the organization; 2) those whose intrinsic task motivations are satisfied outside the organization; and 3) those who do not have the potential for task motivation.[42] Of individuals with strong task motivation, two types have been identified by Hackman:[43] 1) *accomplishment seekers*, who are primarily interested in accomplishment, confidence, pride, and recognition; and 2) *responsibility seekers*, who are pri-

[39] Robert J. House and Lawrence A. Wigdor, "Herzberg's Dual-Factor Theory of Job Satisfaction and Motivation: A Review of the Evidence and a Criticism," *Personnel Psychology*, 20, no. 4 (Winter 1967), 369–89.

[40] Thomas J. Sergiovanni and Fred D. Carver, *The New School Executive. A Theory of Administration* (New York: Dodd, Mead & Company, 1973), pp. 56–67.

[41] *Ibid.*, pp. 62–63.

[42] *Ibid.*, p. 80.

[43] Ray Hackman, *The Motivational Working Adult* (New York: American Management Association, 1969), pp. 128–30.

marily interested in responsibility (supervising others) and personal growth.

Another individual whose early research supported and extended the findings of Herzberg is M. Scott Myers.[44] In a study of 1,344 managers at Texas Instruments, Myers[45] found that "highly motivated managers rather consistently characterize their superiors as persons who are approachable and open-minded, maintain high expectations, provide ready access to company information, encourage initiative and risk taking, help them learn from mistakes, and give credit for top performance." On the other hand,

> Poorly motivated managers, though less consistent in describing their supervisors, more often describe them in terms that match Theory X, or reductive supervision. Their supervisors are typically authority-oriented, not usually receptive to conflicting ideas from subordinates, tend to over-supervise and discourage initiative and risk taking, are intolerant of mistakes (particularly those that might embarrass them), are prone to look for someone to blame for mistakes, tend to overlook successes and stress failures.

The findings of Myers are useful because they point out that motivations tend to be related to the kinds of supervisory relationships experienced. They suggest that if a school superintendent develops good interpersonal relationships, the principals in the school system will tend to be more highly motivated; and if the principals develop good interpersonal relationships, the teachers will tend to be motivated. The interpersonal relationships which promote high motivation in a school organization are those which are work oriented and which free individuals to become self-actualized in their work. They are not ordinary social relationships but are those which enable an individual to grow and to do the best possible work, and which provide recognition for work well done.

The provision of desirable supervisory relationships is thus central to the task of educational administration. Motivation is necessary in order for an organization to be effective, and such motivation tends (at least at the managerial and professional levels) to be related to the kinds of supervisory relationships experienced. For a school administrator, the development of interpersonal relationships which enable the staff to become highly motivated toward organizational accomplishment can be a strong satisfier because such relationships are central to successful task performance in educational administration.

---

[44] M. Scott Myers, "Who Are Your Motivated Workers?" *Harvard Business Review*, 42, no. 1 (January–February 1964), 73–88.

[45] M. Scott Myers, "Conditions for Manager Motivation," *Harvard Business Review*, 44, no. 1 (January–February 1966), 58–71.

A slightly different approach from that of Herzberg was taken by David C. McClelland and John W. Atkinson, and a formal theory or model of motivation was developed by Atkinson.[46] As revised and extended, the Atkinson model takes account of three types of motivation based upon three types of needs: 1) need for achievement; 2) need for power; and 3) need for affiliation. The model assumes that motives are latent until aroused, and that once a motive is triggered by some characteristic in the situation, it releases energy for the purpose of satisfying a need.[47]

The Atkinson model has been set forth succinctly as follows:[48]

The Atkinson model holds that *aroused motivation* (to strive for a particular kind of satisfaction or goal) is a joint multiplicative function of (a) the *strength of the basic motive* [M], (b) the *expectancy* of attaining the goal [E], and (c) the *perceived incentive value* of the particular goal [I]. In other words, a person's aroused motivation to behave in a particular way is said to depend on the strength or readiness of his motives, and on two kinds of perceptions of the situation: his expectancies of goal-attainment and the incentive values he attaches to the goals presented. The model can be summarized as follows:

$$\text{Aroused Motivation} = M \times E \times I$$

Based upon the model and related research, Litwin and Stringer posit four critical elements in motivated performance of organizational members:[49]

1. The motives and needs the individuals bring to the situation;
2. The organizational tasks that must be performed;
3. The climate that characterizes the work situation; and
4. The personal strengths and limitations of the operating manager.

Particular emphasis is placed by Litwin and Stringer upon organizational climate as a factor in motivation. Climate is seen as affecting which worker motivations are aroused, and hence as being the mediating influence between task requirements and individual needs. Litwin and Stringer state[50] that "because climates can affect the

[46] John W. Atkinson, *An Introduction to Motivation* (Princeton, N.J.: D. Van Nostrand Company, Inc., 1964).

[47] George H. Litwin and Robert A. Stringer, Jr., *Motivation and Organizational Climate* (Boston: Division of Research, Graduate School of Business Administration, Harvard University, 1968), pp. 12-13.

[48] *Ibid.*, pp. 11-12. Based upon John W. Atkinson, "Motivational Determinants of Risk-Taking Behavior," in *A Theory of Achievement Motivation*, eds. John W. Atkinson and Norman T. Feather (New York: John Wiley & Sons, Inc., 1966), pp. 11-29.

[49] Litwin and Stringer, *Motivation and Organizational Climate*, p. 168.

[50] *Ibid.*, p. 169.

motivation of organization members, changes in certain climate properties could have immediate and profound effects on the motivated performance of all employees. . . . The *manager's leadership style is a critical determinant of organizational climate.*"

The various theories and research findings on motivation have led to emphasis upon job enrichment, that is, to delineating positions so that they provide opportunity for individuals to take initiative and to carry greater responsibility. Job enrichment involves the restructuring of positions so that they provide greater intrinsic satisfactions.

For example,[51] radios were being assembled by twelve women in a large plant on a production-line basis with each woman doing one small part of the assembly. Upon the recommendation of an industrial consultant (Chris Argyris), it was decided that each of the women "would assemble the total product in a manner of their (sic) own choice. At the same time they would inspect, sign their name to the product, pack it, and handle any correspondence involving complaints about it." Though production dropped at first, "By the end of the fifteenth week production was higher than it had ever been before. And this was without an inspector, packer, or industrial engineer. More important than increased productivity, costs due to errors and waste decreased 94 per cent; letters of complaint dropped 96 per cent."

Job enrichment for teachers necessitates opportunities for each teacher to perform roles which are deeply satisfying. Many teachers need opportunities to relate to individual students in some degree of depth. Although teacher specialization is necessary, especially at the secondary and college levels, such specialization may decrease motivation if it results in estrangement of the teacher and student. To be highly motivated, many teachers need to witness the impact of their work upon the lives of individual students. Some teachers want opportunities to pursue particular interests in order to develop a high level of expertise in some aspect of their teaching field. For such teachers, job enrichment means assigned responsibilities which legitimize and encourage such growth.

Differentiated staffing in a particular situation may contribute either to job enrichment or job impoverishment. If a teacher is limited to specific duties such as giving lectures and constructing tests, differentiated staffing can result in job stultification. On the other hand, differentiated staffing can lead to job enrichment if teacher interests are taken into account.

The concept of job enrichment suggests that in central-office as

[51] Paul Hersey and Kenneth H. Blanchard, *Management of Organizational Behavior* (Englewood Cliffs, N.J.: Prentice-Hall, Inc., 1969), p. 45.

well as school roles, the motivations of the individual need to be acknowledged. When individuals are expected to perform only a small part of a complete task, the loss in motivation may more than offset possible gains derived from specialization of function.

Setting Goals

Any organization has both official and operative goals. The official goals are those which appear in writing and which have been formally adopted. Official goals may be stated for the school system as a whole, for some part of the school system, or for a particular program. Operative goals, on the other hand, are seldom stated but can be inferred from organizational activities. The best way to discern operative goals is to examine the decisions made by the top-ranking administrators, particularly those concerning the use of organizational resources.

The official goals of school systems usually concern learning on the part of the children. Yet the pressures which some teachers and administrators bring to bear on children suggest that their operative goals are to turn children into quiet and obeisant automatons who will not think for themselves either in the school or in the society at large. The actions of some administrators suggest that the goal is to make financial profits on athletic teams to the neglect of educational considerations. In resisting court orders, some school systems seem to have as operating goals a demonstration of their own power and denial of the constitutional rights of minority groups. To be effective, an administrator needs to be realistically aware of both official and operative goals.

If an organization is to survive, its goals must be consistent with its primary task or mission. An organization cannot survive if it fails to take into account the societal needs which call for its services. Schools must therefore identify and respond to the needs of students and the larger society if they are to continue as a viable institution.

One of the major problems of motivation in a school organization is the conflict which so often occurs between the goals of an individual and those of the organization. Such conflicts are inevitable as organizational members try both to maintain their individuality and to be part of an educational enterprise in which the goals are formulated at least to some extent by someone else. For an educational organization to be most effective, individual and organizational goals need to be improved through interaction with each other. While organizational goals must necessarily be consistent with the organization's primary task, they can often accommodate the individual's goals as well. Conversely, individual goals can often be tailored so as to contribute also to the goals of an organization. Some of the most effective schools are those in which each teacher follows his own interests and does things his own way. Unless such individual activities are integrated with the goals of the school as a whole, however, a school's efforts tend to become diffused, with the result that major educational purposes are neglected.

For many years the need for organizational consistency was presumably met through the line-and-staff organization. Goals were set by those at the top of the organizational hierarchy, and orders were then passed down the line to obtain action directed toward achievement of the goals. The major difficulty with attempts to achieve consistency through commands, especially in dealing with professionals, is that an individual who is not committed to a goal will often ignore the goal completely or at best give it lip service or half-hearted allegiance.

A more recent concept of management control through goals has been called management by objectives (MBO) or management by objectives and results (MBO/R, an admittedly redundant term).[52] This method seeks to provide management control through commitment to objectives for the organization as a whole and for parts of the organization. Since objectives can provide the discipline which is necessary for consistent action, detailed direction for each individual becomes unnecessary. Policies may still be necessary, but detailed rules and regulations can be minimized if there is a genuine commitment to objectives.

Management by objectives has been dehumanizing when the objectives emanated from the top of the organizational hierarchy and were then used for appraisal purposes. However, management by objectives can provide for improved organizational effectiveness and greater self-actualization of individuals if: 1) individual staff members and staff groups are involved in formulating objectives at various levels in the organization; 2) the administrator recognizes that absolute consistency and coherence in objectives are not essential; 3) the staff (including the administrator) recognizes that creativity often emerges from confusion; and 4) the staff members (including the administrator) trust one another to act in good faith.

Goals need to be developed at three levels:

1. Goals for the organization as a whole
2. Goals for each unit in the organization
3. Goals for each individual

[52] Stephen J. Knezevich, *Management by Objectives and Results* (Arlington, Va.: American Association of School Administrators, 1973). Peter F. Drucker, *Managing for Results* (New York: Harper & Row, Publishers, 1964). G. S. Odiorne, *Management by Objectives. A System of Managerial Leadership* (New York: Pitman Publishing Corp., 1965).

These three types of goals can develop simultaneously since each should influence the others. Any written statements should be reviewed periodically and modified. Goal setting should, where possible, resolve tensions between the goals of the individual and those of the organization, and where such resolution is not possible, should attempt to strike a balance between organizational and individual goals so that neither seriously detracts from the legitimate goals of the other.

Some of the processes which may be used in goal setting follow.

1. The Group Conference

Of the participatory methods of goal setting, the most traditional is the group conference or meeting. Using the discussion method, the group deliberately works out a logical statement of goals and subgoals. In such meetings, a combination of informal and parliamentary procedures is often used.

2. The Confrontation Meeting

The confrontation meeting, designed by Beckhard,[53] is a special type of group conference designed to utilize individual needs and goals in identifying organizational problems and priority actions. The total management group from all levels of an organization may be involved. The meeting may run for a day or longer. Based on Beckhard's experience as a management consultant, a sample design and schedule for the meetings have been developed.

3. The Objective-Strategy-Tactics System

A system was developed at Texas Instruments that requires a yearly review of the annual goals of individual managers in relation to ten-year goals of the business areas of the corporation. Over one hundred managers convene for this review of their goals by peers and officers of the company. Selected strategies and programs are also presented monthly to the office of the president or a vice-president who is usually several organizational levels above the person reporting. This procedure allows for interchange relative to goals between executives at different hierarchical levels, provides top-level executives with firsthand information on specific projects and programs, and provides recognition and incentive to the project directors.[54]

---

[53] Richard Beckhard, "The Confrontation Meeting," *Harvard Business Review*, 45, no. 2 (March-April 1967), 149-55.
[54] M. Scott Myers, *Every Employee a Manager. More Meaningful Work Through Job Enrichment* (New York: McGraw-Hill Book Company, 1970), pp. 50-52.

4. The School of the Future

A technique used by Paul Mort was to suggest that staff members plan a school in terms of what they think schools will be like at some specific time (about ten or fifteen years in the future).[55] Such a school would then be planned, constructed, and put into operation, the assumption being that the innovations in the school would spread to surrounding schools. In a sense, the operation of the innovative school was expected to sharpen the goals of other nearby schools. A variation of the school of the future concerns room design. Teachers are asked first to visualize the room or space in which they would like to work, and second, to state what they would like to accomplish that they are not doing now.

5. Contrasts

Teachers or other staff are asked to develop lists of contrasts. For each item describing the school or organization as it now is, a contrasting statement is listed indicating how the individual would like it to be. When grouped in categories, the contrasts readily lend themselves to the formulation of specific objectives.

6. Questionnaires

Questionnaires can be used to elicit the thinking of individuals about goals, and the results from the total group can then be disseminated to the individuals as a basis for another round of responses or for group deliberation. For example, in order to formulate goals for an inservice education program, a questionnaire might ask teachers if they have difficulty with any one of a half dozen human relations problems, such as teaching an underachieving or overaggressive child, and request that they add other problems from their experience. The list from the total group can then be referred to the individual group members so that each may add problems to the total list and rate the importance of each item in the list. The resulting list can again be referred to the individuals for final rating. The final list of items and ratings can readily be transformed by a planning group into a list of goals and objectives for the program.[56]

---

[55] Paul R. Mort, "Studies in Educational Innovation from the Institute of Administrative Research: An Overview," in *Innovation in Education*, ed. Matthew B. Miles (New York: Teachers College Press, Teachers College, Columbia University, 1964), pp. 317-28.

[56] For a description of use of the Delphi method in goal formulation see Richard A. Schmuck and Philip J. Runkel, *Handbook of Organization Development in Schools* (Palo Alto, Cal.: National Press Books, 1972), pp. 115-16. Barry M. Richman and Richard N. Farmer, *Leadership, Goals, and Power in Higher Education* (San Francisco: Jossey-Bass Publishers, 1974), pp. 317-19.

7. Individual Conferences

Individual conferences relative to goals may be undertaken at any time. The purposes of such conferences are: 1) to provide the individual and the administrator with a clear conception of the *individual's* goals; 2) to provide for a discussion between the individual and the administrator of *organizational* goals; and 3) to explore relationships between the individual's and the organization's goals. Formal individual conferences are not necessary if adequate communication concerning goals takes place between individuals and the administrator in the conduct of the regular organizational activities. Unfortunately, many administrators know little about the professional goals of individuals in the organization and thus promote organizational goals which tend to stifle individual initiative.

8. Peer Evaluation

Periodic evaluation (perhaps once every five years) by a committee of two or three peers can be effective if such evaluation is desired by the staff and if the purpose of the evaluation is to help each staff member to clarify his or her goals and to grow in the capacity to attain them. An evaluative report by colleagues to an administrator implies operative goals more closely related to staff appraisal than to staff growth. Peer evaluation can be counterproductive when the official goal is to promote the professional growth of faculty members but the operative goal is to provide an appraisal of the competence of individual faculty members for the administration. However, peer evaluation can be helpful if the procedures are consistent with a stated purpose of individual goal clarification and professional growth.

Decision Making

Democratic values imply that persons who are affected by a decision will be consulted. This idea is a logical corollary of the Revolutionary motto: No taxation without representation.

In a school system, the right to participate in decision making has not only an ethical basis but yields practical advantages as well. The people who are affected by a decision know best what the needs are and to what extent the existing policies have been effective in meeting them. They are closest to the situation and know or can find out about existing conditions. Because they are affected, they have a special stake (which sometimes becomes a vested interest) in seeing to it that the decision will not affect them or their interests adversely.

Participatory decision making may be expected to result in better decisions because the thinking of a number of people is brought to bear on a problem.[57] Moreover, when people are involved in making a decision, they are more likely to implement it effectively, and the increased understanding resulting from participatory involvement helps to unify the group or organization. Participatory procedures help to integrate the goals of an individual with those of the organization. When wisely used, participatory decision making can be a means for individual growth, not only in terms of the substantive problems under discussion, but also in terms of self-functioning, group process skills, and leadership competence. Perhaps the greatest value of participatory decision making is the sense of power which it conveys to individuals. Participants need not feel helpless with respect to organizational policy, but instead can utilize policy making as another area for self-actualization.

Research findings in general support the desirability of participatory decision making. Findings have shown that individuals lose interest in problem solving unless they participate actively;[58] that *group decision* as a component of group discussion brings about considerable behavioral change whereas *group discussion* as such brings about very little change;[59] that participatory decision making reduces resistance to change;[60] that groups can continue to function effectively despite the loss of the status leaders if leadership has been shared with the members of the group;[61] that participatory supervision is associated with higher task motivation and job satisfaction;[62] that group interaction often leads to greater risk taking on the part of the group members;[63] that group decision reinforces in the be-

[57] For some research evidence on this point, see Donald L. Piper, "Decision-making: Decisions Made by Individuals vs. Those Made by Group Consensus or Group Participation," *Educational Administration Quarterly*, 10, no. 2 (Spring 1974), 82-95.

[58] Harold J. Leavitt, "Unhuman Organizations," *Harvard Business Review*, 40, no. 4 (July–August 1962), 90-98.

[59] Kurt Lewin, "Group Decision and Social Change," in *Readings in Social Psychology*, eds. T. M. Newcomb and E. L. Hartley (New York: Holt and Co., 1947), pp. 330-44.

[60] Lester Coch and John R. P. French, Jr., "Overcoming Resistance to Change," in *Group Dynamics: Research and Theory*, 3rd ed., eds. Dorwin Cartwright and Alvin Zander (New York: Harper & Row, Publishers, 1968), pp. 336-50. Harold J. Leavitt, "Unhuman Organizations," pp. 90-98.

[61] M. Dean Havron and Joseph E. McGrath, "The Contribution of the Leader to the Effectiveness of Small Military Groups," in *Leadership and Interpersonal Behavior*, eds. Luigi Petrullo and Bernard M. Bass (New York: Holt, Rinehart & Winston, Inc., 1961), pp. 167-78.

[62] Floyd C. Mann, Bernard P. Indik, and Victor H. Vroom, *The Productivity of Work Groups* (Ann Arbor, Mich.: Survey Research Center, Institute for Social Research, University of Michigan, 1963).

[63] M. A. Wallach and N. Kogan, "The Roles of Information, Discussion, and Consensus in Group Risk Taking," *Journal of Experimental and Social Psychology*, 1 (1965), 1-19. J. A. F. Stoner, "A Comparison of Individual and

ɔf group members the values which are commonly accepted in ture;[64] and that decisional participation is a major factor influ-, teacher satisfaction.[65] Research has found that an increased a decision making for individuals and groups results in increased activity, in greater self-actualization, and in greater satisfaction higher management and the organization. It was found also that eases in the role of upper management in decision making can in-ase productivity, but only at the cost of increases in dissatisfac-ɪn and turnover of personnel.[66]

Somewhat different findings were obtained in the research of Alutto and Belasco.[67] They were able to identify three decisional states of teachers: deprivation (teachers who desire more participation), equilibrium (teachers who want no change in current rate of participation), and saturation (teachers who desire less participation). It was found that young men teaching in secondary schools in rural areas felt most deprived in terms of decisional participation, and that these same teachers "reported the highest levels of role conflict and the most favorable attitudes toward such militant activities as collective bargaining, strikes, and unions."[68] Older women teaching at elementary levels in urban areas tended to experience the greatest decisional saturation.

The research findings as a whole seem to indicate that participatory decision making is highly desirable, but that the structure for such decision making should be flexible enough to allow for varying rates of participation.

Because of the importance of participatory decision making, a school system should create an organization for policy development as well as policy execution. Such an organization implies policy-making bodies at various levels including the school system as a whole, the various schools, and individual departments. These bodies

---

Group Decisions Involving Risk" (unpublished Master's thesis, School of Industrial Management, Massachusetts Institute of Technology, 1961).

[64] F. Nordhoy, "Group Interaction in Decision-Making Under Risk" (unpublished Master's thesis, School of Industrial Management, Massachusetts Institute of Technology, 1962). A. I. Teger and D. G. Pruitt, "Components of Group Risk Taking," *Journal of Experimental Social Psychology*, 3 (1967), 189-205.

[65] James A Belasco and Joseph A. Alutto, "Decisional Participation and Teacher Satisfaction," *Educational Administration Quarterly*, 8, no. 1 (Winter 1972), 44-58.

[66] Nancy C. Morse and Everett Reimer, "The Experimental Change of a Major Organizational Variable," *Journal of Abnormal and Social Psychology*, 52 (1956), 120-29.

[67] Joseph A. Alutto and James A. Belasco, "Patterns of Teacher Participation in School System Decision Making," *Educational Administration Quarterly*, 9, no. 1 (Winter 1973), 27-41. See also Belasco and Alutto, "Decisional Participation," pp. 44-58.

[68] Alutto and Belasco, "Patterns of Teacher Participation," p. 38.

may include all the members of a given group or may include elected staff members, student representatives, and some administrators *ex officio*. For some policy-making purposes, the line-and-staff organization represents a natural grouping. However, not all needs are related to specific parts of an organization. Thus, in addition to the line-and-staff organization, there are needs for large group meetings, interdepartmental committees, student-faculty-parent groups, committees with members from different hierarchical levels in the organization, and other groups. Groups such as these should be provided for through planned organization.

The specific structure which will be developed to provide for decision making will doubtless be related to a school system's history, purposes, and personnel. The less traditional a school system, the more the line-and-staff organization for decision making will be supplemented by other decision-making groups representing various parts and hierarchical levels of the organization.

Regardless of other factors, the structure should be appropriate for the functions to be performed. Function implies structure. Furthermore, available evidence suggests that the conditions for effective problem solving vary with the task at hand and that problem solving is affected by many variables.[69] In addition, there is strong evidence to indicate that different types of tasks call for different types of organizational structure.[70]

Like so many aspects of organizational life, participatory staff action which is good in itself may be poorly administered. Too much emphasis is sometimes given in participatory plans to providing representation of all groups which could possibly have an interest in a policy, with the result that the policy-forming group is too large to function effectively and an excessive expenditure of staff time is involved. In some staffs, committees are appointed as a means of postponing decision making. In others, the motivations for effective decision making may be real, but the cost in staff time is prohibitive.

Because the evidence suggests that group problem solving may take as much as eight times longer than individual problem solving,[71] and because it seems to indicate also that individuals are more interested in having opportunities for participation available rather than in actual participation itself,[72] smaller decision-making groups with

[69] Leavitt, "Unhuman Organizations," pp. 90–98.

[70] Peter M. Blau and Richard Scott, *Formal Organizations* (San Francisco: Chandler Publishing Co., 1962), chap. 5.

[71] V. H. Vroom and L. D. Grant, "The Consequences of Social Interaction in Group Problem Solving," *Organizational Behavior and Human Performance*, 4, no. 1 (1969), 77–95.

[72] L. R. Hoffman and N. R. F. Maier, *The Use of Group Decision to Resolve a Problem of Fairness* (Ann Arbor, Mich.: Willow Run Laboratories, University of Michigan, 1959).

channels of communication to other persons who are or might be interested are often useful. "Organizations will always require meetings," says Drucker,[73]

> ... because the knowledge and experience needed in specific situations are never available in one head; they have to be pieced together out of the knowledge and experience of several people. But whenever a time log shows the fatty degeneration of meetings—wherever, for instance, people find themselves in meetings a quarter of the time or more—the system needs to be corrected.

Drucker suggests that every administrator ask himself:

> (a) *What am I doing that really does not need to be done at all—by me or anyone else?*
> (b) *Which of the activities on my time log could be handled by somebody else just as well, if not better?*
> (c) *What do I do that wastes the time of others?*

A specific example is then cited as follows.

> The senior administrator of a large government agency learned from his subordinates that meetings in his office wasted a lot of their time. This man asked all his direct subordinates to every meeting—whatever the topic. As a result, the meetings were far too large. And because everyone felt that he had to "show interest," everybody asked at least one question—usually irrelevant. The meetings stretched on endlessly. The administrator had feared that any uninvited men would feel slighted, but when he found out that everyone felt the meetings a waste, he began sending out a printed form which reads:
> "I have asked (Messrs. Smith, Jones, and Robinson) to meet with me (Wednesday at 3:00), to discuss (next year's capital appropriations budget). Please come if you think that you need the information or want to take part in the discussion. In any event, you will immediately receive a full summary of the discussion and of any decisions reached, together with a request for your comments."
> Where formerly two dozen people met all afternoon, four men and a secretary now get the matter over with within an hour or so.

Because of considerations such as those mentioned by Drucker, it is often useful to think of groups as being of two types: representative and working. A *representative* group is useful as a means of involving other groups and organizations, to obtain a variety of viewpoints, and to disseminate information back to the individuals or to

---

[73] Adapted from pp. 44, 36–39 ("Organizations will always . . . within an hour or so") in *The Effective Executive* by Peter F. Drucker. Copyright © 1966, 1967 by Peter F. Drucker. Originally appeared in Harper's Magazine, and reprinted by permission of Harper & Row, Publishers, Inc.

the agencies represented. On the other hand, a *working* group is useful to get work done expeditiously. When new groups are initiated, they may be organized as either of the two types or a combination of both.

Competition and Conflict

If decision making is to be participatory in nature, competition and conflict will occur. Through the give and take of participation, competition becomes more open, and latent conflict becomes active.

It is important to an organization that the individuals and units in the organization vigorously propose their own programs and express their own particular perceptions. If all participants seek in their presentations to be concerned about the organization as a whole, much of the value of widespread participation is lost. The various problems and conditions in the different parts of an organization need to be taken into account in order that sound administrative decisions can be made. While individuals and units should be encouraged to present the case for their own programs, they should be encouraged also to recognize the need for decisions to be made in the interest of the organization as a whole.

Some administrators fear conflict and believe that it should be held to an absolute minimum. In fact in some instances, administrators have told their staff members that anyone who becomes involved in intrastaff conflict will be fired. Such administrators fail to realize that conflict, though sometimes destructive, is an essential aspect of constructive organizational behavior.

The Nature of Conflict

Contrary to popular opinion, conflict is necessary for the development of strong interpersonal relationships and hence for strong group loyalties.[74] Through conflict, interpersonal tensions and differences which otherwise would be continually expressed in indirect ways can be resolved. Such resolution increases mutual feelings of confidence and trust among the contending parties and provides greater confidence that future differences can be resolved successfully.

Conflict establishes conditions which may enable a group to modify its goals, values, norms, structures, programs, and procedures.

---

[74] While including my own thinking in this section, I have drawn freely from Lewis A. Coser, *The Functions of Social Conflict* (New York: The Free Press, 1956). See also E. B. McNeil, *The Nature of Human Conflict* (Englewood Cliffs, N.J.: Prentice-Hall, Inc., 1965).

Conflict is more readily tolerated when the contenders sense that they are committed to common purposes and that only their means differ. If group members can express to one another the idea that they are engaging in conflict not only to resolve a specific issue but for the more long-range purpose of strengthening interpersonal relationships, feelings sometimes become less intense and differences more easily resolved.

When there is conflict with an outside group, the identity and boundary lines of a group are clarified and strengthened. Whether the outside enemy is real or imagined, this kind of conflict promotes a group's cohesion. Group members tend to sense the common danger to them and their group and to realize that group unity provides the strongest defense.

Conflict is most intense when it arises out of close relationships. Thus conflict between two persons within a unit in an organization tends to be stronger than a similar conflict in an organization as a whole; and by the same token, two persons who are close to one another can develop an especially strong relationship if they learn how to resolve conflict between themselves. Conflict is especially great when one side is perceived by the other as threatening the integrity or survival of the group. Also conflict tends to be more intense when it occurs after a period of apparent harmony. In such situations, negative feelings as well as differences of opinion on various matters accumulate and the issue over which the conflict has developed tends to symbolize all the previously unexpressed differences and hostilities.

One must admit that conflict is sometimes dysfunctional and destructive. If a relationship has not been strengthened through resolution of prior conflicts, it is more vulnerable to disruption. Likewise, conflict which represents a desire to express rage or to get revenge rather than to achieve resolution of a social issue may lead to counterfeelings and increasingly irrational group action. A relationship is threatened if a conflict challenges the basic assumptions upon which the relationship is based.

When conflict with an outside group becomes intense and prolonged, a group tends to become more intolerant and to require more conformity within. Then the group is likely to invent or find a dissenter in its midst who becomes a scapegoat and an object for the rage and hostilities of the group members.

Undoubtedly, the society in general and organizations in particular will continue to experience frequent and intense conflicts. Conflict is inevitable in a period of changing values and may be expected to occur on many fronts. Such conflict may signal the end of our traditional institutions, at least as we have known them, or it may signal a transition to a fuller realization of our democratic ideals.

Conflict and the Administrator

In responding to conflict, administrators should continuously analyze the conflict to identify the real issues. The surface issues may be symbolic of more basic differences, may be used to accomplish hidden purposes, or may be a vehicle used by one or both sides to express hostility to the other.

On the basis of the analysis, administrators can then examine their own purposes to determine what they really want. If attacked or otherwise threatened, the administrator may be tempted to try to demolish the opposition. If the opposition are alienated, however, they may become implacable enemies who vigorously oppose the administrator on a variety of issues. The administrator may decide that what he or she really wants is not so much to annihilate the opposition or win on a specific point as to achieve educational goals and, if possible, to enlist the opposition over a period of time in helping to achieve them.

The capacity of an administrator to cope with conflict, including situations in which the administration is under attack, is related to the capacity to maintain open communication within the administrative team. Unanimity of opinion concerning what ought to be done is not essential, but open discussion of the situation and of strategies for coping with it can be a powerful instrument in conflict resolution. When feelings of resentment develop among the members of an administrative team with each blaming the others for what is happening, the capacity for creative approaches to the problem is sharply reduced, and the disarray of the team is frequently sensed by the opposition.

In any conflict, the various ideas and forces are constantly in flux. A position which at one time represented the middle ground may later become an extreme. The unwritten rules governing the combat may change. Individuals' perceptions of one another change, and people who have identified with one person may shift their allegiance to another. An administrator needs to obtain as much information as possible concerning what is happening and to develop strategies which enable the administrator to move with changing events. In being flexible in moving toward solutions, an administrator should not compromise personal integrity or values. An administrator needs to think about the possible reactions and strategies which may be employed by the opposition, and to develop a fallback position to which retreat is possible. The administrator needs to know what resources can be summoned to resolve the conflict and may sometimes find it useful to let the opposition know what power he can bring to bear in the situation.

In responding to conflict within an organization, whether in a conference or in some other form, an administrator needs to be active enough to maintain rational processes in the situation. The resolution of conflict is possible only when there can be rational discussion. The administrator needs also to utilize communication skills to insure that the people involved have an opportunity to express not only their ideas but also their feelings. The administrator should help adversaries to understand the position and feelings of their opponents and should, where possible, help the opposing individuals or groups to negotiate their own decisions. Finally, when faced with a judicial type of decision, the administrator should make what he or she considers to be the right decision rather than one designed to placate one side or the other in the controversy.

If conflict results in improved communication, it can be a constructive force resulting in improved solutions to organizational problems. On the other hand, if conflict results in poorer communication, with people becoming defensive and accusatory rather than really listening to one another, it can be a destructive force resulting in disruptions and violence. Whether conflict becomes constructive or destructive depends upon the human relationships involved. If a genuine effort is made by the schools to improve human relationships, the unrest and factionalism which pervade contemporary society may be turned to advantage in the educational process.[75]

CONCLUSION

In this chapter various aspects of organizational relationships have been considered. The nature of formal and informal organizations was discussed, and attention was then directed specifically to motivation in organizations, goal setting, decision making, and competition and conflict. One important aspect in all these matters, however, has been omitted from consideration. That aspect concerns role relationships, and to this matter we now turn our attention.

SUGGESTED READINGS

Ackoff, Russell L., *A Concept of Corporate Planning*. New York: Wiley-Interscience. A Division of John Wiley & Sons, Inc., 1970.

[75] Because societal conditions involve the school in relation to the community, these matters are considered in Chapter 9, "School-Community Relationships."

Argyris, Chris, *Integrating the Individual and the Organization.* New York: John Wiley & Sons, Inc., 1964.

——, *The Applicability of Organizational Sociology.* London: Cambridge University Press, 1972.

Behling, Orlando and Chester Schriesheim, *Organizational Behavior. Theory, Research, and Application,* chap. 8, "Organizational Purposes." Boston: Allyn and Bacon, Inc., 1976.

Etzioni, Amitai, *A Comparative Analysis of Complex Organizations. On Power, Involvement, and Their Correlates,* rev. and enlarged ed. New York: The Free Press, 1975.

Gross, Bertram M., *The Managing of Organizations. The Administrative Struggle,* chap. 5, "The Ancestors," chap. 6, "The Pioneers: The Gospel of Efficiency," chap. 7, "The Pioneers: New Beginnings." New York: The Free Press of Glencoe, 1964.

Hall, Richard H., *Organizations, Structure and Process.* Englewood Cliffs, N.J.: Prentice-Hall, Inc., 1972.

Harrison, E. Frank, *The Managerial Decision-Making Process.* Boston: Houghton Mifflin Company, 1975.

Katz, Daniel, "The Motivational Bases of Organizational Behavior," in *Organizational Behavior. Readings and Cases,* ed. Theodore T. Herbert. New York: Macmillan Publishing Co., Inc., 1976, pp. 121–42.

Likert, Rensis and Jane Gibson Likert, *New Ways of Managing Conflict.* New York: McGraw-Hill Book Company, 1976.

Lutz, Frank W. and Laurence Iannaccone, *Understanding Organizations: A Field Study Approach.* Columbus, Ohio: Charles E. Merrill Publishing Company, 1969.

Robbins, Stephen P., *Managing Organizational Conflict. A Nontraditional Approach.* Englewood Cliffs, N.J.: Prentice-Hall, Inc., 1974.

Sergiovanni, Thomas J. and Fred D. Carver, *The New School Executive. A Theory of Administration,* Part II, "The Human System." New York: Dodd, Mead & Company, 1973.

Simon, Herbert A., *Administrative Behavior. A Study of Decision-Making Processes in Administrative Organizations,* 3rd ed. New York: The Free Press, 1976.

Wynn, Richard, *Theory and Practice of the Administrative Team.* Washington, D.C.: National Association of Elementary School Principals, National Association of Secondary School Principals, American Association of School Administrators, and National School Public Relations Association, 1973.

ADMINISTRATIVE ROLES IN EDUCATION

7

Over the past quarter of a century a great deal of progress has been made in the development of role theory and research, and new role concepts, which help to explain behavior, have been developed. These concepts have important implications for enabling administrators to function more effectively.

CURRENT STATUS OF THE BODY OF KNOWLEDGE

The many hundreds of studies that have been conducted with reference to roles add up to an impressive body of knowledge. Research on roles has been conducted with reference to many occupational groups including the role of "the teacher, school administrator, school board member, school counselor, and pupil. . . ."; with reference to deviancy including "the juvenile delinquent, prisoner, drug addict, alcoholic, handicapped, the dying, and even the fool"; the family; role playing as a technique for training and therapy; and "processes such as learning and socialization. . . ."[1]

All this activity has resulted in a substantial body of research find-

[1] Bruce Biddle and Edwin J. Thomas, eds., *Role Theory: Concepts and Research* (New York: John Wiley & Sons, Inc., 1966), p. 14.

ings. As a consequence, "The concept of role is one of the central elements in sociological thinking."[2] Though the research literature in the field still consists of discrete research findings which have not been fully integrated into a comprehensive body of knowledge, and although the instrumentation in research studies on role is not always as sophisticated as would be desirable, the field of role is one of the most advanced among the behavioral sciences. As a consequence, role theory and research provide considerable information concerning administrative roles and promise to be a fruitful source for improving administrative practice.

This chapter will explain some role terms and concepts, suggest implications of some important research findings for administration, delineate different types of administrative roles, and interpret the impact of symbolic roles in administration.

SOME DEFINITIONS AND CLARIFICATIONS

The new role concepts have resulted in a somewhat technical language in which common terms are used in a special sense. While it is not our purpose to become deeply involved in the extensive terminology of role analysis, an understanding of a few basic terms and concepts is essential to a meaningful discussion of roles in organizations.[3]

Two companion terms, "position" and "role," describe two corresponding concepts.

Position

The first of these two concepts was originally identified by the term "status," which referred to the position of an individual in relation to other persons in a society. Although as a means of designating the status of a person's relationships to other people, the word "status" seemed entirely appropriate, it created difficulty because

---

[2] Alex Inkeles, "Sociological Theory in Relation to Social Psychological Variables," in *Theoretical Sociology: Perspectives and Developments*, eds. John C. McKinney and Edward A. Tiryakian (Englewood Cliffs, N.J.: Prentice-Hall, Inc., 1970), p. 412.

[3] For definitions of terms used most frequently in role analysis, see Neal Gross, Ward S. Mason, and Alexander W. McEachern, *Explorations in Role Analysis: Studies in the School Superintendency* (New York: John Wiley & Sons, Inc., 1958), p. 67. Primarily for persons becoming acquainted with role theory for the first time, Biddle and Thomas have developed a table with 18 terms, giving for each term both the Common Language Meanings and Selected Meanings in Role Theory. See Biddle and Thomas, *Role Theory*, pp. 10-12.

many people thought that "status" meant the extent to which an individual enjoyed *prestige*, whereas sociologists involved in the study of roles intended a broader meaning. As a result, the term "status" often confused matters and is now sometimes avoided in connection with role theory; instead, the word "position" has been suggested to designate "the location of an actor or class of actors in a system of social relationships."[4] Sometimes the words "niche" or "office" are also used.

Position may be either assigned or achieved. Whether position is assigned or achieved, however, it is indicative of a person's place or location in relationships to others. A person's position may be that of mother, son, middle child in the family, blind man, widow, church deacon, old man, baby, plaintiff, or referee. Some of these positions are high in prestige and some are low. Some relate to one kind of category and some to another. Yet all of these positions are indicative of relationships between and among people.

Role

The second of the two companion terms, "role," has undergone transformation of a different sort. "Role" is the behavioral equivalent of "position" and includes both behavior itself and the attitudes and values inherent in the behavior. A crossing guard who is directing traffic in order that children going to school may safely cross a busy street is in a *position* (i.e., crossing guard) which describes this individual's relationship to others. This position has implications for the individual's behavior or role. The crossing guard wears a uniform so that others recognize this person's authority to direct traffic. The guard does not hesitate to walk into the street to signal the cars to stop and the children to cross the street. Not only does the crossing guard know what a person in this position is supposed to do but everyone else who identifies the crossing guard expects this behavior.

However, the term "role" as defined by early authorities also created problems, for "role" seemed to imply that only one kind of behavior is appropriate for a person in a particular position, this behavior presumably being determined by society or by the culture. Later investigation revealed that disagreements often exist as to what is appropriate behavior in a particular position. In order that the concept of role may encompass the many differences of opinion, it has been suggested that "role" be defined as "a set of expectations

---

[4] Gross, Mason, and McEachern, *Explorations in Role Analysis*, p. 67.

applied to an incumbent of a particular position."[5] These expectations may be held by a wide variety of individuals, including the individual who occupies the position, and hence they invariably express differing perceptions and include disagreements concerning the desired behavior. Every role expectation has two dimensions: direction, that is, something should or should not be done; and intensity, that is, each expectation "can be placed somewhere on a continuum which ranges from the completely permissive, through the preferential, to the mandatory."[6] "A *role behavior* is an actual performance of an incumbent of a position which can be referred to as an expectation for an incumbent of that position."[7]

Thus, "position" and "role" express different concepts. An individual may have a *position* but may not understand what constitutes appropriate *role behavior* for the position. For example, a young teacher just out of college had a great deal of trouble with discipline. The whole class became so uncontrollable that a crisis developed. Later in discussing her problems, she said: "I tried everything to get them quieted down, but to no effect. I laughed with them, pleaded with them, scolded, became angry. I even cried. But nothing had any effect." This highly talented young woman had obtained the position of teacher but had to go through some very unhappy experiences before she learned appropriate role behavior. An individual newly appointed to the position of school superintendent made public statements indicating racial bias, failed to prepare reports requested by the board of education, and competed with the board president for public attention in the discussion of matters relating to the schools. This individual had assumed a *position* as school superintendent but had not fully assumed the *role*.

ROLE INTERRELATIONSHIPS

One of the major concepts in role theory is that roles are interrelated: a person's roles cannot be understood in isolation from the roles of others with whom the person relates. Thus roles constitute complementary and interlocking sets of behaviors. Behavior is an expression not only of an individual but of a social system as well. The concept of role interrelationships is thus an aspect of systems theory.[8]

[5] *Ibid.*, p. 67.
[6] *Ibid.*, p. 60.
[7] *Ibid.*, p. 67.
[8] See Chapter 3.

Role Systems

In a research study on roles with specific reference to the school superintendency, Gross, Mason, and McEachern concluded that three basic ideas are included in most role conceptualizations, namely, "that individuals: 1) in *social locations* 2) *behave* 3) with reference to *expectations.*"[9] Interrelationships among roles are emphasized as follows: "A position can be completely described only by describing the total system of positions and relationships of which it is a part. In other words, in a system of interdependent parts, a change in any relationship will have an effect on all other relationships, and the positions can be described only by the relationships."[10]

To designate a particular position under study or consideration Gross, Mason, and McEachern use the term *focal position*, and to designate another position related to a *focal position*, they use the term *counter position.*[11] Not only do relationships with the *focal position* need to be considered, but the interrelationships among the *counter positions* also are important in determining the behavior of the occupants of these positions and hence the behavior of the individual in the focal position. To make the situation still more complicated, the focal position may be involved in more than one system of interrelationships, so that two or more sets of counter positions may be included in relation to the focal position.[12] A school superintendent, for example, is typically involved in many systems, some of which are within the local community and some of which are not. A diagram representing some of these relationships is shown in the accompanying model.

The chart shows the school superintendent occupying the *focal position* in relation to some sets of *counter positions*. If an accurate analysis of a position is to be made, one must also take into account many situational factors.

Since positions are interrelated, the roles attached to them are interrelated. The behavior of an individual is not only affected by the expectations of others, but these expectations are largely an outgrowth of others' roles. If someone is already expected to perform a task, expectations that a third person will perform the task are diminished, and on the other hand, if a task perceived as being necessary has not been performed, expectations for someone to

---

[9] Gross, Mason, and McEachern, *Explorations in Role Analysis*, p. 17.
[10] *Ibid.*, p. 53.
[11] *Ibid.*, p. 51.
[12] *Ibid.*, pp. 51–55.

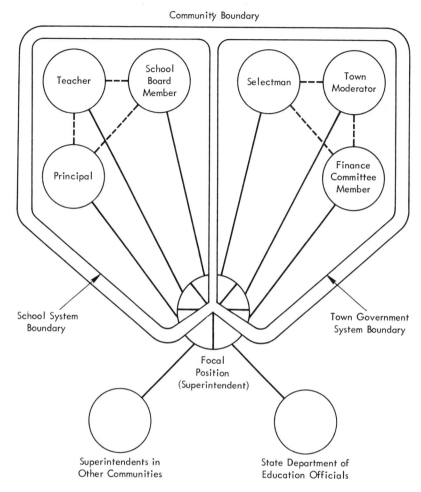

The Gross-Mason-McEachern Multiple Systems Model*

*Neal Gross, Ward S. Mason, and Alexander W. McEachern, *Explorations in Role Analysis: Studies in the School Superintendency,* p. 55.

perform the task will grow. Roles are not separate but are inter-related to create patterns or structures of interpersonal relationships.

The conception of roles as constituting multiple systems points up the power of administrators, for it suggests that a change in adminis-trative role behavior can have far-reaching implications. Different role behavior by an administrator calls for different role behavior on the part of persons in counter positions, and change on the part of these persons can in turn affect role behavior in the role systems of which they are part. The behavior of an administrator thus has a ripple effect, influencing most strongly the role behavior of persons with whom he associates most directly and intensively, and through these people, influencing in lesser degree the role behavior of others as well.

Multiple role theory suggests also that the needs which are evident in a situation are a powerful ally of the administrator in getting jobs done. If the need to have a task performed is evident, the social system will tend to respond by creating a readiness for task performance. In many instances the system will respond through action on the part of an individual or a group without any action on the part of the administrator. Because of role interrelationships, change in individual role behavior can persist only if other role behaviors in the system change also, and hence change efforts on the part of an administrator are usually more successful when they involve a group rather than separate individuals.

Role Complexity

As a social system becomes more complex, there is a corresponding increase in complexity in the positions, roles, and role systems which are necessary to that social system. In a simple society the number of roles to be performed is limited. Only a small number of occupations is needed, and hence the number of occupational roles is limited. Furthermore, the occupational roles in a simple society tend to specify the social roles. Thus, for example, a shoemaker in the Middle Ages knew not only that he was to make shoes, but also the kinds of behavior which would be expected of a shoemaker on social occasions.

In modern societies, however, roles constitute a highly complex phenomenon. Role complexity results from: 1) an increase in the number of different roles in a modern society, with the result that each person must perform many different roles; 2) a proliferation of the duties and behaviors attached to each role, to the extent that many times the individual in a position cannot possibly perform all the behaviors which may be implicit in a particular role; 3) constant change in purposes, methods, and relationships, so that behavior which met expectations in the past is no longer appropriate in the present; 4) ever-increasing differences in perceptions with resulting disagreements among both individuals and groups concerning the role expectations for an individual in a specific position; and 5) interrelationships between and among the various roles and role systems.

As roles proliferate, they tend to be assigned to different people, and the need for coordination of the various roles arises. The coordination of a complexity of roles is the executive function and defines the essence of the administrative role.

Role Conflict and Ambiguity

Empirical evidence indicates that an individual's roles may be activated intermittently, one after another, or sometimes simultaneously. An administrator may spend the morning in the role of superintendent, may at noon be in the role of service club member, may go home after work to the roles of spouse and parent, and on Sunday may assume the role of church member.[13] These and the many other roles of an individual may occur in some kind of sequence. On the other hand, an individual may perform several roles simultaneously. It has been found, for example, that the behavior of school board members may be affected by their church affiliation,[14] and it stands to reason that a school administrator's behavior may be affected by parental concerns and attitudes or by other roles, many of which may be outside the administrative position. Furthermore, an administrative position itself calls for a variety of roles such as those of supervisor, consultant, counselor, board representative, faculty representative, educational leader, financial officer, building planner and maintenance officer, and many others.

It is impossible to perform a variety of different administrative roles without the roles being at times in conflict. A school administrator is indeed "the man in the middle." Among other things, the administrative role requires that, on the one hand, administrators represent the governing board or their administrative superiors in carrying out school system policies and, on the other, that they represent the staff to their superiors in efforts to change existing policies and procedures; that they represent various concerned groups such as students, teachers, parents, and community groups to one another even though the concerns of one group may run counter to those of another; and that they keep the organization running smoothly while simultaneously upsetting its equanimity by promoting change. An administrative role represents many diverse needs and interests, and when these needs and interests are in conflict, role conflict for an administrator ensues.

Four different types of role conflict have been identified:

1. Interrole conflict — resulting from two or more conflicting roles
2. Intrasender conflict — resulting from conflicting role expectations from a single individual

---

[13] For a much more detailed and somewhat humorous example see Ralph Linton, *The Cultural Background of Personality* (Englewood Cliffs, N.J.: Prentice-Hall, Inc., 1945) reprinted in *Readings in Social Pscyhology*, rev. ed., eds. Guy E. Swanson, Theodore M. Newcomb, and Eugene L. Hartley (New York: Henry Holt and Co., 1952), p. 264.

[14] Gross, Mason, and McEachern, *Explorations in Role Analysis*, p. 323.

3. Intersender conflict — resulting when role expectations of some persons are in conflict with the role expectations of others

4. Person-role conflict — resulting when role requirements are not consistent with the values, interests, or beliefs of the individual in the role.

The first three types have been called *objective role conflict* because they exist in the objective environment, and the fourth may by called *subjective role conflict.*[15]

A problem of role ambiguity arises when the role expectations are not clear, that is, when individuals do not know what is expected of them or how their work is evaluated by their administrative superiors and others. Both role conflict and role ambiguity tend to result in "low job satisfaction, low confidence in the organization, and a high degree of job related tension."[16]

Some major studies relative to role conflict in educational administration have resulted in findings which provide some useful leads for administrative action. One of the most important studies concerns the role behavior of 105 Massachusetts school superintendents and their 508 school board members. This study, conducted by Gross, Mason, and McEachern,[17] found that school superintendents disagreed with school board members on all items concerning division of labor, and that the two groups disagreed on over half the items pertaining to superintendent performances, superintendent attributes, and school board performances. There was more agreement on the items concerning superintendent participations, and most agreement on superintendent friendships.

School board members and superintendents, in defining the division of responsibilities between their two positions, would each assign greater

---

[15] Daniel Katz and Robert L, Kahn, *The Social Psychology of Organizations* (New York: John Wiley & Sons, Inc., 1966. Reprinted by permission of John Wiley & Sons, Inc.), pp. 184–85.

[16] *Ibid.,* p. 190. For a "Theoretical Model of Factors Involved in Adjustment to Role Conflict and Ambiguity," see Robert L. Kahn and others, *Organizational Stress: Studies in Role Conflict and Ambiguity* (New York: John Wiley & Sons, Inc., 1964), p. 30. For a model which predicts the way in which a position incumbent will resolve role conflict, see Gross, Mason, and McEachern, *Explorations in Role Analysis,* pp. 300–301. For a test of the Gross-Mason-McEachern model, see Donald L. Sayan and W. W. Charters, Jr., "A Replication Among School Principals of the Gross Study of Role Conflict Resolution," *Educational Administration Quarterly,* 6, no. 2 (Spring 1970), 36–45. For an expansion of the Gross-Mason-McEachern model see G. Ritzer and H. M. Trice, *An Occupation in Conflict* (New York: W. F. Humphrey, 1969). For a study on role conflict resolution see Richard V. Hatley and Buddy R. Pennington, "Role Conflict Resolution of High School Principals," *Educational Administration Quarterly,* 11, no. 3 (Autumn 1975), 67–84.

[17] Gross, Mason, and McEachern, *Explorations in Role Analysis,* p. 116.

responsibility than the other to his own position. . . . School board members would be more likely than superintendents to accept by-passes of the superintendent, and superintendents more likely than school board members to accept by-passes of the school board.[18]

Of the 105 school superintendents, 91 percent perceived that they had been exposed to role conflict on budget recommendations, 88 percent on teacher salary recommendations, 71 percent on personnel hiring and promotion, and 53 percent on time allocation.[19]

A related study was conducted in a community in upstate New York to compare the perceptions of community residents with those of the teaching staff relative to control over decisions affecting the schools.[20] Disagreements between citizens and teachers were found concerning increased control over *economic issues* (money expenditures) by the community as opposed to increased control by the school staff, and final control over *administrative* decisions by the school board as opposed to control by the superintendent and other school administrators. Teachers believed that final control over *educational* issues should rest with the profession whereas community representatives were not in agreement on this matter. The Belasco-Alutto-Glassman study found a definite schism between the opinions of citizens and professionals concerning who *has* final control over school decisions and also who *should* exercise control over such decisions. The data indicate that there is potential for sharp conflict between citizen and teacher groups on issues relating to control. Citizens want greater control for themselves and the school board whereas teachers want more control for the professional staff. Since both citizens and professionals desire change in control over *educational* and *economic* (money) matters, these two areas appear to have the greatest potential for conflict.

In studying *Role Conflicts of School Principals*, Dodd found[21] that "secondary school principals were more exposed to conflict than elementary school principals for all sets of counter positions." At the elementary school level, "Men principals (as compared to women principals) reported more frequent exposure to conflict for all three sets of counter positions (teacher-parent, teacher-administra-

[18] *Ibid.*, pp. 141–42.
[19] *Ibid.*, p. 259.
[20] James A. Belasco, Joseph A. Alluto, and Alan Glassman, "School-Community Relations," in *Educational Administration and the Behavioral Sciences: A Systems Perspective*, eds. Mike M. Milstein and James A. Belasco (Boston: Allyn and Bacon, Inc., 1973), pp. 479–92.
[21] Peter C. Dodd, *Role Conflicts of School Principals*. Final Report No. 4, National Principalship Study (Cambridge, Mass.: Graduate School of Education, Harvard University, October, 1965), Chap. 9, pp. 4–5.

tor, and teacher-teacher conflict). Their reaction was more intense than that of women to teacher-parent conflict only."

A study of the role of the elementary school principal was conducted by Foskett and Wolcott in a single school district in a West Coast city.[22] When comparisons were made between the actual views of elementary principals concerning their role and the actual views of other groups, it was found that the superintendent and the school board members differed from the principals in their views even more than did the citizens, parents, and community leaders. Although principals believed that the superintendent's views would be closer to theirs than the views of any of the other groups, in actual fact the superintendent's views were farther than any other group from the views of the principals. The actual views of teachers were more closely in agreement with the actual views of principals than were those of any other group. In their perceptions of the views of others, the principals were least accurate with reference to the school superintendent. Their highest accuracy was in their perceptions of the views of teachers.

A study of role conflict experienced by department chairmen in a university system was conducted by Carroll.[23] Data were obtained for 148 of the 305 department chairmen in the seven university organizations making up the university system of the state of Florida. It was found that the type of role conflict experienced most frequently was perceived by the department chairmen to be intersender role conflict, that is, conflict resulting from incompatible expectations of the chairman's behavior on the part of two or more people. The greatest amount of role conflict was perceived in the areas of faculty salary decisions and faculty promotion decisions. In amount of role conflict perceived, these two areas ranked well above the other four areas, which in rank order were academic tenure, faculty hiring, departmental budget, and faculty time allocation.

Taken together these studies indicate that role conflict and ambiguity are both inevitable and pervasive. They are a phenomenon experienced by everyone and especially by administrators.

Role conflict and ambiguity are not necessarily evils, but they need to be considered and worked with or they can have destructive consequences. Numerous studies have found that they tend to be

---

[22] John M. Foskett and Harry F. Wolcott, "Self-Images and Community Images of the Elementary School Principal," *Educational Administration Quarterly*, 3, no. 2 (Spring 1967), 162–82.

[23] Archie B. Carroll, "Role Conflict in Academic Organizations: An Exploratory Examination of the Department Chairman's Experience," *Educational Administration Quarterly*, 10, no. 2 (Spring 1974), 51–64.

associated with low satisfaction and morale.[24] On the other hand, role conflict and ambiguity can allow behavior which would not be tolerated if roles were precisely defined, and they can provide a creative tension which stimulates new ideas and greater effort in an organization.

The complexities of the administrative role pose many problems which cannot easily be resolved. An understanding of role phenomena can be helpful in enabling an administrator at least to recognize the kinds of dilemmas he or she is facing. In addition to an understanding of the nature of role conflicts and ambiguities, an understanding of professional ethics provides an ethical basis for decision making, and familiarity with the code of ethics of the appropriate professional organization is a necessity for every administrator. Sound decisions on matters relating to role conflict and ambiguity call imperatively for administrators with a strong sense of self and respect for others. Such administrators are in the best position to arrive at workable solutions for the many role conflicts and ambiguities which are inherent in any administrative position.

Role conflict and ambiguity necessitate continual attention to the problem of role delineation, for if neglected, these conditions may precipitate a crisis. The goal in role delineation is to prevent conflict and ambiguity from becoming destructive and to use them in such a manner that they become a creative force. Open communication in which differences in perceptions are freely shared is essential if role conflict and ambiguity are to be constructively utilized. For example, an administrative team can be helpful to an administrator by discussing with him openly their disagreements with his conceptions of his role. To some extent roles can be clarified by administrative decisions that assign responsibility for specific tasks to specific people. In addition, administrators should continually explain their perceptions of their own and others' roles. When appropriate, they should invite others to state their own role perceptions. Occasionally a full-fledged analysis and revision of roles should be made,[25] perhaps but not necessarily involving a complete staff reorganization. The adoption of policies can enable an individual to make specific decisions in an impersonal way; when decisions relative to role conflict or ambiguity are made on the basis of policies, they are more impersonal and more likely to be accepted. It is often

---

[24] Katz and Kahn, *The Social Psychology of Organizations*, p. 190 (as cited earlier). Dodd, *Role Conflicts*, chap. 9, pp. 6-7. Carroll, "Role Conflict."

[25] For some practical procedures see Richard A. Schmuck and Philip J. Runkel, *Handbook of Organization Development in Schools* (Palo Alto, Cal.: National Press Books, 1972), pp. 157-60.

possible through policy-making or other types of meetings and conferences to bring together people with conflicting role expectations in a situation where the conflicting expectations can be aired. People can often learn from one another in such a situation and, if nothing else, can gain some understanding of the reasons why subsequent administrative decisions may not fully accommodate their viewpoints.

SOME ADMINISTRATIVE ROLES

Because interpersonal relationships are central to administration, the administrative roles involving interpersonal relationships warrant special attention. Any administrator may perform several such roles. In the field of education, these roles are usually subsumed under the term "supervision." Other terms such as "consultant," "helping teacher," "counselor," and "coordinator" are used also, but the differences in meaning which these terms designate are not always clear.

In a number of the professions such as medicine, clinical psychology, and social work, and in business and industry as well, several different terms are used to designate different types of helping roles. These other fields widely use three terms: consultation, counseling, and supervision. All three terms frequently but not always refer to a one-to-one relationship. All three relate to enterprises in which people are paid salaries and fees, to voluntary enterprises, and to relationships in private life. With the exception of consultation, which sometimes involves a single conference, the terms refer to relationships which develop over a rather extended period of time.

Consultation

Consultation is initiated by someone who seeks advice on a problem from someone else whom he or she considers to be an expert. The person seeking the advice may be designated as the "consultee," and the helping person as the "consultant." The consultee not only initiates but also terminates the relationship. The consultee may be a physician who wants the advice of another physician on a particularly difficult case, an administrator who needs advice on how to deal with an organizational problem, or a business head who calls in an efficiency expert to suggest how economies can be effected in production. As indicated earlier, a consultation relationship usually develops through time but might last for the duration of a single conference only.

Because a consultation is initiated to obtain advice, the consultee is free either to accept or to reject the suggestions and recommendations. The consultee has full control over what he or she will do.

It is important to note also that consultation implies no evaluation of the consultee. The individual's competence is not in question. A request for consultation does not indicate a weakness on the part of the consultee, but only a desire for an expert opinion in an area of specialty.

Individuals employed as full-time consultants are not easily placed in the administrative hierarchy of an organization. Normally they are located in a staff position outside the line of authority — they neither wield administrative authority nor evaluate those who do exercise it.

Counseling

As is true in consultation, so also in counseling the person seeking help both initiates and terminates the relationship. The persons in the counseling relationship are called the "counselee" (who seeks the help) and the "counselor" (who provides the help).

The counseling relationship is distinctive because it is initiated when an individual has a problem which is personal in nature: perhaps he strongly dislikes his supervisor; perhaps he dislikes his work hours or working conditions; perhaps he has a choice to make between his present position in the organization and another position. When counseling help is given within an organization, the problems for which an individual seeks help are ordinarily personal but nevertheless related to the work situation. Problems which go beyond the work situation can be dealt with elsewhere, but are usually not covered by the counseling services which an organization provides for its own staff.

In a counseling relationship, the counselee works out his or her own solutions. If suggestions or recommendations are offered by the counselor, the counselee is free to accept, reject, or modify them. An effective counselor, however, usually offers a minimum of advice, preferring instead to help the counselee identify relevant considerations which the counselee would otherwise be inclined to neglect.

In this type of relationship the counselee is not evaluated by the counselor, for the purpose of the relationship is to help the counselee to work out solutions which are acceptable to the counselee — not to someone else. Furthermore, the counselor must keep the discussions confidential if the counselee is to have complete freedom in discussing the problems at hand; otherwise the counselee may not mention pertinent facts out of fear that such revelations will result in repercussions from the counselor or will be exposed to others.

Although the counselee has the right to terminate the relationship

at any time, it is assumed that the relationship will not go on endlessly, and if the counselee does not move to terminate the relationship, the counselor may initiate a discussion resulting in a joint
decision to bring the relationship to a close.

Because the counselor does not seek to evaluate the counselee and
because the discussions must be kept confidential, the counselor does
not hold a line position (one with administrative authority) in the
organizational hierarchy.

Supervision

The word "supervision" is used by a number of the helping professions, and by many businesses and industries as well, to refer to
relationships in which one person has authority over another, that is,
to the usual boss-employee relationship.[26] These relationships are
explicit in the structure of an organization, and the supervisor's position can readily be identified on an organizational chart. The relationships continue through time and are not initiated or terminated
except when there is a change in the organizational structure.

Relationships of this type are required by the organization as a
means of achieving organizational goals. Supervisors are responsible
for the work done by each employee under their supervision, and it
is usually expected that the suggestions and recommendations of the
supervisor are to be carried out by the employee.

In this type of relationship, either the supervisor or the employee
may bring up problems related to the work situation. The decisions
which are made on these problems are made or approved (explicitly
or implicitly) by the supervisor.

Comparisons Among the Three Types
of Relationships

All three kinds of relationships are developed to deal with problems relating to the work situation and may continue through a
period of time. However, consultation and counseling relationships
develop on the initiative of the person to be helped, and focus on
the individual's needs or those of the organization as the individual
sees them. By way of contrast, supervision develops to help the
organization maintain control and focuses on the needs of the organization whether the individual being supervised is concerned about

---

[26] For a description of supervision as a boss-employee relationship see James
M. Black and Guy B. Ford, *Front-Line Management: A Guide to Effective
Supervisory Action* (New York: McGraw-Hill Book Company, 1963).

these needs or not. In the consultation and counseling relationships, there is no attempt to evaluate the person who is seeking help, but in a supervisory relationship, the supervisor evaluates the employee to assure that the work is being competently performed. There is a contrast also in the matter of decision making, for in the consultation and counseling relationships, the person asking for help continues to hold the full power of decision making whereas in the supervisory relationship, the power of decision making rests with the supervisor.

Differences among the three types of relationships exist, too, with reference to the intimacy of the two people involved in the relationship. The supervisory relationship involves the least intimacy, for discussion centers upon the needs of the organization with relatively little emphasis upon the perceptions of the individual employee. Next in intimacy is the consultant relationship, for this relationship centers upon needs which have been identified and felt by the consultee, even though these needs may also be needs of the organization. The counseling relationship is the most intimate, for here the discussion focuses specifically upon the needs and perceptions of the individual.

A somewhat different question is that of fraternization; whereas intimacy refers to the relationship during the hours specifically devoted to supervision, consultation, or counseling, fraternization refers to relationships not necessitated by the work situation. For the very reason that counseling is the most intimate relationship, it is least well adapted to fraternization, for as emotional involvement increases, the counselor loses objectivity and hence is of less use to the counselee. The supervisory relationship does not lend itself to fraternization because fraternization seems to imply equality, which is the very antithesis of supervision (in the sense in which the term is used here). The consultant relationship is best suited for fraternization because it assumes relative equality of the two persons, both in terms of prestige and of professional competence.

Implications for Educational Administration

All three types of relationships are needed in the administration of schools and school systems. In the past, the emphasis has been almost exclusively, in many schools and school systems, upon supervision. The other two types of relationships — consultation and counseling — have for the most part been neglected.

In recent years, there has been increasing recognition of the need to break away from old patterns of supervision. The emphasis of the profession upon democratic attitudes; the accumulation of research findings on the nature of human relationships; the experimentation which has characterized administration in some schools, industries, and agencies; and finally, the growing militancy of the teaching profession — these and other forces in society and the profession have led to a modification of the old patterns of supervision.

Use of the single term "supervision," however, has tended to confuse thinking in this area. Whether a single term or three different terms are used to refer to helping relationships is not as important as differentiating among the three kinds of relationships, for only as differentiations among the three are understood can the relationships be adequately provided for and practiced in an organization.

The three different types of roles, all of which need to be utilized in administration, require different types of administrative behavior and hence imply internal role conflicts.

These implicit role conflicts in the three types of relationships have led some organizations to provide three different types of positions. Administrators in these organizations are relieved largely of consultant and counseling roles through the provision of staff specifically for these functions. Such provisions can assist in making the various helping roles effectual. However, provisions of this type do not completely eliminate helping-role conflicts of administrators because all three roles are still needed by an administrator in interpersonal relationships. If administrators will learn the uses and skills of each of the helping roles and how to move readily from one role to another as necessary, they will be able to deal more effectively with the role conflicts involved and at the same time will be able to relate to others in more useful and helpful ways.

SYMBOLIC ROLES

Before leaving our consideration of roles, we should note that roles are experienced by everyone to greater or lesser degree in symbolic terms, that is, to the persons experiencing them, role behaviors represent something above and beyond the reality of the role itself.

Symbolism occurs when a present experience calls up feelings which relate to a past experience. This substitution is made because a person perceives some elements in the present situation that are associated with similar elements experienced in the past. As a result, an individual may react in terms of the past situation rather than in terms of the present. Feelings which were appropriate in a past situation tend to prompt behavior which relates to the past and which may not be appropriate in the present.

Because relationships in a family are emotionally intensive, family experiences often color later experiences outside the family. School phenomena symbolize to many people a family in which the administrator (at different times and in varying degrees) acts as head of the family. This image stirs up feelings — both positive and negative — which people had in their families, with the result that the feelings toward administrators and others are often stronger than is appropriate in relation to the facts of the situation. Although legal authority is conferred by legislative action or delegation, much of the psychological power of an administrator is derived from the fact of symbolic roles.

Administrators are thus not responsible for all feelings directed toward them. If such feelings are negative, administrators may want to examine their actions to see what they are contributing to the problem. Human relationship problems are usually created by the people on both sides. Yet administrators may discover that their actions are inherently a part of their role, and that their symbolic role rather than any specific behavior is responsible for the strong negative feelings of some people.

Occasionally, a woman administrator may be seen in a mother role, as was doubtless the case when a child who had just come home from his first day at school referred to the school principal as "that big mommy who owns the whole school and everything." Women administrators are often cast in a father role, however, and a woman cast in this symbolic role is expected to act as if she were a man.

Family symbolism is expressed in the prejudice of many people that only a man is fit to be principal of a school, especially of a secondary school, or to be a school superintendent, a state governor or president of the United States. Although the prejudice against women administrators is symptomatic of prejudice against the female sex, it goes deeper in that it is also an expression of symbolization of roles, which is to say that many people feel that it is only right and proper that a man should be the head of the family. As prejudice against women as a sex declines and as women increasingly share the role of executive and bread winner within the family unit, the role of mother will become more similar to the role of administrator, with the result that in the future women will be accepted more readily as administrators.[27] People will then *feel* that a woman administrator can function successfully.

When faculty members perceive a faculty group as a family, their

---

[27] For a research study concerning administrators by sex see Neal Gross and Anne Trask, *The Sex Factor and the Management of Schools* (New York: John Wiley & Sons, Inc., 1976).

feelings about faculty members and occurrences are considerably heightened. If the feelings tend to be positive, the faculty may be more cohesive and may work together effectively in order to delineate and move toward common goals. However, faculty members are likely to be highly sensitive to favoritism. The "promotion" from within a faculty group to an administrative position almost always stirs up strong positive and negative feelings which go beyond the reality of the situation and might be more appropriate in a family situation in which one of the siblings is promoted to the position of father. These loyalties, jealousies, resentments, and tensions, which stem from feelings related to family, profoundly affect the ways in which a faculty functions.

It is not unusual to observe an administrator who believes that his position gives him the right to make arbitrary decisions consonant with his own personal desires. He does favors for those who are part of *his* "family." Nepotism and favoritism, as has already been pointed out elsewhere, are the modern equivalent of hereditary privilege.[28] Actions such as these are sometimes engaged in by administrators who feel inadequate and therefore symbolically recreate the family unit as a means of affording themselves security and protection.

Not only are school administrators symbolized as parent figures, but many citizens see the whole school in symbolic terms as a parent figure. To them the school seems all-powerful, just as their parents once seemed all-powerful, and hence their feelings toward the school and its staff members, both individually and as a group, are likely to be stronger than is warranted by the observable facts in the immediate situation.

These symbolizing tendencies serve to heighten feelings in all aspects of school-community relationships and often lead to inappropriate behavior. A citizen may bitterly resent school taxes because, as a result of her childhood relationships with her own parents, she resents all organizations representing authority. A parent may feel that a school is not concerned about his child and may become belligerent or may be afraid to express his feelings because he himself felt unloved by his parents as a child.

Symbolization affects all relationships and must be taken into account if interpersonal relationships of any kind are to be understood. Symbolization heightens feelings; it emphasizes the human elements in any situation; and it increases the potential for good or evil in all human relationships.

[28] John W. Gardner, *Excellence. Can We Be Equal and Excellent Too?* (New York: Harper Colophon Books, Harper & Row, Publishers, 1961), pp. 5–10.

CONCLUSION

Role theory provides a useful way of conceptualizing human behavior. Each individual has a position in relation to others in society or in an organization, and the expectations which people hold for the behavior of an individual in a particular position delineate the person's role. Roles consitute complementary and interlocking sets of behavior, and an individual's roles are defined in relation to the positions and roles of others in the various systems of positions and relationships of which the individual is a part.

Administrators are often involved in role conflict and ambiguity, conditions which generally lead to low satisfaction. Role conflict and ambiguity, however, are not necessarily bad because they provide tension which is potentially creative. Administrators need to understand role conflict and ambiguity and learn how to utilize them to constructive ends.

In education, the administrative roles pertaining to interpersonal relationships are generally subsumed under the word "supervision." Yet there are different kinds of such roles which need to be performed. Unless these roles are differentiated, consultation and counseling tend to be neglected. Administrators need to be able to choose which of the roles they intend to activate at a particular time.

The concept of symbolization of roles helps to explain much human behavior which would otherwise be unintelligible. Because the symbolization of roles heightens feelings, it permeates administrative relationships whenever it occurs. It may be either a constructive or destructive force in a particular situation.

Related Questions

Although role theory and research findings and their implications for administration have been presented in this chapter, a number of questions relative to administrative roles remain unanswered. In subsequent chapters the following role-related questions are considered.

1. What is the role of a school administrator in improving school climate? What is a wholesome climate like? What are the major dysfunctions in interpersonal relationships which lead to unwholesome school climates?
2. What is the role of a school administrator in improving school-community relationships?
3. How can a school administrator fulfill the role of educational leader?

SUGGESTED READINGS

Berger, Peter L., *Invitation to Sociology: A Humanistic Perspective*, chap. 5, "Sociological Perspective — Society in Man." Garden City, N.Y.: Anchor Books, Doubleday & Company, Inc., 1963.

Biddle, Bruce J. and William J. Ellena, eds., *Contemporary Research on Teacher Effectiveness*. New York: Holt, Rinehart and Winston, Inc., 1964.

Biddle, Bruce J. and Edwin J. Thomas, eds., *Role Theory: Concepts and Research*. New York: John Wiley & Sons, Inc., 1966.

Borgatta, Edgar F., ed., *Social Psychology: Readings and Perspective*, Part 1, Sec. 7, "Roles and Reference Groups." Chicago: Rand McNally & Company, 1969.

Carkhuff, Robert R., *Helping and Human Relations. A Primer for Lay and Professional Helpers*, vols. 1 and 2. New York: Holt, Rinehart and Winston, Inc., 1969.

Combs, Arthur W., Donald L. Avila, and William W. Purkey, *Helping Relationships: Basic Concepts for the Helping Professions*. Boston: Allyn and Bacon, Inc., 1971.

Grace, Gerald R., *Role Conflict and the Teacher*. Boston: Routledge & Kegan Paul, 1972.

Gross, Neal, Ward S. Mason, and Alexander W. McEachern, *Explorations in Role Analysis: Studies in the School Superintendency*. New York: John Wiley & Sons, Inc., 1958.

House, Robert J., "Role Conflict and Multiple Authority in Complex Organizations," in *Organizational Behavior. Readings and Cases*, ed. Theodore T. Herbert. New York: Macmillan Publishing Co., Inc., 1976, pp. 216-28.

Johnson, David W., *The Social Psychology of Education*, chap. 3, "Role Theory, the Role of the Teacher, and Role Conflict," chap. 4, "The Role of the Student." New York: Holt, Rinehart and Winston, Inc., 1970.

Kahn, Robert L. and others, *Organizational Stress: Studies in Role Conflict and Ambiguity*. New York: John Wiley & Sons, Inc., 1964.

Katz, Daniel and Robert L. Kahn, *The Social Psychology of Organizations*, chap. 7, "The Taking of Organizational Roles." New York: John Wiley & Sons, Inc., 1966.

Orwell, George, "Shooting an Elephant," *Shooting an Elephant and*

Other Essays. New York: Harcourt, Brace & World, Inc., 1950, pp. 3-12.

"Role: Psychological Aspects; Sociological Aspects," *International Encyclopedia of the Social Sciencies*, 13, 546-57.

Sergiovanni, Thomas J. and Fred D. Carver, *The New School Executive: A Theory of Administration*, chap. 9, "School Executives and Role Relationships." New York: Dodd, Mead & Company, 1973.

Wolcott, Harry F., *The Man in the Principal's Office*. New York: Holt, Rinehart and Winston, Inc., 1973.

ORGANIZATIONAL CLIMATE

8

Many research findings point to the importance of interpersonal relationships in affecting an individual's development and behavior. These influences are often so subtle and pervasive, however, that they may be hard to identify. It is almost as if they were part of the atmosphere. To take such influences into account, a new construct was needed—that in any group or organization there exists a system of subtle and pervasive interpersonal affective relationships. Some word was needed to identify the new construct, and that word is "climate." Climate as used in an organizational context consists of the total affective system of a human group or organization, including feelings and attitudes toward the system, subsystems, superordinate systems, or other systems of persons, tasks, procedures, conceptualizations, or things. Climate thus refers to the relationships in any situation as these are affectively experienced by the people in the situation.

Variables which have been used to determine managerial effectiveness have never been able to account for much more than half of the variability in managerial effectiveness. The assumption is that what remains must be a function of the differences in environmental or situational characteristics.[1] The concept of climate encompasses such differences.

---

[1] John P. Campbell and others, *Managerial Behavior, Performance, and Effectiveness* (New York: McGraw-Hill Book Company, 1970), pp. 385-86.

170

Earlier (in Chapters 1 and 6) the importance of considering the *human* in relation to the *task* dimension was emphasized. It was stressed that one cannot be considered adequately except in relation to the other. In this chapter, special attention is devoted to one aspect of the human dimension — the organizational climate. As is pointed out both explicitly and implicitly from time to time, however, a wholesome climate is not simply one which helps individuals to feel secure; on the other hand, it is one which enables individuals to function effectively, that is, among other things, to perform work that needs to be done. In any specific situation, the organizational climate and task are inseparable; they permeate each other.

In this chapter consideration will be given first to the importance of school climate and the ways in which a school affects a child. The influence of administration on climate is then considered. Next attention is devoted to the status of organizational climate as it presently exists in the schools. The school as a feeling system and some types of interpersonal dysfunctions are then described. Finally, suggestions are made for improving organizational climate.

IMPORTANCE OF SCHOOL CLIMATE

The importance of the climate in a school can hardly be overstated, for the school's climate as it is experienced by each child has a powerful impact upon the formulation of a child's concept of self, his ability to work effectively, and his capacity to develop mutually satisfying relationships with others. Only the home has a more powerful impact upon a child's personality development, and in the case of some children, the school is the nearest approximation to a home that the child will ever experience.

The emotional climate is important to adults also, for although their personality structures are more fully developed and more stable than those of children, adults also are affected by their experiences. The difference between adults and children in this respect is only one of degree rather than kind. An adult's self-concept, work habits, and interpersonal relationships have developed over a considerable number of years, and hence an adult is not as readily affected by surrounding conditions as is a child. Nevertheless adults' personalities are affected by the daily events in their lives, especially by those which they experience as being emotionally intensive.

An individual's self and self-concept develop as a result of interpersonal relationships through time, especially those relationships experienced at an early age. The self consists of an individual's characteristic and potential mental processes and the meanings which the individual infers from experiencing the environment. An individual's self-concept consists of feelings and conceptions about self derived from relating the self to other persons, groups of persons, and physical objects and phenomena in the environment. Each individual self is unique, and each self acts as a selecting, organizing, and interpreting force, governing the individual's perceptions. An individual places a positive value on those experiences which enhance his self-concept. Some experiences are perceived, accepted, and organized into the self structure. Other aspects of the environment cannot be perceived with any reasonable degree of accuracy by the individual because they are inconsistent with his concept of self.

Because the self (including the self-concept) governs an individual's perceptions and hence affects his interpersonal relationships, an individual's self and his interpersonal relationships are inseparable. A person does not have a self plus interpersonal relationships with other people; instead a person's self and his interpersonal relationships are each implicit in the other. Implicit in a change in self is a change in interpersonal relationships, and implicit in a change in interpersonal relationships is a change in self. If a person can be integrated into a new system of interpersonal relationships, his self will inevitably change; and by the same token, if one person in a system changes as a self, the system and the other selves comprising it will necessarily change.

To the extent that a system is *emotionally intensive*, interpersonal relationships are part of the *core* of each individual *self*, that is, they are deeply locked into the individual's values, strengthening commitment to the values on the one hand and serving as a behavioral expression of the values on the other. A system which is not emotionally intensive is relatively easy to change, but change in such a system will not affect the selves of the people involved as deeply as will change in a more emotionally intensive system. Thus, interpersonal relationships in a small school faculty in which relationships are emotionally intensive can strengthen common values and thus significantly affect the behavior of the various faculty members. In contrast, interpersonal relationships in a large school in which such relationships are not as intensive emotionally will not affect the values as deeply and thus will have less effect upon individual behavior. A change in an emotionally intensive system is the more difficult but it is also the more significant for the individuals involved.

The importance of a strong self is one of the major findings in modern behavioral science. Self-concept is a permeating influence which affects all of a person's experiences, profoundly influencing his ability to function effectively, his competence in coping with life's problems, and his capacity for developing satisfying and productive relationships with others.[2] Research studies in general support the theoretical generalizations in this area. A number of research studies have found an empirical relationship between self acceptance and acceptance of others.[3] Studies support the belief that children's feelings about themselves are affected by their relationships with their parents.[4] Another finding is that there is a relationship between an individual's self concept and his or her achievement motivation[5] and goal-setting behavior.[6] Research has discovered a positive relationship between an individual's desire for change and the wishes of others concerning the individual's growth.[7]

---

[2] Rudolf Dreikurs, *Social Equality: The Challenge of Today* (Chicago: Henry Regnery Company, 1971). Don E. Hamachek, ed., *The Self in Growth, Teaching, and Learning* (Englewood Cliffs, N.J.: Prentice-Hall, Inc., 1965). Prescott Lecky, *Self-Consistency: A Theory of Personality* (Garden City, N.Y.: Anchor Books, Doubleday & Company, Inc., 1951. Anchor Books Edition, 1969). Erich Fromm, *Escape from Freedom* (New York: Rinehart & Company, Inc., 1941, 1969). Karen Horney, *New Ways in Psychoanalysis* (New York: W. W. Norton & Company, Inc., 1939). Harry Stack Sullivan, *Conceptions of Modern Psychiatry* (Washington, D.C.: The William Alanson White Psychiatric Foundation, 1947). A. H. Maslow, *Motivation and Personality*, 2nd ed. (New York: Harper & Row, Publishers, Inc., 1970). Carl R. Rogers, *On Becoming a Person* (Boston: Houghton Mifflin Company, 1961).

[3] K. T. Omwake, "The Relationship Between Acceptance of Self and Acceptance of Others Shown by Three Personality Inventories," *Journal of Consultant Psychology*, 18 (1954), 443-46. E. L. Phillips, "Attitudes Toward Self and Others: A Brief Questionnaire Report," *Journal of Consultant Psychology*, 15 (1951), 79-81. R. D. Trent, "The Relation Between Expressed Self-Acceptance and Expressed Attitudes Toward Negroes and Whites Among Negro Children," *Journal of Genetic Psychology*, 91 (1957), 25-31.

[4] J. B. Thomas, "A Study of the Self-Concepts of Pupils in Their Final Year at a Streamed Junior School" (Unpublished Master of Education dissertation, University of Wales, 1971). W. C. Washburn, "Patterns of Protective Attitudes in Relation to Differences in Self-Evaluation and Anxiety Level Amongst High-School Students," *California Journal of Educational Research*, 13, no. 2 (1962), 84-94. Gene R. Medinnus and Floyd J. Curtis, "The Relation Between Maternal Self-Acceptance and Child Acceptance," in *Readings in the Psychology of Parent-Child Relations*, ed. Gene R. Medinnus (New York: John Wiley & Sons, Inc., 1967), pp. 103-105.

[5] B. N. Mukherjee, "Some Characteristics of the Achievement-Oriented Person: Some Implications for the Teacher-Learning Process," *International Journal of Educational Sciences*, 3, no. 3 (1969), 209-16. J. G. Martire, "Relationship Between the Self Concept and Differences in the Strength and Generality of Achievement Motivation," *Journal of Personality*, 24 (1956), 364-75.

[6] I. D. Steiner, "Self-Perception and Goal-Setting Behavior," *Journal of Personality*, 25 (1957), 344-55.

[7] A. M. Crovetto, L. L. Fischer, and J. L. Boudreaux, *The Pre-School Child and His Self-Image* (New Orleans: Division of Instruction and Division of Pupil Personnel, New Orleans Public Schools, 1967). S. Rosen, G. Levinger, and R. Lippitt, "Desired Change in Self and Others as a Function of Resource Ownership," *Human Relations*, 13 (1960), 182-92.

HOW THE SCHOOL AFFECTS A CHILD

Although children are affected by all their experiences both in and outside of school, the people who directly affect them most in a school are undoubtedly their teacher (or teachers) and their peers. It is not surprising that when 110 seventh-grade boys and girls were asked in informal interviews to list the people significant in their personal lives and those significant in their academic lives, parents were named by nearly all the pupils, and teachers and peers were also named.[8]

While the principal does more than any other one person to create the climate of a school, the teacher more than any other person sets the climate in the classroom[9] and is the most significant person in the school experience of most children. To some extent all children experience the teacher as symbolizing a parent, and often the teacher's influence on a child is second only to that of the real parent with whom the child lives.

A number of studies specifically concern the child's self-concept in relation to the school. A statistically significant relationship has been found between pupil self-concept and organizational climate in the classroom.[10] Another finding is that "children's perception of their teachers' feelings toward them correlate positively and significantly with self-perception, . . . and the more positive the children's perception of their teachers' feelings, the better was their academic achievement and the more desirable their classroom behavior as rated by the teachers."[11] In addition, it has been found that a student's

[8] Wilbur Brookover, Ann Paterson, and Shailer Thomas, *The Relationship of Self Images to Achievement in Junior High School Subjects.* Cooperative Research Project No. 845 (Washington, D.C.: U.S. Office of Education, Department of Health, Education, and Welfare, 1962).

[9] For research evidence on this point see a summary of research conducted by H. H. Anderson and colleagues in Ned A. Flanders, "Some Relationships Among Teacher Influence, Pupil Attitudes, and Achievement," in *Contemporary Research on Teacher Effectiveness*, eds. Bruce J. Biddle and William J. Ellena (New York: Holt, Rinehart and Winston, Inc., 1964), pp. 196-231.

[10] Henry H. Wiesen, "An Investigation of Relationships Among Intelligence, Organizational Climate in the Classroom, and Self-Concept as a Learner Among Ten-and-Eleven-Year Olds" (unpublished Doctoral Project, University of Maryland, 1965). A similar finding, though not statistically significant, is reported by Franklin Pumphrey, "Relationships Between Teachers' Perceptions of Organizational Climate in Elementary Schools and Selected Variables Associated With Pupils" (unpublished Doctoral Project, University of Maryland, 1968). For a college-level study see Rebecca Vreeland, "Organizational Effects on Student Attitudes: A Study of the Harvard Houses," *Sociology of Education*, 38, no. 3 (Spring 1965) 233-50.

[11] Helen H. Davidson and Gerhard Lang, "Children's Perceptions of Their Teachers' Feelings Toward Them Related to Self-Perception, School Achieve-

self-concept of his own abilities is positively correlated with the image which he perceives as being held of him by significant others, that is, by mother, father, favorite teacher, and best friend.[12] Furthermore, it has been found that if children who have been selected purely by chance are identified for a teacher as being on the verge of marked intellectual growth, the prediction becomes self-fulfilling, that is, the children who are expected by a teacher to improve in intelligence usually do so even though they have been selected solely at random.[13] Another study found that a positive relationship between the child and the teacher is effective in the socialization of the child.[14] Numerous studies with similar findings have been reported in the professional literature.[15]

In summarizing research findings relative to "Desirable Behaviors of Teachers," Gage has written as follows:[16]

It seems safe to say that the teacher-pupil relationship in our society is such that warm teachers are more effective, by and large, in eliciting favorable attitudes from pupils. Social-psychological theory suggests that our tendencies toward consistency and homogeneity in our ideas, i.e., toward cognitive balance, push us toward liking someone whom we perceive as liking us. Pupils realize that the warm teacher likes them, and they tend to like him in return. And when they like him, they tend to identify with him, to adopt his values more readily, and even to learn subject matter from him more effectively. Whatever it may lack in surprise value, the finding that teacher warmth is desirable must be considered to be fairly well established.

---

ment and Behavior," *Journal of Experimental Education,* 29 (December 1960), 107-18.

[12] Wilbur B. Brookover and Shailer Thomas, "Self-Concept of Ability and School Achievement," *Sociology of Education,* 37 (Spring 1964), 271-78.

[13] Robert Rosenthal and Lenore Jacobson, *Pygmalion in the Classroom* (New York: Holt, Rinehart and Winston, Inc., 1968). For additional research on this problem see Jere Brophy and Thomas Good, "Teachers' Communication of Differential Expectations for Children's Classroom Performance," *Journal of Educational Psychology,* 61, no. 5 (1970), 365-74. Jeremy D. Finn, "Expectations and the Educational Environment," *Review of Educational Research,* 42, no. 3 (Summer 1972), 387-410.

[14] R. A. Schmuck and E. VanEgmond, "Sex Differences in Relationship of Interpersonal Perceptions to Academic Performance," *Psychology in the Schools,* 2 (1965), 32-40.

[15] See the series of articles on "A Key to Learning: Good Teacher-Student Relationship," *NEA Journal,* 57 (April 1968), 14-24. See also Herbert A. Thelen, *Classroom Grouping for Teachability* (New York: John Wiley & Sons, Inc., 1967).

[16] Nathan L. Gage, "Desirable Behavior of Teachers," in *Teachers for the Disadvantaged.* The Report of the School-University Teacher-Education Project of the Research Council of the Great Cities Program for School Improvement in Cooperation with Northwestern University, eds., Michael D. Usdan and Frederick Bertolaet (Chicago: Follett Publishing Co., 1966).

Teachers also have great influence on the kinds of experiences which children will have with their peers and on the meanings which they will attach to these experiences.

Some understanding of the many ways in which emotional climate affects children can be gleaned from the "Framework for Analyzing a Human Being" developed by Prescott and his associates on the basis of sixteen years of experience in studying school children. A thoughtful reading of the processes listed is suggestive of the many ways in which schools deeply affect the personality development of children. The headings which Prescott includes are listed below:[17]

1. Physical Factors and Processes
2. Love Relationships and Related Processes
3. Cultural Background and Socialization Processes
4. Peer-group Status and Processes
5. Self-developmental Factors and Processes
6. Self-adjustive Factors and Processes

Children are affected by the total environment of the school. They may relate not only to teachers but to other professionals such as counselor, principal, nurse, or curriculum coordinator. In many schools the custodian is a major influence. Sometimes the school secretary or cafeteria director will be a person of influence. Children may have a meaningful encounter with parents other than their own. Relationships with peers and the acceptance or rejection which a child experiences in such relationships, together with the feelings of adequacy or inadequacy which these events engender, affect a child deeply. As children attempt to maintain and enhance their self-respect in trying to cope with the school situation, their feelings about themselves are influenced by what they perceive others' feelings to be toward them.

Through all their relationships children develop perceptions relative to their own adequacy, and these are an outgrowth of their feelings concerning their acceptance or rejection by others. They develop feelings about themselves as individuals, about their capacity to achieve success, about their academic abilities, about their physical adequacy, about their own ethnic or cultural group, about the nation of which they are a part, about their capacity to win and perform in desired roles, about their ability to cope with difficult situations, about their ability to deal with strong personal feelings and frustrations. The climate includes all interpersonal relationships

---

[17] Daniel A. Prescott, *The Child in the Educative Process* (New York: McGraw-Hill Book Company, 1957), pp. 205-208.

in a school and affects every aspect of a child's development as a maturing person.

CLIMATE AND ADMINISTRATION

The school superintendent does more than any other single person to create the climate of the school system. Teachers tend to function effectively in an open climate in which ideas and feelings can be openly expressed, ideas are judged on their own worth rather than on the basis of who offered them, the staff as a whole works together rather than as small cliques or separate compartments of the organization, respect for individual personality is reflected in the professional behaviors of the organization, and zest for living is sensed in the atmosphere. Teachers tend to function less effectively in a closed or repressive climate. Thus, a research study on the role of the elementary school principal discovered a positive relationship between teachers' morale and teachers' professional performance.[18] Another study found that when school principals shared power with teachers, the teachers shared power with their students,[19] while a study of educational innovation "found that innovative (school) districts were more similar to the open climate than the closed. . . ."[20]

A major study in industry discovered that workers tend to develop the same kinds of relationships with others that they experience with their superiors in the organizational hierarchy. Thus, foremen who worked under supervisors who tended to be more considerate were generally found to be more considerate in attitudes and behavior toward the men working under them; and likewise, foremen who worked under supervisors who emphasized task-related matters tended themselves to score higher in their "structuring" attitudes and behavior. Even after a leadership training course, these tendencies were observable. The attitudes and behavior of the foremen were thus clearly influenced by the leadership climate which they themselves were experiencing.[21]

[18] Neal Gross and Robert E. Herriott, *Staff Leadership in the Public Schools* (New York: John Wiley & Sons, Inc., 1965).

[19] Ronald Bigelow, "Changing Classroom Climate Through Organization Development," in *Organization Development in Schools*, eds. Richard Schmuck and Matthew Miles (Palo Alto, Cal.: National Press Books, 1971), pp. 71–86.

[20] Larry W. Hughes, "'Organizational Climate'—Another Dimension to the Process of Innovation?" *Educational Administration Quarterly*, 4, no. 3 (Autumn 1968), 21.

[21] Edwin A. Fleishman, "Leadership Climate, Human Relations Training, and Supervisory Behavior," *Personnel Psychology*, 6, no. 2 (Summer 1953), 205–22.

A number of studies reported by House indicate that[22] "there is evidence that subordinates tend to: act as their superiors act, have attitudes similar to those of their superiors, and act in response to their perception of their superiors' desires." In a widely cited study, Sykes found[23] that although leadership training for ninety-seven supervisors resulted in the intended change in role expectations on the part of the trainees, the change eventuated in so much resentment toward senior management that, during the first year after the training program, nineteen supervisors resigned and an additional twenty-five were trying to move to other positions. When the supervisors refused to accept the attitudes of senior management, life in the organization apparently became intolerable for many of them. The organizational factors which result in human relations training having either functional or dysfunctional consequences are explained by House.[24]

In another study, important relationships were found to exist between an administrator's personality and administrative practices, communications patterns in the school, and the school's emotional atmosphere.[25] After conducting a research study centering on the use of simulated materials, Hemphill, Griffiths, and Fredericksen came to the conclusion that there are many relationships which doubtless exist between personality tendencies and performance variables.[26] A study by Wilhelms in experimental teacher education found[27] that "students learned mentally healthy ways to act because they were treated in mentally healthy ways. One becomes mentally healthy by experiencing mental health." Conversely, the administrator's limitations have been found to be reflected in the limitations of the school.[28]

[22] Robert J. House, "Leadership Training: Some Dysfunctional Consequences," *Administrative Science Quarterly*, 12, no. 4 (March 1968), 560-61.

[23] A. J. M. Sykes, "The Effect of a Supervisory Training Course in Changing Supervisors' Perceptions and Expections of the Role of Management," *Human Relations*, 15 (1962), 227-43.

[24] House, "Leadership Training," pp. 556-71.

[25] David H. Jenkins and Charles A. Blackman, *Antecedents and Effects of Administrative Behavior*. School-Community Development Study Monograph, No. 3 (Columbus, Ohio: The Ohio State University Press, 1956). Leonard Lee Murdy, "Perceptions of Interpersonal Relationships Among Secondary School Administrators" (Doctoral dissertation, University of Southern California, 1962).

[26] John K. Hemphill, Daniel E. Griffiths, and Norman Fredericksen, *Administrative Performance and Personality* (New York: Bureau of Publications, Teachers College, Columbia University, 1962).

[27] Fred T. Wilhelms, *Teacher Education and Mental Health*. Report of the Teacher Education Project Supported by Training Grant No. 2M-6625 from the National Institute of Mental Health. (August 1963).

[28] Winfield S. Christiansen, "The Influences of the Behavior of the Elementary School Principal Upon the School He Administers" (unpublished Doctoral Project, Stanford University, 1953).

In addition to evidence such as that just cited, the idea that an administrator and the climate which an administrator helps to create have profound effects upon the people in an organization is implicit in many behavioral science findings.

STATUS OF ORGANIZATIONAL CLIMATE

Both research evidence and direct observations provide a basis for asserting that in the public schools in the United States, the organizational climate generally leaves much to be desired. Pupils are often bossed, bored, berated, and belittled. In many schools and classrooms, guilt feelings are created and intensified, anxiety is increased, and disrespect of self is fostered. The United States probably has the finest school system ever created on a very large scale, yet the school experience of individual children is often unwholesome. The continued development of a vigorous and well-educated citizenry adequately equipped to deal with the problems of the times necessitates schools which are more humane institutions.

After being involved in two studies lasting six years in a large urban school system and four other systems, one observer developed the premise "that school bureaucracy infantilizes both students and staff from kindergarten through high school, from school secretary to superintendent." This observer adds: "The effects of this infantilization are disastrous whether one looks at them from the point of view of educational, psycho-dynamic, or socio-political goals."[29] The writer goes on to present "A Baker's Dozen of Examples," some of which follow.

A supervisor to a group of new elementary school teachers explains the methods and purpose of an arithmetic unit and ends asking, "Do you have any questions?" One young teacher speaks up. "I was confused about the presentation of fractions." She is pointedly ignored as silence reigns. "Anyone who has anything to say, raise hands and when addressing me, my name is Miss Paris."

A pre-school program for "culturally disadvantaged" *four*-year-olds is designed to make for greater success once the children get to kindergarten, come next fall — 15 minutes daily is devoted to making these four-year-olds sit quietly in their chairs at desks without getting up until a signal, whereupon they are taught to form a line. Grades are given for quiet sitting and neat line formation.

A teacher has set up a busy energetic room. Samples of everyone's work are gaily hung about. An art supervisor arrives and in front of the

[29] Ruth Newman, "The School: The Effects of an Institution in Infantilizing Students and Staff," mimeographed (Washington, D.C.: Washington School of Psychiatry, March 1967).

class she says to the teacher, "My, what an unattractive color scheme you have for your bulletin board, Miss L. Isn't it time you learned that one display looks better than all those papers? You certainly haven't read the manual for bulletin boards — when will you learn?"

A teacher after much struggle got a slow-learning class excited about an astronomy project. The children, all at least two years behind grade-level in reading, are busy making planets, labeling them and writing stories about them. At 10:15 the Principal enters. "Mrs. K. this is reading period, how can you deprive these children from their reading experience?" Mrs. K. tries to explain. "That is no excuse," the principal says in front of the class. "The plan requires reading from 10:00 to 10:30. I don't like to think of your rating next term — some people have no sense." The teacher flushes and says to her class, "Put the planets away, take out readers." Later to the consultant she says, "You know only two of them can read in the reader. But with the Amidon plan interpreted by a rule-following principal — able or not able they must use the readers if it's reading time. So readers it will be."

A boy who has done well in math has failed to hand in math homework for two weeks. He is sent to the counselor's office where, having sat for half the morning because the counselor has been busy, he finally sees her and explains he hasn't understood the math unit now going on so has been unable to do the work. "Did you ask Mrs. D?" "I asked her last week, and she says I should know — that I didn't listen. I told her I did listen and I still didn't get it. She said I must be stupid; other people got it." Tears — "I asked my Father — he didn't know either." More tears. "So I gave up, I'll get an F for the unit, I guess."

One teacher of a special class is found in her room rocking herself at her desk, holding her hand and staring at the clock. Her children are wide eyed, silent and sober. Trouble? She has slammed her finger in the desk drawer. She needs first-aid. She has been instructed by the principal not to leave this difficult class alone at any time. She has not sent for help because previous to the finger slamming incident, she has lost her temper at the class (which has something to do with slamming her finger). She has told her class that no one may budge from his seat for ten minutes. When consultant entered, six minutes of pain had passed.

Anyone who is familiar with schools can bring to mind many comparable examples. Perhaps most discouraging of all is the fact that in many classrooms, most of the children are bored, and order is maintained not through a lively absorption in learning, but rather through the authority of the teacher.

Although there has been no nationwide study of organizational climates in schools, a representative sample of seventy-one elementary schools in six different regions in the United States was studied by Halpin and Croft. On the basis of responses to a questionnaire by 1,151 respondents in these seventy-one schools, Halpin and Croft arrived at the categorizations shown in the following table.[30]

Since the Halpin-Croft study, there have been many research

[30] Andrew W. Halpin, *Theory and Research in Administration* (New York: The Macmillan Company, 1966), pp. 171–73.

Seventy-One Elementary Schools Categorized by Climate
As Measured by the Organizational Climate Description Questionnaire

Type of Organizational Climate		Number of Schools
Open		17
Autonomous		9
Controlled		12
Familiar		6
Paternal		12
Closed		15
	TOTAL	71

studies in which organizational climate was measured. Although one can only speculate as to the distribution of schools by climate types in the nation as a whole, these later studies confirm the finding that there is a wide range in school climates[31] and lead one to the conclusion that, while many schools have open climates, there are literally thousands of schools in the United States with closed organizational climates. There are thousands of schools in addition with climates which cannot accurately be characterized as being closed but which are far from being open. Thus, although the climate in some schools in the United States is wholesome, the climate in many schools is unwholesome in a number of respects. In every school the organizational climate can undoubtedly be improved. The many dropouts or perhaps more appropriately the many pushouts from the schools, the general boredom on the part of many students, the fact that many students can at most name no more than one really "good" teacher in their whole school experience, the discipline problems, the vandalism and defacing of school buildings, the use of grades and parental pressures "to get students to study," the sarcasm and derogation with which students are often treated — these are a few of the evidences for believing that the learning climate in schools needs to be markedly improved.

THE SCHOOL AS A FEELING SYSTEM

Organizational climate is usually measured in terms of the reported or observed behavior in a social system. To obtain an index of climate, a researcher usually attempts to measure the kinds of

---

[31] For example see unpublished Doctoral dissertations, University of Maryland, by Angeline G. Boisen (1966), Adrian DeWitt (1975), John G. Gist (1972), Joseph Grant (1973), Maynard E. Keadle (1976), Anthony G. Marchione (1972), Francis J. Masci (1975), Wallace K. Pond (1974), Franklin Pumphrey (1968), Robert F. Redmond (1975), Doris S. Sewell (1973), Richard Thomas (1975), and C. Monica Uhlhorn (1972).

relationships in an organization as they are expressed in specific behaviors. Behaviors lend themselves to assessment because they can readily be identified and to some extent measured.

Yet the climate or atmosphere in an organization is made up of the feelings of the people. Feelings are more fundamental to climate than behaviors but are far more difficult to measure. Behaviors are significant as a measure of climate simply because they are related to feelings. It is the feeling systems in which individuals are involved which constitute the group or organizational climate which they are currently experiencing.

A feeling system consists of patterns of feelings experienced by persons in a social system. The feelings of each person in such a system contribute to and result from the total feeling system. Thus the behavior of an individual with masochistic feelings is directed toward promoting actions by others which trigger and enable the individual to rationalize feelings of pain, humiliation, and suffering. Similarly, in the system as a whole, the myriad feelings experienced by various individuals in the feeling system result in behaviors which trigger and enable the various individuals to rationalize characteristic feelings.

Careful and sustained observation, together with a wealth of indirect empirical evidence, indicates that a school functions as a feeling system.[32] To the extent that feelings are present and are communicated, however indirectly or subtly, each group in a school becomes a feeling system. The feeling system in an individual classroom, especially when the children are with a single teacher for the entire school day, is relatively intensive as compared to the feeling system in a school. Because the various groups in a school are not separate and discrete but are joined together by overlapping memberships, the school as a whole is a feeling system which, except when feelings are aroused, is loosely knit and of relatively low emotional intensity. The kind of feeling system which comes into being results from the extent of acceptance or nonacceptance of the right of each individual to be an autonomous person with percep-

---

[32] See, for example, W. R. Bion, *Experiences in Groups* (New York: Basic Books, Inc., 1959). James L. Framo, ed., *Family Interaction. A Dialogue Between Family Researchers and Family Therapists* (New York: Springer Publishing Company, Inc., 1972). Harold Guetzkow, "Differentiation of Roles in Task-Oriented Groups," in *Group Dynamics: Research and Theory*, 3rd ed., eds. Dorwin Cartwright and Alvin Zander (New York: Harper & Row, Publishers, 1968), pp. 512-25. William G. Hollister, "The Risks of Freedom-Giving Group Leadership," *Mental Hygiene*, 41, no. 2 (April 1957), pp. 238-44. Theodore M. Newcomb, "Stabilities Underlying Changes in Personal Attraction," in Cartwright and Zander, *Group Dynamics*, pp. 547-56. A. K. Rice, *Learning for Leadership. Interpersonal and Group Relations* (London: Tavistock Publications, 1965).

tions, feelings, values, interests, and behaviors which are unique rather than prescribed by the norms of the group or enmeshed with the selves of the other group members.

Since emotional relationships are ordinarily of only moderate intensity in a school, there is some latitude in a school for the behavior of each individual. It seems clear, however, that faculty members are soon "typed" by their fellows, and various faculty members begin to play distinctive roles in the group. They adopt characteristic styles of behavior and levels of functioning. Various individuals compete for leadership roles, and a "pecking order" develops. Students also are soon "typed" by their fellows as they assume various roles and differing statuses.

A case of a faculty member who works in a small department will serve as an example. This faculty member is generally agreeable and pleasant. Upon meeting a colleague, he usually smiles and says something socially acceptable. Professionally he expresses himself freely within the limits of acceptable opinion tacitly agreed upon by the group. He feels free to wear unusual, nonconforming clothes, and often makes risque comments. In general among the faculty, he is adaptive to the behavior of others. It is significant that the nonconforming aspects of this individual's behavior are accepted by the group in the areas of dress and conversation. Let him try to change from his adaptive type of behavior or from a passive to a more active role with reference to professional matters, however, and the whole group becomes uneasy. If he persists in any genuine change, the group members make sarcastic remarks, avoid social relationships with him, and use whatever other pressures are necessary to get him to give up the change.

Initially, the feeling system in a school or classroom results from the behavior of individuals expressing their needs and feelings in a developing network of interpersonal relationships. Once a feeling system has developed, it powerfully conditions the behavior of the individuals who comprise it as well as that of individuals entering the system.

Children first develop characteristic patterns of functioning in the home. By the time they come to school, they have already learned ways of relating to other people. They will seek out other boys and girls with complementary behavioral patterns and will attempt intuitively to manipulate teachers to accommodate their characteristic functioning. A child who is used to vertical relationships in the home, to being dominated by or to dominating others, will seek out other children whose interpersonal relationships tend to be vertical in nature. A child who is overdependent at home will try to be dependent (or possibly overaggressive) in relation to the teacher.

On the other hand, a child who is respected at home as a person will typically seek to develop interpersonal relationships based upon mutual trust and respect.

It should be noted, however, that the behavior patterns of children in a school have not been permanently established by the family but can be greatly influenced by a competent teacher, especially if the teacher is supported by competent administration and supervision. For many children, the school is the only stable influence in their lives. For all children, the relationships in school are important.

The system of interpersonal relationships in a school is highly complex. The organization of the school necessitates the development of specialized positions such as teacher, principal, custodian, lunch room supervisor, nurse, and the like, and the assignment of specific roles to specific individuals. Many of these roles require professional preparation. The expectations which people have in relation to specific positions as compared to the actual performance of the individuals in these positions have much to do with their feelings toward one another. Conflict tends to be created to the extent that there is a discrepancy between role expectations and performance; if such conflict is not resolved through communication, it can lead to increasing tension throughout an organization.

Each person's feelings are part of a larger feeling system, and any change in one part of the feeling system affects all the other parts of the system. In an intense feeling system, some individuals become so involved in the feelings of others that they do their feeling for them, as when a child suffers a setback in the form of a low grade and a friend or a parent feels the disappointment. In a feeling system, the feelings of one person may be unconsciously transferred to another individual in the system, and functioning is affected accordingly.

Considerable evidence has accumulated to show that systems usually perpetuate rather than change an individual's level of functioning. The reason has already been indicated, namely, that individuals seek out roles and enter into interpersonal-relationship systems which enable them to perpetuate their own functional level and style.

A system typically develops an equilibrium in which the various roles, interrelationships, and functional level of the system are held constant. The system as a whole resists functional change. If one person in a system changes his level of functioning (that is, his level of self-actualization), the whole system mobilizes its resources to force the individual back to his former functional level. If the individual persists in a higher level of functioning, the system may eject him physically or psychologically. If group members believe that ejection of the individual is not feasible, the system will typically compensate through a lower level of functioning on the part of someone else in the system. Such compensation is a form of initial resistance to change in the system. When an individual can change his functional level and persist in the change despite the mobilization of pressures from the rest of the system, however, the system can change and the individual's functioning at a higher level will come to be accepted. Change in the functional level of a system can come about through change in the system's mission or purposes; changes in task delineation; changes in the system's external environment; the addition of new persons to the system or the loss of present members; or persistent change on the part of one individual, especially if the individual carries authority at the top of the system hierarchy. Functional level and feeling system are inseparable, and any significant change in functional level signifies a change in the feeling system.

The primary figure in the feeling system of a school is the administrator, and the surest way to change a feeling system in a school is through a change in the behavior of the principal. In addition to delegated authority, a principal symbolizes a parent figure to many children and staff, and thus has power to affect the school which goes far beyond actual delegated legal authority. By the same token a teacher is the primary figure in the feeling system of a classroom, with power to affect the feeling system in the classroom far beyond actual delegated authority. An individual teacher who is strong enough can develop a wholesome climate in a classroom even though the overall climate in the school is not wholesome. Because of the authority with which a school principal is endowed legally and psychologically, however, the emotional climate created by most teachers is affected by the climate in the school as a whole. It takes a rare teacher to feel joyous and energetic in a school in which the principal lacks respect for teachers and takes administrative actions which are generally upsetting to them.

SOME INTERPERSONAL DYSFUNCTIONS

Automatic response mechanisms come into play in all types of groups and organizations, and to the extent that they replace rational action, the feeling system in the particular group or organization tends to be dysfunctional. Automatic response phenomena can be observed when the same response to a particular behavior invariably occurs. They are expressed in a variety of administrative behaviors. In many schools and other organizations, administrators are not decisive; they typically procrastinate in making a decision and invariably appoint a committee as a means of deferring the decision indefinitely or of getting someone else to make it. The making of a decision creates anxiety, especially if the decision is negative, and many administrators prefer the temporary relief of anxiety to the greater relief which eventually results from resolving the problems. Situations which are the converse of the foregoing also occur. In such situations, through acting arbitrarily (i.e., giving the appearance of strength), through consistently providing resources to support some innovations but not adequately considering others, or through automatically giving subtle hints such as facial expressions, the administrator indicates the limits within which freedom of expression and self-actualization of staff members will be tolerated.

Although automatic response phenomena develop in varying degrees in all groups and organizations, a school is not functioning effectively if automatic responses characteristically replace considered action. Examples of automatic response phenomena in a faculty group are: 1) when a staff member presents a problem to an administrator, the administrator "automatically" responds by giving advice; 2) when hostility toward the administration is expressed, for whatever reason, the other faculty members "automatically" enter into the feeling of hostility and give it verbal expression; 3) when a problem arises, it is "automatically" referred to a committee, and the committee "automatically" is a large one; 4) when a particular faculty member who has sometimes demonstrated poor judgment speaks, he is "automatically" tuned out by the other faculty members; 5) when a particular individual tells a "joke," however lacking in humor, the whole group laughs; 6) when a clerical task is to be performed, the group gets a woman to do it; 7) when a major administrative post is to be filled, the group seeks a white man (not a black man or a woman) for the position. Many organizations will not tolerate open conflict even when it is directed toward the resolution of interpersonal and task-related problems. The fact that so-called democratic organizations sometimes turn out to be colorless, unimaginative, and frustrating to the persons involved, implies that such organizations are characterized by automatic response mechanisms. The problem is that, in a real sense, organizations of this type are not actually democratic.

In schools and other organizations which are functioning more effectively, automatic responses are less characteristic. The behavior in meeting problems in such organizations is characterized by spontaneity and ingenuity. Old patterns are not followed automatically. Divergent views are respected and considered. Each person feels free to express his or her own thoughts, and the climate is characterized by an ever-deepening level of communication, that is, by more and more open and appropriate expression of feeling-level and intuitive responses. In this type of school, conflict is utilized constructively because solutions which are effective over the long run are preferred to temporary relief from anxiety through customary responses.

Another type of feeling-system dysfunction occurs through the development of triangular relationships. The simplest type of triangular relationship exists when two persons conspire against rather than communicate with a third person in an attempt to resolve interpersonal problems; more complex variations of triangular relationships develop when several persons or a group occupy one of the positions in the triangle. Such relationships are represented by the following figures or possibly by a triangle with still more persons occupying point "A", "B", or "C".

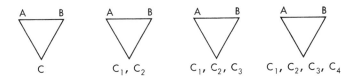

In each instance in the figures above, "A" represents the initiator of the dysfunctional configuration, "B" represents the person against whom the feeling system is being mobilized or in whom it is invested, and the others in each figure (designated by "C" with each subscript designating a different person) are those who are drawn into the emotional configuration by "A", that is, they are the ones to whom "A" expresses resentments or problems concerning "B". A closely related phenomenon, represented by the same geometric figure, is illustrated when a point on the triangle represents not a single person but a group or an organization.

Examples of triangling are as follows: 1) one person draws another into feelings of hostility toward a third person or group; 2) one person talking to another is able to evoke feelings of sympathy concerning his troubles with somebody else; 3) two persons feeling hostile toward one another transform their mutual hostility into shared hostility toward a third person (or group or cause) or into shared emotional investment in a third person (or group or cause). Triangular relationships in which a point on the triangle is occupied by a group or an organization are illustrated by a situation in which one person tells a "joke" which demeans blacks, Jews, or some other minority group, and draws his nonobjecting listeners into a feeling system in which prejudice and hostility are shared and approved.

Exchanges of the type just described typically reduce the anxiety level of the persons involved in the feeling system. Becoming part of a feeling system with one or more other persons can be used as a means of gaining approval; and becoming an undifferentiated part of a group alleviates the feelings of loneliness which at times an authentic person must endure.

Realistic planning and the discussion of problems with colleagues or consultants can serve useful and necessary purposes and are not necessarily a form of triangling. Triangling implies that one person or group draws someone else into a common nonrational emotional field. If a consultant continues to be rational rather than becoming emotionally involved with the consultee, triangling does not occur even though the consultee's relationship with a third person is the subject of discussion.

Exchanges become dysfunctional whenever they become a substitute for appropriate action toward the resolution of real problems. Discussion of a problem with someone else may be used as a means of relieving tension instead of facing and attempting to resolve the real problem. If an individual is having an interpersonal problem with his boss, the only person with whom the problem can be resolved is the boss — not the individual's spouse or a colleague. By the same token, an individual who is drawn into a feeling system of prejudice and hostility in order to relieve personal anxieties at the expense of his or her authentic self is becoming involved in a dysfunctional system rather than moving in the direction of more effective functioning. Examples of triangling abound in conversations which may be heard in faculty lounges or over the faculty lunchroom table.

Another dysfunctional response phenomenon is the stereotyping of faculty members by one another. Stereotyping of the members of minority groups is an obvious phenomenon. In faculties the major type of stereotyping which is not generally recognized is the categorization of faculty members as either "caring" or "task" oriented. These stereotypes develop as defense mechanisms. For example, when an argument involving the human and the task dimensions of education or organization ensues, a staff member who feels that he has had a difficult time upholding his side of the argument can conveniently stereotype the other as being "soft" ("caring") or as "not caring" (being "task" oriented). The tendency to stereotype faculty members in these two categories exists to some extent in all faculties. It is less characteristic as faculties develop their capacity to tolerate conflict and to utilize it constructively.

IMPROVING THE ORGANIZATIONAL CLIMATE

Any brief statement on how to improve the organizational climate in schools is inevitably an oversimplification. In the final analysis, improvement in the organizational climate in a school is possible only to the extent that there is improvement in the school as a whole, including the learning of subject matter, skills, procedures, and attitudes; the quality and quantity of books, supplies, and equipment; the buildings and grounds; the lunches; and the transportation. The school climate cannot be separated from the rest of the school. The task of improving climate is thus complex. Because schools mirror the strengths and weaknesses of society as a whole, the improvement of climate in the schools touches upon all that is known and believed about how people learn, upon scientific methods and processes, and upon the nature and values of the whole society. However, some comments can be made relative to the human aspects of the problem.

If school administrators want to improve the ways in which boys and girls are developing in school, if they want to improve the learning climate in the classroom, they must consider carefully the relationship between their own behavior and the functioning of others in the school. An administrator may feel dissatisfied if experienced teachers allow too much noise and general disorder in the classrooms, hold disparaging attitudes toward students, gossip maliciously about one another, or are lax in discharging special assignments. When dissatisfied with the behavior of others, administrators are well advised to analyze the functioning of the social system as a whole and specifically to see what their own behavior may be contributing to the problem. Perhaps they themselves are engaging in the types of behavior to which they object. Perhaps they are forcing their viewpoints upon the faculty and not allowing genuine freedom in the discussion of important issues. Perhaps they are making demands upon teachers which are felt to be unreasonable and which are resented. Perhaps they undertake too much of the work themselves rather than delegate it to assistants. Possibly they are lax in making demands upon themselves. Maybe they are trying to please everybody rather than get on with the tasks at hand. When the behavior of organizational members is not satisfactory, the administrator is often contributing to the problem.

An administrator sets the tone for a school organization. An administrator's values, attitudes, and practices influence behavior throughout an organization. Some people in an organization will tend to accept an administrator's ideas and behavior uncritically and to adopt them as a model for their own viewpoints and behavior. Some will openly or surreptitiously oppose an administrator. But no one in the organization will be completely indifferent because all are affected by administrative action.

Administrators are endowed both legally and symbolically with powerful sanctions, and their approval and disapproval are of concern in varying degress to every organizational member. Their beliefs and expectations have widespread impact. An administrator may promote originality and creativity, or may run a school as a factory. The administrator may or may not demonstrate constructive ways of clarifying goals, opening up communication, utilizing conflict, conducting meetings, and involving others in decision making. What an administrator does or fails to do affects organizational climate because: 1) administrative decisions affect everyone in the organization, in relation to both job-related satisfactions and dissatisfactions; 2) other organizational members invariably react to administrative actions, some copying them and others opposing them; and 3) administrative actions are instrumental in determining the procedures and conditions which facilitate the resolution of organizational problems or which impede effective organizational action. A competent administrator who respects human personality, who believes in the scientific method, and who trusts cooperative thinking and action, can set an organizational tone which enables others in the organization to learn efficiently and to develop in effective functioning.

While the statement may seem obvious, it bears emphasizing that administration needs to be concerned first and foremost with the curriculum of the school. The curriculum should affirm the inherent dignity of each person — regardless of race, color, creed, or sex. This ideal implies the need for greater emphasis upon intrinsic motivations. Students can learn effectively if they are motivated — if the material and the processes to be learned are important to them. All students are motivated to learn something, but the motivations may be expressed in either constructive or destructive ways. The problem for education is to identify and utilize students' motivations. Grades provide extrinsic rather than intrinsic motivation. They may provide a useful record, but the better the students and faculty know each other, the less grades are needed. A student studying music under a master teacher (outside a school) does not receive a grade; instead the teacher learns the student's likes and dislikes, strengths and weaknesses, accomplishments and areas of need, and then nurtures the student's growth. The schools rely too much on rewards and punishments as means for achieving educational ends; frequently the control function takes over and becomes an end in itself; and then busy work, which may appear to be educational but which actually is motivated by the need to control, contributes to the students' aversion to "school."

Although in general greater emphasis upon intrinsic motivation is needed, such an emphasis does not obviate the need for children to have direction, advice, and limits set by adults. The point is not that adult direction and guidance are unnecessary, but rather that they are so often overused to the neglect of intrinsic motivations. In some situations, contingency reinforcement can be used to advantage. For example, if a teacher or principal who wants to change relationships in a classroom or school has been thinking in terms of social systems, he may not know how to change a whole system and hence may not know where to begin. In such a situation, contingency reinforcement may be useful because it suggests that the individual identify a specific behavior which he wants changed, and then develop specific ways of modifying his own behavior in order that the desired change may come about. Teachers who want less noise in the classroom often reward more orderly behavior. By indicating approval through smiles and friendly comments when children are courteous and orderly and by withholding such rewards when they are unnecessarily noisy, teachers are often able to improve the learning situation in the classroom. On the other hand, too great a reliance on external methods of control tends to curb initiative, originality, and the development of individual potentialities through inner motivation and self-discipline. It is to be noted that the use of contingency reinforcement can be consistent with systems theory if it is utilized as a means of effecting change in a system rather than as a means of accomplishing change in one or more individuals only.

If the inherent dignity of the individual is to be affirmed, the influence of status factors in inhibiting student learning must be recognized and ameliorated. Status factors presently affect teaching in various ways. Many teachers are biased by a student's socioeconomic status. Many hold strong prejudices concerning race, color, or ethnic group. In general, teachers in the early grades favor girls (though teachers sometimes strongly favor children of the opposite sex), but as the students progress to high school and college, the educational program increasingly favors men. Many teachers are strongly biased in favor of students who are superior academic achievers, and teachers generally favor children who are enterprising. Similarly, the students themselves develop status systems based upon some of these same factors as well as upon peer group norms and mores, including opposition to authority, physical prowess, dress, personal attractiveness, and special skills such as social or artistic capabilities. Students who rank low in prestige with their teachers and peers and whose low grades imperil their relationships with their parents, are handicapped in learning. They tend to develop poor self-concepts, and because they feel that they are poor learners, their capacity for learning is reduced. Moreover, there is evidence that such children tend to be neglected by the teacher in the classroom.[33]

[33] R. S. Adams and B. J. Biddle, *Realities of Teaching: Explorations with Videotape* (New York: Holt, Rinehart and Winston, Inc., 1970). R. Rist, "The Self-Fulfilling Prophesy of the Ghetto School," *Harvard Educational Review* (Summer 1970).

In order to enable students to learn, the emotional climate must provide acceptance for all students, by both teachers and peers. Such acceptance does not mean approval of poor work, but rather means recognition of the worth of the individual and trust in the capacity of every person to learn and to grow. It means that students are heard, not only with respect to their ideas and interests but also with respect to their feelings, both in reference to their personal concerns and the school program as a whole. This acceptance of students requires that teachers and administrators develop competencies in communicating to students in a manner which enables students to know that they are being heard.

Administrators should recognize that they perform no function of greater importance than selection of staff. Because of the importance of staff, staff selection warrants adequate investment of the administrator's time. A truly wholesome climate necessitates administrators and teachers who have a strong sense of self-identity which is enhanced through personal and professional growth. Boys and girls need to experience relationships with persons who are true educators in the sense of being interested in growth rather than in the achievement of preconceived and irrelevant goals. They need to experience relationships with persons who feel secure in their own worth, with individuals who can communicate openly on the one hand and act decisively on the other, with persons who understand the joys and frustrations of growth because they themselves are trying to grow. Staff recruitment and selection should therefore place greater emphasis upon the individual person's capacity to relate effectively to others than has been typical in the past.

If teachers and administrators are to provide a program in which students feel accepted, they need appropriate learning opportunities in the affective domain to become increasingly aware of their own biases and to grow in their ability to provide an enabling climate. Furthermore, they themselves need to experience this type of climate. A wholesome climate for students cannot be provided in a school with an unwholesome climate for staff. Teachers need to be enabled to grow in relation to their own motivations rather than in relation to the needs of someone else. Community relationships likewise should reflect mutual respect and open communication if they are to contribute to a wholesome climate in the school. *Teachers and administrators can learn to communicate effectively with students and citizens and can resolve many of the current school-community problems only if they learn to communicate openly in appropriate ways and at appropriate times in their relationships with one another. They can learn to respect boys and girls only to the extent that they learn to respect each other.*

The quality of the interpersonal relationships on a staff is closely related to the extent to which the group or organization and the individuals comprising it rely upon automatic response mechanisms. The use of such mechanisms as a substitute for rational processes invariably limits a school's potential for helping students and faculty to grow in their capacities to function effectively. In my opinion, administrators who are nonconformists[34] owe their successes not only to their ideas, but to the fact that their nonconformity tends to destroy automatic response mechanisms and thus frees others in the organization to think creatively. By refusing to function in accordance with the implicit assumptions underlying a social system infused with automatic response mechanisms, an administrator can change the social system so that all persons involved in it can function more effectively and can respond to new problems and situations thoughtfully and with zest and spontaneity. If the organization is to be lively, the administrator needs to respond fairly and honestly to the persons in the situation rather than resorting to triangling. The administrator must be able to help a staff to get conflict out into the open and to utilize it constructively. The administrator must not resort to the stereotyping of persons in minority groups or of faculty members by categorizing them as either a "caring" or "task" type of person. Because the school consists of a number of systems, an effective administrator will take a systems approach to change and will become competent in working with the system as a whole, rather than trying to change small segments of the system as if they were separate and discrete parts.

A relationship means that the various individuals involved are party to the relationship. A master-slave relationship can exist in a truly free society only through the explicit or implicit collusion of two people — the one agreeing to be the master and the other agreeing to be the slave. An idiosyncrasy on the part of one person in a relationship is possible only if the other is willing to tolerate the idiosyncrasy. Because mutual consent is necessary, a school administrator or teacher in a free society can change his relationships with others if he himself is capable of change.

If you want to help someone with whom you are involved to learn to function more effectively, stay in the relationship but get out of the problem.

The play *And Miss Reardon Drinks a Little*[35] by Paul Zindel

---

[34] For an example of the nonconforming type of administrator see Robert Townsend, *Up the Organization* (New York: Fawcett World Library, 1970).

[35] Paul Zindel, *And Miss Reardon Drinks A Little* (New York: Dramatists Play Service, Inc., 1971). Reprinted by permission of Curtis Brown Ltd. Copyright 1971, 1972 by Paul Zindel.

centers around three sisters: a teacher, an assistant school principal, and an administrator in the central office (presumably an assistant school superintendent). The teacher (Anna Reardon) is psychotic and is on leave from the school system. She lives with her sister (Catherine Reardon), the one who is an assistant principal and who "drinks a little." A central element in Anna Reardon's psychosis is that she abhors many things because they seem to her to represent corpses. She cannot stand anything made of leather because leather is part of a dead animal. So is fur in any form. To her, telephone poles are dead trees. She is utterly revolted by the idea of eating fresh meat, for to her, the eating of meat is the devouring of a corpse. Because Anna is disturbed by such things, Catherine keeps them out of the house (though she does occasionally eat raw red meat on the sly). At the end of the play (as I interpret it), Ceil, the assistant school superintendent, is so disgusted with both Anna and Catherine that she breaks off the relationship. In contrast, Catherine is going to continue to live with Anna, but she makes it clear that she intends to order large amounts of meat, that she will no longer cater to Anna's idiosyncrasies. In other words, Catherine intends to stay in the relationship but to get out of the problem. Because of Catherine's action, one has reason to believe that Anna will be enabled to find her way back to a better life.

A young teacher who was appointed to a school principalship found after a few months in the position that he was working extremely hard but that the staff was shirking its duties. His visits to classes had convinced him that many of the teachers were not effective in the classroom. The irresponsibility of the teachers led him to make increasingly frequent tours through the building to get the teachers to do a better job of teaching and to keep the students under control. In connection with general faculty meetings and the faculty committees which had been established by the young man's predecessor, the new principal had found that he had to do more than his share of the work in preparing materials between meetings and sustaining the discussions. When special events were to be held at the school, only minimal help had been provided by the faculty. Meanwhile, teachers had been coming to the principal for advice on specific matters of classroom procedure. When the principal finally took stock of the situation, he realized that he was serving the faculty as a school flunky rather than as an administrator. At this point, he decided that he was going to be an administrator in fact as well as in name. He began to discuss with individual teachers and faculty groups the ways in which the school program could be improved. When teachers came to him with inconsequential matters, he refused to become involved or helped them to arrive at their own decisions. When he attended meetings of the general faculty or of faculty committees, he spoke less and quit doing so much of the preparatory work. In addition, he deliberately missed some of the committee meetings and stopped running (almost literally) through the building to keep things under control. Gradually the faculty responded to the change; some faculty members became more responsible and others became more irresponsible. When the principal persisted in this change in behavior, the faculty as a whole became more responsible; teachers began to do a better job in the classroom; they began to make more decisions affecting their own classrooms; they did more work in relation to faculty and committee meetings; and a few even began to volunteer to help the administrator on special tasks.

Change in any social system carries with it an element of danger, for when one individual improves his or her level of functioning, the system mobilizes its energies to resist change, and a lower level of functioning on the part of others often develops. However, the healing power of deep-level communication should not be underestimated. To get out of the problem, to refuse to cater to another's idiosyncracies, may mean to the other that one does not really care, but a deeper kind of caring can be shown through feeling-level communication. Teachers or administrators can help themselves and others — whether one person or a social system — only by developing and maintaining relationships. Breaking off a relationship or continuing to be part of the problem is seldom if ever helpful.

CONCLUSION

Organizational climate affects every individual in an organization. It is particularly influential in the lives of children, who are still at an impressionable age. The type of climate which develops in a school is induced to a considerable degree by the administrator, who typically wields more influence than any other single individual in a school, while the climate in a classroom is largely induced by the teacher. Unfortunately, the climate in many schools and classrooms is not what it ought to be.

The importance of school climate calls attention to the relationships within the school organization. Complementing these relationships are those with individuals, groups, and agencies outside the school. To be effective, administrative leadership must encompass the relationships outside as well as within the school organization. These relationships which cross the boundaries of the school organization receive attention in the next chapter.

SUGGESTED READINGS

Appleberry, James and Wayne K. Hoy, "The Pupil Control Ideology of Professional Personnel in 'Open' and 'Closed' Elementary Schools," *Educational Administration Quarterly*, 5, no. 3 (Autumn 1969), 74–85.

Dreikurs, Rudolf and Loren Grey, *Logical Consequences: A New Approach to Discipline.* New York: Hawthorn Books, Inc., 1968.

Dreikurs, Rudolf, Bernice B. Grunwald, and Floy C. Pepper, *Maintaining Sanity in the Classroom. Illustrated Teaching Techniques.* New York: Harper & Row, Publishers, 1971.

Ginott, Haim, *Teacher and Child. A Book for Parents and Teachers.* New York: The Macmillan Company, 1972.

Glasser, William, *Schools Without Failure.* New York: Harper & Row, Publishers, 1969.

Halpin, Andrew W., *Theory and Research in Administration*, chap. 4, "The Organizational Climate of Schools." New York: The Macmillan Company, 1966.

Moustakas, Clark and Cereta Perry, *Learning to be Free.* Englewood Cliffs, N.J.: Prentice-Hall, Inc., 1973.

Otto, Henry J. and Donald J. Veldman, "Control Structure in Public Schools and the Decision and Influence Roles of Elementary School Principals and Teachers," *Educational Administration Quarterly*, 3, no. 2 (Spring 1967), 149–61.

Schmuck, Richard A. and Patricia A. Schmuck, *A Humanistic Psychology of Education. Making the School Everybody's House.* Palo Alto, Calif.: National Press Books, 1974.

Simon, Sidney B. and Howard Kirschenbaum, *Readings in Values Clarification.* Minneapolis, Minn.: Winston Press, Inc., 1973.

Steinhoff, C. R., *Organizational Climate in a Public School System.* ERIC systems accession number ED003681. Syracuse, N.Y.: Syracuse University, 1965.

Weinstein, Gerald and Mario D. Fantini, eds., *Toward Humanistic Education. A Curriculum of Affect.* New York: Praeger Publishers (Published for the Ford Foundation), 1970.

SCHOOL- 9
COMMUNITY
RELATIONSHIPS

Schools are maintained by a society to achieve certain purposes. They do not exist in a vacuum. They are part and parcel of the society which maintains them, and in a democracy, they perform the essential function of preparing the people for responsible citizenship.

Public schools in the United States hold a unique place in the governmental structure. They are operated as a public service, paid for by public monies, and controlled by public boards of education to which authority has been delegated by the state. The local board of education is a unique legal agency created for the purpose of enabling the people to hold close control over the public schools, and the parent-teacher association is a unique voluntary organization which seeks improvement in the conditions for each child through promoting closer cooperation between the parents and the schools. Although the structure is designed to provide close working relationships between the schools and the community, schools need to become more sensitive to their role in society and to meet individual and community needs more effectively if they are to come nearer to the realization of their full potential.

A modern school typically functions in a community of extraordinary complexity, and the local community is affected not only by neighboring communities but by the world at large. Any sizeable community includes numerous types of organizations, and these organizations seek to achieve purposes which range all the way from missions conceived in the public interest to those which are inimical to the very existence of the educational institutions.

Attention in this chapter is directed initially to the changing community conditions as they are expressed through student protest, teachers' organizations, citizen control, and role changes of administrators and others. The implications of these conditions for programs of school-community relationships are then explored, and suggestions for improving school-community relationships are made.

CHANGING CONDITIONS

Within any given culture and especially in a highly differentiated society, conflicting values develop, and these conflicting values legitimize a wide variety of norms.[1] Under conditions of rapid social change, special strains are placed upon value integration.[2] Such strains, while always present to some extent in a complex society, may become so severe that a new integration of values is essential if the society is to endure.

At present in the United States and indeed throughout the world, opposing value systems are resulting in interpersonal conflict, parliamentary disagreement, and actual physical conflict including the use of armed force. These conflicts in value systems are reflected in many issues and strains in contemporary society. Many people in the United States seek to maintain a caste system in which blacks, Jews, women, and others are not granted the full rights of citizenship; on the other hand, many citizens are working actively to promote equal rights for all. The environment is being polluted at a rate which poses an imminent threat to the life of everyone on this planet; yet there are citizen groups and governmental agencies engaged in vigorous efforts directed toward environmental protection. Many businesses seek profits without maintaining more than a pretense of honesty; yet there are honest businessmen, and many groups have been organized to protect consumer interests. Many physicians and attorneys are more interested in making money than in providing professional service; yet more students are entering the medical and legal professions because of humanitarian interests than ever before.

---

[1] Robin M. Williams, Jr., "The Concept of Values," *International Encyclopedia of the Social Sciences*, 16, 286. Talcott Parsons, "An Overview," in *American Sociology: Perspectives, Problems, Methods*, ed. Talcott Parsons (New York: Basic Books, Inc., 1968), p. 329.

[2] Williams, "The Concept of Values," p. 286.

Some persons and groups want governmental action which would weaken the schools; yet many believe that effective schools are the nation's best hope. The listing of issues growing out of conflicts over values could be extended at length.

In these conflicts the real question is not whether the ideals of liberty, equality, and fraternity will foster change. Such change is inevitable. The real question is whether the needed changes can be accomplished within the limits of the present system. Some people are advocating that change be brought about through anarchy and violence, but the trouble with anarchy and violence is that they are not only initially destructive but nobody ever knows where they will lead.

In a democracy every citizen is responsible for doing whatever is possible to help promote constructive community action. However, a school administrator has a special responsibility for leadership and can be a powerful force in helping a community to identify and develop the human resources which will enable it to cope with its problems.

Student Protest

Student protest may be observed in many forms in today's schools. Elementary and secondary pupils in many classrooms are virtually uncontrollable.[3] In a large high school at a single point in time there may be several hundred students roaming through the halls when they should be in class. Pupils at school steal from and assault one another. In one large suburban school system, over a fourth of the high school students are absent from school for over a month (twenty school days) each year. In another large system, students have organized a revenge day for getting even with school officials. Teachers and administrators in various school systems are viciously assaulted, and occasionally one of them is killed. Student publications in many schools direct a continuing barrage of criticism against the respective schools and their administrations. The dollar costs of vandalism in the schools have become alarmingly high.

What is the meaning of actions like these? Is there no end to them? What do students want?

If the actions of students are looked at as being a form of communication, the messages which they are sending seem to be that

---

[3] For a research study on student brinkmanship in the classroom see Joseph W. Licata and Donald J. Willower, "Student Brinkmanship and the School as a Social System," *Educational Administration Quarterly*, 11, no. 2 (Spring 1975), 1-14.

they are demanding: 1) the respect which they believe is due to them as human beings; 2) communication with an older generation including faculty members and administration; 3) educational experiences which have meaning for them; and 4) a society whose practices are more consistent with its stated ideals.

The student movement as a whole includes strong neurotic as well as wholesome elements. Some students show evidence of serious emotional problems in various ways such as the use of drugs, sexual promiscuity, suicide attempts, and use of violence. Some want to destroy the very fabric of our way of life by destroying the institution of the school. Some want to wreak vengeance on administrators or faculty members for all the unhappy experiences they have ever had. Such students may simply want an excuse for indulging their own masochistic and sadistic tendencies.

Student protests are likely to become destructive when there is a lack of constructive leadership. When there is no leadership directed toward constructive action, a student group may become open to almost any suggestion, and then accept leadership directed toward destructive action. On the other hand, leadership such as that exercised by President Kingman Brewster of Yale University a few years ago in accompanying over a thousand students to Washington, D.C., to discuss societal problems with members of Congress helps students learn to utilize their energies constructively in resolving problems.

In the past, students in schools and universities have often been treated like workers at the lowest level in the organization. They have been expected to follow orders and have had little prestige. Today students are asking to be treated more like clients, employers who come to specialists (the school) for help but who can leave one specialist to employ another whenever the desired help is not forthcoming. Until the learning experience itself becomes more meaningful and students are accorded more respect, substantial student resentment and dissatisfaction may be expected to continue.

Teachers' Organizations

Teachers' organizations in recent years have become increasingly powerful and militant. Teachers who have organized in professional associations as well as those who have joined teachers' unions have engaged in negotiation proceedings with boards of education and in many cases have gone on strike. These activities are a far cry from those of teachers' organizations prior to 1960 when the great majority of teachers believed that teachers' strikes were unethical and that negotiations should be engaged in only by nonprofessionals.

Teachers' organizations are not only a part of the school community, but their militance and the resulting negotiations frequently involve the community. Implicit in the concept of system is the idea that the community at large is always involved with teacher organizations; the relationships between the two have simply been highlighted by teacher militancy.

Despite the fact that many factors over which administrators have no control have contributed to teacher "unionization," it is doubtful that teachers would ever have become so tightly organized had it not been for the type of administration employed in many school systems. Although some administrators have functioned with regard for staff, many of them have not respected teachers as professionals, have been unwilling to listen to them, and have been highly autocratic.

The exercise of bargaining rights represents a decision on the part of many teachers to use collective power in place of petition and persuasion. Many teachers have become convinced that they cannot expect fair treatment from society or from its representatives (such as boards of education, school superintendents, and city councils) unless they exert concerted power to obtain their demands.

Citizen Control

Citizen control has of course been a tradition dating from the early settlements in North America. When education was a responsibility of the family and even when it was a function normally performed by the church, the right to control the education of a child was always closely guarded by the parents. With the advent of public schools and compulsory education, citizens continued to exercise control through the state legislatures, local boards of education, and other public bodies, and they retained the prerogative of sending their children to either public or private schools.

The traditional citizen control, however, has been largely negative in character; that is, citizens usually have not interfered with school policies as long as the schools have seemed to be running smoothly. It has only been when the citizens were dissatisfied that they have become active in attempting to influence school policies.

Since World War II, citizens have begun to take a more positive role in the direction of educational policies. School board elections, bond-issue campaigns, and other educational issues have stirred the people as never before. Parent-teacher associations, study groups, advisory councils, coordinating groups, citizen surveys, cooperative surveys, women's organizations, pressure groups, and other types of affiliations have enabled thousands of citizens to have an active part in the direction of education.

As citizens have taken a more active role, however, the actual control over educational policies has in some respects been slipping away from them. Power structures have developed and have evolved with the changing times. School districts have become larger and larger, both in terms of geography and population, so that the individual citizen often has a smaller voice in relation to the whole. Procedures within school systems have become increasingly technical and complex, so that a citizen experiences difficulty in comprehending all that is involved. Change is coming with increasing speed, and a citizen finds difficulty in keeping up with events and ideas. Financing of the schools has been transferred to some extent to the state and federal governments and, in limited measure, in some cases even to private foundations. State and federal laws and decisions of the courts dictate to a considerable extent what the schools can and cannot do.

Although many citizens are more active on policy questions than ever before, there are even more who are apathetic and ignorant on issues confronting education. As Mann has pointed out,[4] local newspapers and the other media deal largely with disjointed school happenings rather than with policy questions. Professional books and journals are not readily accessible and are not written for the layman. Official information from the school system is not readily available in understandable terms to most citizens. Many people, especially those of low socioeconomic status, do not know how to use the information which is available; others believe that educational policies are too complicated for them to understand. Many citizens lack the motivation to understand educational issues and to take an active part in decision making, and the motivation which citizens do have for participation is often diluted by the competition from noneducational problems for citizen attention. Because of the lack of information and the inability of many citizens to conform to a rational model of decisional participation, school administrators have often excluded citizens from an active role in policy decision making.

More active participation on the part of many citizens is essential if the schools are to be more effectual. In the past, the purpose of educators in promoting citizen involvement has often been to get citizens to pay for what the educators think is necessary. Such an approach is not related to the motivations of many citizens. Citizens are strongly motivated toward exerting "more direct control over institutions which affect their lives." Citizen involvement can be

---

[4] This paragraph is based upon Dale Mann, "Public Understanding and Education Decision-Making," *Educational Administration Quarterly*, 10, no. 2 (Spring 1974), 1–18.

more effectual if based upon this motivation, if adequate information is provided, and if administrators really want to involve citizens on a realistic basis.[5]

In some instances the desire of citizens to exercise greater control over the schools has come into conflict with growing teacher militance. Such was the case in New York City where opposition on the part of the United Federation of Teachers developed against the plan for decentralization of school control. Conflicts of this type are basically a result of disagreements over the role of the citizen and of governing boards on the one hand, and the role of the professional educator and of teachers' associations and unions on the other.

The meeting ground of lay and professional concerns is the education of the children. To the extent that citizens regard the education of their children as a matter of paramount importance, they will willingly pay the taxes necessary to support good schools. And by the same token, if teachers will place the education of the children in proper perspective as their paramount concern, they have the best chance over a long period of time of obtaining substantial increases in salaries.[6] This argument does not suggest that taxpayers need not be concerned about the amount of their taxes or that teachers should not fight for a stronger profession and for better salaries. It suggests only that taxpayers and teachers, along with the children, will be better off in the long run if values are kept in appropriate perspective, with financial considerations assuming a secondary position to the primary consideration, which is the education of the children.

Role Changes

The roles of administrators and others are presently undergoing changes as radical as the changes occurring in society itself, and there are currently a great many speculations and predictions as to what the roles of superintendents, principals, supervisors, teachers, and others in school systems will become. The movement toward collective bargaining on the part of teachers, the disenchantment of an increasing number of students, and the developing involvement of citizens in school programs, all reflect the changing nature of society and imply changing roles for individuals who are engaged in education.

Many people believe that collective bargaining will result in a distinct split between teacher organizations on the one hand, and super-

---

[5] *Ibid.*

[6] For a parallel argument concerning profits as related to performance of tasks in private enterprise, see Robert L. Katz, "Toward a More Effective Enterprise," *Harvard Business Review,* 38, no. 5 (September–October 1960).

visors, principals, superintendents, and school board members on the other. Some believe that principals and supervisors will form their own bargaining units. Some believe that there will be three major bargaining organizations or unions, representing faculty, students, and administration, respectively, with the students generally allying themselves with the administration against the faculty, and the governing boards losing much of their power to the three groups. Some believe that school principals will lose the role of educational leadership, which will be taken over by leaders in small groups within the faculty or by the "shop steward" (faculty association representative) for the faculty as a whole; others believe, however, that collective bargaining will free school principals from many administrative routines, thus enabling them to perform more adequately their major role of educational leadership. Some believe that the personalities involved will determine whether the role of educational leadership is performed by the "shop steward" or by the school principal.

The ways in which roles in education will develop will depend considerably upon whether collective bargaining in the schools is based upon the model developed in business and industry, in which labor and management engage in a test of power, or whether it is based upon a new model in which the parties involved agree upon a common goal, namely, to seek to improve the educational opportunities of the children.[7] Such a goal implies concern in the bargaining process for all involved — students, teachers, and citizens.

Of one thing we can be sure — the tasks of teaching and administration will need to be performed as long as schools continue to exist. Students will still need opportunities to learn, teachers will be selected, instructional materials will have to be provided, buildings to be constructed, maintained, and operated, schedules to be developed, opportunities for staff growth to be made available, budgetary resources to be allocated, and countless other tasks will have to be performed and decisions made. While these tasks will remain, the positions of the people who perform them may change. The roles of principal and supervisor will change or may even be eliminated; the role of the superintendent will change; students, teachers, and citizens will exercise more power; but nevertheless someone will perform the essential organizational functions.

The role changes which are in process and the dissatisfactions

[7]See Gerald E. Dart, "Educational Negotiations: Downhill All the Way," *Educational Leadership*, 30, no. 1 (October 1972), 9-12. William A. Vantine, "Toward a Theory of Collective Negotiations," *Educational Administration Quarterly*, 8, no.1 (Winter 1972), 27-43. George Madden, "A Theoretical Basis for Differentiating Forms of Collective Bargaining in Education," *Educational Administration Quarterly*, 5, no. 2 (Spring 1969), 76-90.

evidenced in the current scene emphasize the need for greater understanding and competence on the part of administrators. Because of the unrest among students, teachers, and citizens, it is imperative that administrators improve their understanding of the behavioral sciences, including the ways in which people function not only as individuals, but as members of groups, organizations, and communities.

IMPLICATIONS FOR SCHOOL-COMMUNITY RELATIONSHIPS

The widespread conflicts in values in contemporary society have already been cited. Society as a whole is in flux, and change is everywhere. Such change may result in the end of the democratic way of life or in a more creative society. The direction in which society moves depends to a considerable extent upon educational leadership.

Because conflicts in value systems are at the root of many controversial proposals for change, communities need moral leadership. When questions of equality or respect for the individual become controversial, educational administrators are responsible for responding in terms of moral commitment. An administrator can rationalize and condone subtle discrimination in the schools but, in so doing, fails the community. In a community leadership role, an administrator need not go looking for trouble; he or she need not try to change a community overnight; but the administrator is responsible for taking a position worthy of a professional educator who seeks to help a community improve education.

A recognition of the human factors involved and the interrelationships implied by systems theory has many implications for school-community relationships. The behaviors which will put these implications into practice cannot simply be mandated. They can come about only through careful staff selection and thoughtful administration which promotes staff growth. Sound programs of staff development are needed.

The following implications, which are not discrete but which interrelate with one another, appear to be particularly important.

A Strong, Humane Educational Program

Effective school-community relationships begin with a sound, humane educational program designed to meet the needs of both the students and the community. If the educational program itself is not reasonably sound in providing wholesome experiences for each child, the school and community relationships will inevitably deteriorate. On the other hand, parents almost always react with strong positive feelings when a teacher or administrator acts out of understanding and caring for a particular child or group of children. The challenge of educational leadership is to help provide educational opportunities for all children which prepare them for the technological advances of modern society and, at the same time, are essentially humanistic in viewpoint and practice.

The educational problems of blacks are similar to those of white students except that they have been exacerbated by racial discrimination in our society. Many blacks are convinced that education will not help them to improve their situation. They may not know anyone who serves as a model of an individual whose status was improved through education. Instead, black children often see their elders unemployed and feeling hopeless, frustrated, and perhaps desperate. In this connection, a study of relocatees from the Southwest area of Washington, D.C., found results which were similar to the findings of other studies of inner city populations, namely, that 71 percent of the respondents suffered from "high anomie," that is, from hopelessness and social dysfunction.[8] These results illustrate the malaise found in many inner cities and help to show why children from inner city populations so often lack motivation for schoolwork.

Many black students see the school as being essentially part of the white establishment. If a black child has a white teacher and if the school administrators also are white, this impression is underscored. It is not surprising that blacks who have been discriminated against all their lives tend to see discrimination in many school practices, whether the discrimination is real or not.

Unfortunately, racial discrimination is real in too many instances. In addition to overt segregation, biases against blacks in schools include segregation through "ability" grouping; racially biased attitudes of teachers expressed in subtle but unmistakable ways; the use of culturally biased standardized tests; the teaching of only slavery and Martin Luther King as constituting black history; the biased allocation of resources such as teachers and supplies on the basis of a school's racial composition or socioeconomic status; and the appointment of few if any blacks to positions of high status in the school system.

The problems of motivation of black students will continue to be

[8] Daniel Thursz, *Where Are They Now?* (Washington, D.C.: Health and Welfare Council of the National Capital Area, 1966). Cited in Daniel Thursz, "Community Participation," *American Behavioral Scientist*, 15, no. 5 (May–June 1972), 733–748.

severe as long as racial discrimination is evident in our society. When individuals who have excelled through obtaining advanced education can readily be seen by black children and taken as models, the motivation of these children toward educational goals can be expected to improve. In the meantime, the best hope is a sound educational program with teachers who have come to terms with their own prejudices.

Some teachers believe that there is such a gulf between blacks and whites in our society that positive relationships between white teachers and black children are virtually impossible. While it is true that some blacks say that they can never fully trust any white person, it should be noted that even when racial differences intervene, feelings of caring and respect are usually sensed, especially when accompanied by adequate communication skills, and that such feelings evoke counterfeelings of affection and belonging.

If education is to be improved, greater attention must be paid to the whole area of affective education, which is the aspect of education that helps individuals in their search for personal identity, significance, and feelings of belonging. Affective education emphasizes the need for psychological safety so that children may sense how they feel and learn to express their feelings appropriately without the need to hide behind masks.

The most important element in affective education is the teacher-child relationship. If teachers really care about children and understand child behavior in depth, the children can develop a stronger sense of self and can pursue educational goals without the distortion of negative authority relationships.

Many exercises illustrative of affective education have been developed.[9] While these exercises may prove helpful just as they are, many teachers will want to modify them to suit their own educational purposes or will develop their own methods of integrating affective education with the other school activities.

Parents oppose affective education when they hear of a label or an exercise which seems to suggest that the school wants to undermine their child's character, religious beliefs, or belief in our governmental system. Yet it would be unusual to find a parent who is opposed to a

[9] For example see Sidney B. Simon, Leland W. Howe, and Howard Kirschenbaum, *Values Clarification* (New York: Hart Publishing Company, Inc., 1972). Louis E. Raths, Merrill Harmin, and Sidney B. Simon, *Values and Teaching* (Columbus, Ohio: Charles E. Merrill Books, Inc., 1966). Harold C. Lyon, Jr., *Learning to Feel — Feeling to Learn* (Columbus, Ohio: Charles E. Merrill Publishing Company, 1971). Gerald Weinstein and Mario D. Fantini, eds., *Toward Humanistic Education. A Curriculum of Affect* (New York: Praeger Publishers, 1970).

school's concern for the wholesome development of each child, which is the core of genuine affective education.

Finally, education needs to be improved through alternative programs. The dissatisfactions with schools have become so intense that suggested alternatives to the public schools are receiving substantial support. Proposals have been made to abandon compulsory school attendance, contracts have been signed with private firms to provide schooling, and public financing is in some instances being arranged to provide support for private and parochial schools. The persistance of these challenges strongly suggests that unless the public schools can develop within the present educational system alternative types of education which will be more effective in meeting individual and community needs, they will be superseded by other types of schooling arrangements. Choices in type of schooling are already being made available to parents and children in some school systems. Some schools within a school system emphasize subject-matter achievement whereas others emphasize process; within an individual school, some classrooms provide uniform procedures while others provide individualized instruction; and parents and children are allowed to choose their type of school or classroom in accordance with their educational preferences. Some of the possible alternatives within the present educational system are attention to objectives (behavioral vs. holistic or personalized), utilization of original discovery, open schools, personalized education, the free university, schools without walls (use of the community as a laboratory), broadening the base of decision-making power in schools, foreign language study in elementary schools, schools freed from subject-teaching programs, and the nongraded elementary school.[10]

Whatever changes are made, the emphasis needs to be on people rather than solely on facets of the organization. Organizational changes in schools are useful when they facilitate meaningful education, but too often administrators become engrossed in organization for its own sake to the neglect of educational considerations.

Open Communication

Open communication among the home, the school staff, and the various segments of the community is necessary if school-community relationships are to be effective. Such communication should be both two-way (in the sense that a continuous interchange of information should occur between the schools and the community) and circular

[10] Articles about most of these innovations appear in *Educational Leadership*, 29, no. 5 (February 1972).

(like a wheel with spokes and rim, in the sense that a number of people both in the school and in the community are involved). In addition to an exchange of information between the schools and all parts of the community, a special relationship is needed between the school and the parents in order that information concerning individual children may be shared freely.

The most effective interpretive agents for communicating between the school and the community are the students, teachers, and parents. They are closest to the school program and in a real sense are the ones who can speak most authoritatively about it. Children and parents do a good deal of talking about what went on at school, and such talk is often accompanied by considerable feeling. Parents may read an article about the schools or hear a speech by the school superintendent, but they are affected more deeply by school reports given by or about their own child.

A problem in many school-community relationships is that the people involved distrust one another. Teachers and principals are often suspicious of the motives of parents, and many parents approach the schools with resentments and fears left from their own school experiences. Many central office administrators believe that reporters deliberately distort school information and hence release it to them reluctantly; at the same time the reporters suspect that they are being deceived and that the schools are trying to hide their mistakes. The result is that the exchange of information often takes place in a guarded, fearful atmosphere.

Many parents feel on the defensive in relating to the school. Reasons for such defensiveness seem clear. Because a teacher or an administrator is relatively highly educated and is in a position of authority, parents often feel inferior by comparison. In addition, parents frequently feel that they are not listened to by the school staff, that the school does not want them to be involved, that the school discriminates in favor of the well-to-do and highly educated, that the school staff will embarrass them by saying confidential or negative things about their child in front of others, that they are not respected. All too often these attitudes receive confirmation from defensive or insensitive teachers and administrators. The feelings of distrust are so strong for some parents that they either stay away from the school altogether or come to the school in a defensive frame of mind. The feelings of distrust which are experienced by many parents are often heightened for parents who are black and who are relating to a school staffed mostly by whites.

The only way that a school can demonstrate its respect for parents is through action. Such action includes both planned communication and the active involvement of parents in school activities. It involves preparation of the staff with training in communication skills, necessary information about the school, and any additional assistance needed so that the staff is ready to welcome rather than reluctantly tolerate the parents.

Informational activities at the local school level may include sending home short notes and samples of work, parent conferences, telephone calls, visiting days at the school, science fairs, open house in the various departments or classrooms, musical and theatrical presentations, video tapes of school happenings, and school handbooks for parents. At the school system level, such activities may include a variety of printed publications such as the superintendent's annual report; news releases and other types of materials (such as films and tapes) for newspapers and the other mass media; programs and speeches for television, radio, and various community groups; and open meetings of the board of education.

An administrator can help to insure that information released to the mass media will be reported accurately to the public if he or she discusses goals, needs, and information with the reporter. Most reporters will act responsibly if they are adequately informed and have confidence in their sources.

Parents can be actively involved in the school in many ways. They can help in the instructional program as paraprofessionals, paid or volunteer, performing many tasks consistent with their competencies, including tutoring, chaperoning field trips, clerical work, and planning and providing help for special events. Parents with special competencies may be willing to serve as expert resource personnel,[11] and a community resource file can assist in the continual identification of parents who are willing to help in particular ways. Community groups may meet in the school facilities. Parents and other citizens who live close to the school may be willing to report any suspicious activities around the building when it is not in use for school or community functions. In addition, as we shall note later, citizens can help to provide feedback to the school and can help to develop school policy.

If the parents do not come to the school, the school should find ways of going to the parents. Some administrators organize coffee hours which are held in various homes for the purpose of informal discussion of the school programs by a staff member and a small group of parents. In some communities, it has been possible to arrange such meetings in the recreation room of an apartment house or in the community room of a library, store, restaurant, or recrea-

---

[11] A notable example of use of the whole community as a working laboratory is the program of the University of Wisconsin at Green Bay.

tion center. Visits by teachers to the homes of their pupils can be successful when they are undertaken by a competent person in a spirit of good will.

A comprehensive plan for school-community relationships should be developed for the school system as a whole and a comparable plan for each school.[12] The plan for the school system as a whole should be based upon specific community needs. To provide direction for the entire effort, the board of education should adopt the plan and allocate resources such as funds, staff, and facilities to support it. In addition, school board policies in general should indicate an awareness of the importance of school-community relationships.

The key person in any program of school-community relationships is the school administrator. Every staff member has a responsibility for school-community relationships, but in a school system as a whole, the key person is the school superintendent, and in an individual school, the school principal. Some responsibilities for school-community relationships can be delegated, but some must be discharged directly by the administrator if the program is to be successful. The administrator must take an active role in large-scale planning and must personally meet with many individuals and groups if the program is to be effective. Perhaps most important, the administrator must provide leadership for the entire program.

A partial indication of the ways in which one administrator met his internal and community responsibilities can be seen from the reported activities of the president of Columbia University during the year 1968-1969. At the beginning of the year, the school was "marked by deep divisions both among the faculty and the student body — divisions often intensified by emotionalism and almost complete polarization of positions on many matters relating to University life and policy." Some of the activities of the president are summarized as follows.[13]

I met with students in my office, on the campus, in residence halls, in fraternity houses, in classrooms, at athletic contests, and invited many to my house. Simultaneously, I met with a great number of faculty members both singly and in groups. In five months, I entertained over 2,000 students, faculty, community people, and others at my home for the purpose of discussing some matter of University or community interest. . . .

I said repeatedly during the year that the University could not forever

[12] For specific suggestions on how to develop a program of effective school-community relationships see Calvin Grieder, Truman M. Pierce, and K. Forbis Jordan, "School-Community Interaction," in *Public School Administration*, 3rd ed. (New York: The Ronald Press Company, 1969), pp. 585–652.
[13] Andrew W. Cordier, *Report of the President for the Year 1968-1969*, Columbia University in the City of New York, pp. 3–9.

live *in* the community if it did not live *with* the community. For some this might be the voice of despair, but for me it is the voice of hope. . . . I had numerous candid talks with many groups and individuals in Morningside Heights and Harlem. I invited many of these groups to my office and to my home to discuss community or community-University questions of interest to them and to the University. . . .

As an outgrowth of these talks, literally hundreds of faculty members and students at Columbia University served as consultants to the community on various concerns including business procedures, legal matters, architectural planning, social work, health and medical services, and other social and educational projects. A program was organized to provide clerical and secretarial training for the people in the community. Business and economic ties with the community were strengthened. Invitations to university events were sent to community members with appropriate interests.[14] Within the university itself, a new university senate was organized, consisting "of 101 members, including representatives of the administration, the tenured faculty, the junior faculty, students, the alumni, and the research staff, as well as representatives of affiliated institutions."[15]

While the foregoing sampling is in no sense a complete description of the activities of the president of Columbia University, it does give an indication of the tremendous amount of community-related activities which an administrator may need to engage in, and seems to imply that these activities would not have served their purpose as well had they been left to someone other than the chief executive of the institution.

Citizen Participation in School
Policy Development

Education becomes increasingly effective as parents and other citizens help appropriately to provide direction for school policy and practice through interpreting the needs of children and the needs of society.

The essence of participatory planning in education may be suggested by a parable. Once upon a time there was a community with children and parents but with no school. Because the parents loved their children, they wanted a school, and so they employed a school staff and designated one of its members to be the school administrator. And he said: "Let us make plans for a school." And they went out together, all the parents and children and school staff, and found

14 *Ibid.,* pp. 10-11.
15 *Ibid.,* p. 15.

a small hill which would make a beautiful place for a school. And they sat down together. And together they planned the school.

Personal involvement in educational planning is greatest when the problems affect a person's own child, and hence citizen planning results in the greatest personal commitment when it involves an individual school. Specific problems and concerns growing out of individual school and community needs are a good place for citizen participation to begin. As people gain more experience in planning, they are more ready to discuss educational goals, objectives, and priorities in the school and community as a whole.[16]

Citizen participation in school policy making implies the need for continuing feedback from the community. Such feedback does not ordinarily take the form of specific proposals, but can provide valuable information concerning the perceptions of citizens as to whether or not the schools are meeting socially approved goals. Feedback may be obtained through informal discussion or conferences; through face-to-face polling by professional pollsters or volunteers; through questionnaires; through interviews which are conducted face-to-face or over the telephone; or through panel discussions, symposiums, or open meetings.

To provide for participatory planning, various types of existing or newly created groups can be utilized, including room parents, grade parents, parent-teacher associations, advisory committees, ad hoc committees, survey committees, policy-forming groups, and others. When such groups center on citizen concerns relative to the development of children, their work can lead logically to consideration of services provided for children by nonschool agencies and thus to coordination of the work of many community agencies. Various types of formal and informal coordinating groups, often including representation of the professional staffs of the agencies involved, have developed in numerous communities.

The utilization of advisory councils has generally proved to be effective both in individual schools and school systems. Sometimes the work of such councils is limited to curriculum matters.[17] Advisory councils typically react to proposals before the school administration puts them into effect. When new proposals are needed, they may suggest policy-forming groups which include citizens as well as students and staff. Advisory councils can be effective at the school system level if they include at least one representative from each school.

[16] For an example see Paula Cramer and Sybil Gilmar, "PPBS: What Should the School Dollar Buy?" *Educational Leadership*, 29, no. 8 (May 1972), 664-67.
[17] See Shirley Jackson, "The Curriculum Council: New Hope, New Promise," *Educational Leadership*, 29, no. 8 (May 1972), 690-94.

One of the major developments in school-community relationships has been the trend toward decentralization. This trend has been going on for many years in the form of staff decentralization.[18] It began with the division of duties within a school system staff on the basis of geographical areas. The trend continued in the larger school systems with the decentralization of the central office, and assistant superintendencies were created in order that the higher levels of decision making in the administrative hierarchy would be more accessible to individual schools and citizens. More recently there has been a trend in large school systems toward the creation of community boards of education in order to provide more direct community control over the schools. The creation of such boards is an expression of the desire of the people to have a greater part in providing direction for the schools and reflects a feeling that they are not adequately consulted now.

To be effective in providing direction for educational policy, an administrator needs to be informed about the power structures of the community. A number of studies have been undertaken for the purpose of characterizing the decision-making processes of entire communities, that is, of finding out what types of people have the greatest power in affecting community decisions, and what kinds of processes and procedures are utilized. Because the public schools are continually in the arena of community decision making, these studies concern the ways in which the basic decisions relative to education are made. Though there are many disagreements among students of the problem over research methods, specific research findings, and interpretation of findings,[19] a substantial body of information has accumulated, and the implications of these findings for school administrators have been indicated in some detail.[20] While much of the research has concerned communities, research has demonstrated that many of the generalizations which can be made about power structures in communities apply to individual schools also.[21]

---

[18] Homer O. Elseroad, "An Evaluation of Central Office Organization and Staff Adequacy in the Baltimore County Public School System with Recommendations for the Decade Ahead" (Doctor of Education Project, University of Maryland, 1961).

[19] Nelson W. Polsby, "The Study of Community Power," *International Encyclopedia*, 3, 157.

[20] Ralph B. Kimbrough and Michael Y. Nunnery, *Educational Administration. An Introduction* (New York: Macmillan Publishing Co., Inc., 1976), pp. 331-65. Ralph B. Kimbrough, *Political Power and Educational Decision-Making* (Chicago, Ill.: Rand McNally & Company, 1964).

[21] Ralph B. Kimbrough, *Political Power*, p. 237.

Studies[22] show that there are five basic types of power structures: 1) monopolistic power structures, in which one or a few individuals in a cohesive leadership group dominate decision making on major issues; 2) multi-group noncompetitive structures, in which several important power groups which are in basic agreement concerning major policies participate in decision making; 3) competitive elite systems, in which there are two or more elite groups of relatively equal strength involved in conflict over policy direction; 4) democratic pluralisms, in which there are many groups which exert power with reference to their own specialized interests, and there is widespread participation of the citizens in decision making; and 5) inert structures, in which various interests do not vie for power but instead individuals have to be found who are willing to assume membership on the school board or to accept other official positions.

In presenting proposals, an administrator needs, through interpersonal relationships, to become aware of the normative processes in a community. If the administrator follows procedures which are not within the limits of community normative processes, the proposals may be rejected, not because of the substantive nature of the proposal, but because of the processes used. If a controversial innovation is to be proposed, it may have the greatest chance for success in one community if it is first mentioned to the head of the monopolistic power structure; in another, if it is first studied by an advisory committee; in another, if it is first mentioned to the president of the school board or discussed with interested board members. Processes such as these represent power structures in action, and change in such processes will not be tolerated if it is perceived as constituting a threat to those who exercise power.

Professional and Lay Roles

If greater trust is to be fostered between schools and their communities, clearer differentiation between professional and lay roles is needed. Many of the functions which are essential for an effective educational program can be best performed by members of the education profession. These functions are those which require professional expertise. They usually require considerable time as well and

---

[22] The first four types of structures are described by Kimbrough and Nunnery, and the fifth by McCarty and Ramsey. See Kimbrough and Nunnery, *Educational Administration*, pp. 338–47. Donald J. McCarty and Charles E. Ramsey, "Community Power, School Board Structure, and the Role of the Chief School Administrator," *Educational Administration Quarterly*, 4, no. 2 (Spring 1968), 19–33.

are often best performed by someone who is a member of a staff which can provide consistency and direction for an entire system.

Aside from a basic lack of faith in people, the biggest single obstacle to more encouragement of citizen participation on the part of professional educators is the fear that citizens will try to take over the professional role. A definition of the professional role is thus as important to the citizen as it is to the professional educator.

Unfortunately, the professional role in education has never been well defined for the simple reason that education has not reached a very high level as a profession. Some individuals enter teaching only as a stepping stone to something else. Some teachers have additional responsibilities such as homemaking or part-time or summer jobs. Many leave to have a family, later returning to the profession. This situation is in sharp contrast to the medical and legal professions, in which the practitioners have such a large investment in their professional preparation and in which the financial rewards are so substantial that they seldom abandon their professional status.

When members of a profession come and go, a definition of the professional role is difficult. The distinctions between the professional and the layman tend to become blurred, and their functions cannot always be differentiated. A parent who has been a teacher may be better grounded professionally than the teacher himself. As staffs become more highly professionalized, however, definition of the professional role becomes increasingly important.

Clearly, parents have a right to be interested in the education of their own children. If they are interested in the welfare of the children, it is only natural that they should be interested in the ways in which the children are being taught, and there is no reason why they should not feel free to inquire about teaching procedures. Parents do not have the right to determine what a teacher or school will do, but they do have a right to give the school information and to express their opinions on the ways in which a school program is affecting their children.

The professional role in education includes any task which requires professional expertise and which involves the education of a child. A teacher should be concerned about a child's total education. Teachers can thus be differentiated from psychologists and psychiatrists, whose central concern is with a child's specific difficulties in learning or emotional development; from church school workers whose central concern is with a child's sectarian religious development; and from social workers and recreation leaders whose central concern is with a child's social or physical development.

Emphasis upon the different roles has resulted in two seemingly contradictory trends: a trend toward more citizen control in school affairs on the one hand, and the strengthening of the education profession on the other. Actually both trends are valid.

If the schools are to meet the needs of children within the context of modern technological society, the thinking of both professional educators and lay citizens is needed. Although it is not practicable, at least at present, to draw any sharp demarcation line between the role of the professional and that of the citizen, thought needs to be given to the differentiation of the professional role in order that the definition of this role may be considerably sharpened through experience. The following principles may be useful.

1. The schools are an instrument of society and should be directed toward achieving society's goals and realizing its ideals. The ultimate control over education should be exercised by the people through legally constituted policy and law-making bodies.

2. Differentiation of the role of the public from that of the professional educator is a complex matter involving judgments relating to the persons, problems, times, and circumstances in the situation, and cannot adequately be set forth in a simple formula.

3. The legal machinery governing public education should be designed to help assure that school policies will be responsive to the considered will (not temporary whims) of the people.

4. The conduct of an educational program is the responsibility of the professional staff. The professional educator is responsible for making educational decisions which are in the best interests of every child. As education becomes more professionalized, the teacher should become the educational authority in the classroom.

5. Parents have a right to be concerned about any aspect of education (including goals and procedures) which affects their children. They have a right to information concerning their children's educational progress, and a responsibility to communicate to the school any important information concerning the effects of the school program upon the development of the child.

6. The professional educator is responsible for synthesizing and applying scientific findings from various academic disciplines. Because professional education draws upon other disciplines, the person or group with the greatest professional competence in a specific area is not always the professional educator employed by the school system. On the other hand, a specialist in a discipline frequently fails to understand the educational processes involved in the utilization of concepts or information from a particular discipline.

7. The function of policy development should be shared by the profession and the lay citizenry. Although all persons are responsible for doing whatever they can to improve education, professional educators are specifically responsible for providing leadership in all aspects of education, including the formulation of goals and the execution of legally adopted policies.

8. Ideas should be evaluated on their merit, not on the source from which they have come. At the same time, the importance of technical proficiency

and professional competence should be recognized, and the information and opinions from professional educators should be carefully weighed.

9. Provision should be made for communications channels to enable citizens to play a positive role in the development and evaluation of educational policy. Such channels should enable citizens to interpret to the schools the needs of the children and of the community. Citizen contributions should be integrated with those of student groups and professional staff.

10. Mutual respect on the part of the lay citizenry and professional educators will help in the resolution of problems through exchange of ideas and information. Conflict from time to time is inevitable, but it should not be allowed to obscure common goals.

CONCLUSION

This chapter has provided an overview of some current community conditions and processes affecting the schools. In particular, student protest, teachers' organizations, citizen control, and resulting role changes have received attention. These conditions imply need for a strong and humane educational program, open communication, appropriate direction of school policy and practice, and clearer differentiation of professional and lay roles.

The role of leadership remains to be considered. What is leadership? What are some leadership theories? How can educational leadership be more effective?

To these questions we now turn our attention.

SUGGESTED READINGS

American Association of School Administrators, *Profiles of the Administrative Team*, chap. 7, "School-Community Relations," chap. 8, "Human Relations." Washington, D.C.: The Association, 1971.

Bagin, Don, Frank Grazian, and Charles Harrison, *PR for School Board Members*, vol. VIII, AASA Executive Handbook Series. Arlington, Va.: American Association of School Administrators, 1976.

Carnegie Commission on Higher Education, *Dissent and Disruption*. New York: McGraw-Hill Book Company, 1971.

Carver, Fred D. and Donald O. Crowe, "An Interdisciplinary Framework for the Study of Community Power," *Educational Administration Quarterly*, 5, no. 1 (Winter 1969), 50–64.

Conway, James A., Robert E. Jennings, and Mike M. Milstein, *Understanding Communities*. Englewood Cliffs, N.J.: Prentice-Hall, Inc., 1974.

Cunningham, Luvern L., "Crisis in School Organization," *Educational Leadership*, 26, no. 6 (March 1969), 551-55.

Dahl, Robert A., *Who Governs?* New Haven, Conn.: Yale University Press, 1961.

Derr, C. Brooklyn and John J. Gabarro, "An Organizational Contingency Theory for Education," *Educational Administration Quarterly*, 8, no. 2 (Spring 1972), 26-43.

Educational Leadership, Journal of the Association for Supervision and Curriculum Development, NEA: "Alternative Forms of Schooling," 29, no. 5 (February 1972); "Community Involvement in Curriculum," 29, no. 8 (May 1972); "Beyond Confrontation!" 30, no. 1 (October 1972).

Fantini, Mario and Marilyn Gittell, *Decentralization: Achieving Reform*. New York: Praeger Publishers, 1973.

Gaynor, Alan K., "Some Implications of Political Systems Theory for Alternative Demand Processing Mechanisms for Public School Systems," *Educational Administration Quarterly*, 7, no. 1 (Winter 1971), 34-45.

Grieder, Calvin, Truman M. Pierce, and K. Forbis Jordan, "School-Community Interaction," *Public School Administration*, 3rd ed., New York: The Ronald Press Company, 1969, pp. 585-652.

Gross, Neal, *Who Runs Our Schools?* New York: John Wiley & Sons, Inc., 1958.

Hunter, Floyd, *Community Power Structure: A Study of Decision Making*. Garden City, N.Y.: Anchor Books, Doubleday & Company, Inc., 1963.

Iannaccone, Laurence and Frank W. Lutz, *Politics, Power, and Policy: The Governing of Local School Districts*. Columbus, Ohio: Charles E. Merrill Publishing Company, 1970.

Levin, Henry M., ed., *Community Control of Schools*. Washington, D.C.: The Brookings Institution, 1970.

Nunnery, Michael Y. and Ralph B. Kimbrough, *Politics, Power, Polls, and School Elections*. Berkeley, Calif.: McCutchan Publishing Corporation, 1971.

Sarthory, Joseph A., "Structural Characteristics and the Outcome of Collective Negotiations," *Educational Administration Quarterly*, 7, no. 3 (Autumn 1971), 78-89.

Saxe, Richard W., *School-Community Interaction*. Berkeley, Calif.: McCutchan Publishing Corporation, 1975.

Walker, Hill M., "The Superintendent's Use of Cooptation in Handling Internal Interest and Pressure Groups: Its Effect and Consequences," *Educational Administration Quarterly*, 4, no. 1 (Winter 1968), 32-44.

LEADERSHIP 10

For many persons the word "leadership" brings to mind a number of leaders who have had impact upon them and upon their world. Any discussion of leadership almost invariably turns to the attributes and methods of some of the world's historic leaders. These leaders may be persons who made their mark in government, such as George Washington, Thomas Jefferson, Abraham Lincoln, Franklin D. Roosevelt, Winston Churchill, Mohandas Gandhi, Golda Meir, Nikolai Lenin, or Adolph Hitler. They may be leaders in the world of thought such as Jesus, Karl Marx, Charles Darwin, Sigmund Freud, Friedrich Nietzsche, Isaac Newton, Marie Curie, or Albert Einstein. They may be creative geniuses in the arts such as Beethoven, Bach, Shakespeare, Dante, Goethe, Michelangelo, or da Vinci. Leaders may be moral, amoral, or immoral; benefactors or malefactors of mankind; individuals who respect other human beings or who disdain them.

Yet all these leaders have something in common. All of them have exercised influence. All of them developed their contributions in response to societal needs, and all were influenced by society.

It is natural then that people should ask: What is leadership? What can be learned about the ways in which leadership functions? How can I be a good leader?

Many attempts to answer these questions have been made. As scientific information accumulates relative to individuals and their relationships with others, leadership is becoming better understood and insights relative to the nature of leadership are increasingly being utilized to advantage.

In this chapter various conceptions of leadership are considered, theory and research findings relative to leadership are presented, and the implications of these ideas for effective educational leadership are explored.

CONCEPTIONS OF LEADERSHIP

In the past, "leadership," "administration," and "management" have often been used interchangeably. As the behavioral sciences have developed, however, the concept of leadership has been increasingly limited to designate a particular aspect of interpersonal relationships. To some authorities, leadership means the role of change agent; to others it means the influence which one person exerts on another.[1] Implicit in both these conceptualizations is the notion of process. Whatever the conception, behavioral scientists typically differentiate leadership from administration. To be effective, however, educational administration must include leadership.

While the concept of leadership has been restricted in one sense, it has been broadened in another. Originally leadership was thought of in terms of the direction or command of a group by its most able member. Leadership and management were considered to be the antithesis of democratic action, for the assumption was that if an organization is to be effective, someone must be in charge and tell others what to do. However, it was found that the foregoing concept, that leadership consists of the ablest person or group telling others what to do, is not comprehensive enough because it fails to include a whole range of leadership phenomena, not only in education but in business, government, and other areas of activity as well. Many administrators have discovered that leadership can be highly effective when they are not directing, but instead are helping individuals and groups to formulate their own goals, identify their own problems, and develop procedures for achieving goals and solving the attendant problems. Often the provision of a wholesome environment is an important aspect of leadership. To be adequate, a concept of leadership must be broad enough to encompass various types of leadership.

Since there are specific types of leadership, it is useful to think of

---

[1] Edgar L. Morphet, Roe L. Johns, and Theodore L. Reller, *Educational Organization and Administration: Concepts, Practices, and Issues*, 3rd ed. (Englewood Cliffs, N.J.: Prentice-Hall, Inc., 1974).

...up as a generic term which refers to processes characterized by interrelationships among people as they work together in the formulation and achievement of common goals. Leadership occurs within an institution or society, and the leaders interact with other persons in the institution and the society. Leadership and isolation are incompatible; a leader may at times feel very much alone, but an individual can function as a leader only through relationships and effective communication with other persons.

A statement by Cartwright and Zander summarizes much of the current thinking on leadership.[2]

Leadership is viewed as the performance of those acts which help the group achieve its preferred outcomes. Such acts may be termed *group functions*. More specifically, leadership consists of such actions by group members as those which aid in setting group goals, moving the group toward its goals, improving the quality of the interactions among the members, building the cohesiveness of the group, and making resources available to the group. In principle, leadership may be performed by one or many members of the group.

This point of view has been stressed by many writers including Barnard . . . Cattell . . . French . . . Gibb . . . Likert . . . Lippitt . . . Redl . . . and Stogdill. . . . The common denominator among these theorists includes the following points: groups differ from one another in a variety of ways, and the actions required for the achievement of valued states of one group may be quite different from those of another. The nature of leadership and the traits of leaders will accordingly be different from group to group. Situational aspects such as the nature of the group's goals, the structure of the group, the attitudes or needs of the members, and the expectations placed upon the group by its external environment help to determine which group functions will be needed at any given time and who among the members will perform them.

Leadership may be defined as a process through which persons or groups intentionally influence others in the development and attainment of group or organizational goals. Leadership includes verbal and nonverbal behavior, which are components of communication in the decision-making processes of individuals and groups. It is exercised when an individual, group, or organization purposely affects the thoughts, feelings, or behavior of others in the formulation or achievement of common or compatible goals through coercion, influence, guidance, supervision, or consultation. To be effective, the nature of leadership must change whenever there are changes in the group's task, the people in the group, or the situation in which the group functions.[3]

[2] Dorwin Cartwright and Alvin Zander, eds., *Group Dynamics: Research and Theory*, 3rd ed. (New York: Harper & Row, Publishers, 1968), p. 304.

[3] For a comprehensive review of "Definitions of Leadership," see Ralph M. Stogdill, *Handbook of Leadership. A Survey of Theory and Research* (New York: The Free Press, 1974), pp. 7-16.

Leadership involves the exercise of power, that is, the capacity to influence events. A leader derives power from the capacity to provide for or to deny need satisfaction to an individual or group. Power may be derived from the ability to grant rewards or impose penalties, or from competence. Authority, or the right to use power, may be attained through position or through competence. Both power and authority are important in effective organizational leadership as well as in the more routine aspects of administration.

Types of Leadership

Two types of leadership can readily be identified: status leadership and emergent leadership. Status leadership is leadership associated with a particular position such as school superintendent, principal, chairman, secretary, consultant, or board president. It is not unusual to hear someone say that Mr. So-and-so has been placed in a position of leadership. Such a comment is simple recognition of the fact that leadership is associated with and expected from persons who occupy certain positions. A superintendent of schools, for example, is expected not merely to provide for the performance of routine tasks but also to provide leadership. Likewise, a chairman, secretary, or other official in a group is expected to perform certain leadership functions. Hence such persons are often referred to as status leaders even though they may or may not exercise real leadership. In addition to status leadership, leadership is often exercised by someone who holds no special position. Because such leadership emerges in relation to particular problems, it is called emergent leadership. A group member who does not hold any special office in a group may express a useful idea, ask a penetrating question, help the group to formulate a plan, or work behind the scenes and make useful suggestions to a status leader. These acts may constitute highly important leadership behavior even though they are not the acts of one of the status leaders.

Emergent leadership has been described in a classic statement by Kilpatrick as follows.[4]

Many seem to think of leadership as if it were only or primarily fixed in advance, either by appointment or election or by special ability and preparation. On this basis those proceed to divide people into two fixed groups, leaders and followers. Such a view seems inadequate, quite denied by observable facts. Actual leadership as we see it comes mostly by emergency out of a social situation. A number of people talk freely about a matter of common concern. *A* proposes a plan of action. *B* successfully voices objection and criticism. *C* then proposes a modified plan. *D, E,* and

[4] William H. Kilpatrick in Samuel Everett, ed., *The Community School* (New York: Appleton-Century Company, Inc., 1938), p. 20.

...tain features of this plan. The group at this point divides, ...y unable to agree. *G* then comes forward with a new plan that ...ines the desired features and avoids the evils feared. The group agree. Here *A*, *B*, *C*, *D*, *E*, *F*, and *G* were successively leaders of the group. And each such act of leadership emerged out of the situation as it then appeared. This is democratic leadership and its success depends on — nay exactly is — an on-going process of education inherent in the situation.

Styles of Leadership

Earlier it was indicated that leadership may be considered a generic term which describes a variety of types of relationships. Through studies of leadership, different leadership styles have been identified.

Autocratic, Laissez-faire, and Democratic Leadership

As an outgrowth of the studies of Lewin, Lippitt, and White,[5] considerable attention has been given to three types of leadership styles: autocratic, laissez-faire, and democratic. While the term laissez-faire leadership is in one sense internally inconsistent, it has nevertheless been used to characterize the behavior of persons in positions of status leadership who often take a passive stance toward the problems of a group or organization.

These styles of leadership have largely been replaced in current thinking by leadership theory and research studies which are typically less ideologically oriented. Nevertheless, the earlier differentiation of styles of leadership is still useful for some purposes.

Actual leadership probably never exists in a pure form as autocratic, democratic, or laissez-faire leadership but to some extent combines them all. Undoubtedly, however, some types of leadership are best characterized by one term and some by another. The different leadership styles may be useful as a means of conceptualizing leadership.

Autocratic leadership is often subdivided to include the "hardboiled autocrat" and the "benevolent autocrat." In both instances, leadership resides in the autocrat. However, the hardboiled autocrat emphasizes production as opposed to human considerations whereas the benevolent autocrat is interested in "his" employees in a paternalistic manner. In the case of laissez-faire leadership, the leadership function may be exercised in a haphazard fashion

[5] Ralph White and Ronald Lippitt, "Leader Behavior and Member Reaction in Three 'Social Climates'," in Cartwright and Zander, *Group Dynamics*, pp. 318–35.

and tends to be ineffectual. In a democratic situation, the leadership process demonstrates respect for every person in the group, and leadership responsibilities are shared. As has been pointed out elsewhere, the decision-making function "resides in the *leader* in the autocratic group, in the *individual* in the laissez-faire group, and in the *group* in the democratic situation."[6]

Idiographic, Nomothetic, and Transactional Leadership

A more recent conception of leadership identifies leadership styles as being nomothetic, idiographic, and transactional. Once again actual leadership probably never exists in a pure form but instead combines all three styles. Nevertheless, leadership in specific instances may be characterized as being primarily of one of these styles or another.

These three styles of leadership can perhaps be best understood in reference to the Getzels-Guba-Thelen model.[7] It will be recalled that this model includes: 1) an organizational or nomothetic dimension, which concerns organizational decision making or legislative action; and 2) a personal or idiographic dimension, which concerns the individual or idea aspect of organization. Three different styles of leadership based upon this model can be conceptualized.

The first and the most commonly practiced type of leadership is nomothetic leadership, which places emphasis upon the nomothetic or legislative aspect of leadership. This style emphasizes organizational goals at the expense of individual needs and motivations. It was expressed in a single sentence by an executive who said, "The best way to identify immature employees is to spot those who have difficulty in identifying their own goals as being the same as those of the organization." By implication this executive was indicating a preference for organizational goals to the exclusion of individual goals. A weakness in nomothetic leadership is that individuals in organizations with such leadership tend to lack motivation because adequate attention is not given to individual goals.

A second type of leadership is idiographic leadership, which places emphasis upon the goals, ideas, and plans of individuals. This style assumes that the organization will get its work done if all of the individuals in the organization are happy and productive. It was expressed in a sentence by a bureau director who said, "The goals of an

[6] Gordon L. Lippitt, "What Do We Know About Leadership?" *Leadership in Action* (Washington, D.C.: National Training Laboratories, National Education Association, 1961), p. 8.
[7] For an explanation of the model see Chapter 3.

organization should be nothing more than the aggregate of the goals of the individuals in the organization." A weakness in this position is that the mission of an organization can be accomplished only if there is planning for the purpose of accomplishing that mission. If all planning is done by individuals in isolation, they will tend to emphasize their own needs and purposes to the neglect of those of the organization as a whole, to duplicate one another's efforts, and to fail to perform some of the necessary organizational tasks.

The third type of leadership is transactional leadership, which may be characterized by its awareness of both the nomothetic and the idiographic dimensions of organization, and its integration of the two. Transactional leadership continually analyzes the situation in relation to organizational and individual needs and purposes. With transactional leadership, the needs and purposes of individuals in the organization are considered as organizational problems are resolved, and conversely, organizational needs and purposes are taken into account as attention is paid to the problems of individuals. Transactional leadership is thus a process through which the task and human dimensions of organization are reconciled and integrated.[8]

THEORY AND RESEARCH

An Overview of Leadership Theories

Because of a persisting interest over a period of years in the phenomenon of leadership, many leadership theories and models have been developed. These theories have been grouped by Stogdill into six major types, briefly described as follows.[9]

Great man theories

These theories suggest that leaders exert power because they possess qualities which differentiate them from and which appeal to the masses. It was thought that through survival of the fittest and intermarriage, a group of leaders biologically superior to the followers developed, and that these leaders naturally rose to positions of power.

---

[8] Transactional leadership in the sense in which the term is used here should not be confused with idiosyncrasy credit theory or social exchange theory, which pertain to transactional leadership in a quite different sense. For an explanation and discussion of these theories see T. O. Jacobs, *Leadership and Exchange in Formal Organizations* (Alexandria, Va.: Human Resources Research Organization [HumRRO], 1971), pp. 93-121.

[9] The material in this section was drawn from Stogdill, *Handbook of Leadership*, pp. 17-23.

Some of the contributors included by Stogdill in this group are F. Galton, F. A. Woods, and A. E. Wiggam. Among the contributors to the trait theories of leadership are L. L. Bernard and O. Tead.

Environmental theories

The environmental theorists believe that leadership is a function of the situation and that leadership is vested in a person by a group, not because this person is inherently a leader, but because he or she can perform needed group functions. A leader does not produce the situation; instead it is the situation which calls forth a leader. Theorists in this group include E. Mumford, E. S. Bogardus, W. E. Hocking, H. S. Person, J. Schneider, and A. J. Murphy.

Personal-situational theories

These theorists represent a synthesis of the *great man* and *environmental* theories and view leadership as the interactive effects between the leader and the situation. Leadership is characterized by relationships among persons rather than by leader traits or situational attributes. The goals and needs of the individual are seen as interacting with those of the group. Among these theorists are E. M. Westburgh, C. A. Gibb, R. M. Stogdill and C. L. Shartle, W. G. Bennis, R. B. Cattell, and E. P. Hollander.

Interaction-expectation theories

These theories emphasize the importance of interactions and the expectations which group members have for the behavior of individual group members, and the ways in which interactions and expectations influence each other. Role structures result from member expectations, and when the structures are seen as serving group purposes, they strengthen expectations that group members will conform to the roles. The leadership potential of any group member is determined by the extent to which the individual initiates and maintains role structure. Theorists included in this group are G. C. Homans, J. K. Hemphill, R. M. Stogdill, B. M. Bass, M. G. Evans, R. J. House, and F. E. Fiedler.

Humanistic theories

These theorists believe that organizations can best achieve their goals when they enable the individuals in the organization to develop their own creative potential. Because human beings are internally motivated, an organization need not create motivation but needs only to harness the already existing motivation. The function of leadership is to free individuals so that they may contribute maximally to organizational goals through their natural tendency to accept responsibility and to develop. Contributors to these theories include Chris Argyris, R. R. Blake, and Jane S. Mouton, R. Likert, and D. McGregor.

Exchange theories

These theories are based on the assumption that social interaction represents a form of exchange in which each group member makes contributions to the group at a personal cost and in turn receives rewards in the form of tangible payment or psychological satisfaction. Interaction continues because it is mutually rewarding to the participants. The leader is rewarded with esteem and prestige satisfactions in return for special contributions to goal delineation and attainment. Theorists cited by Stogdill in this group are G. C. Homans, J. G. March and H. A. Simon, J. W. Thibaut and H. H. Kelley, K. J. Gergen, P. M. Blau, and T. O. Jacobs.

Leader Traits

For a time it was thought that leadership could be explained in terms of certain traits which all leaders were thought to possess. It was believed that leaders were outstanding in traits such as honesty, intelligence, physical size, responsibility, persistence, originality, initiative, and the like. Subsequent research findings, however, cast serious doubts on the validity of the trait theory. It was observed, for example, that honesty might be considered to be a desirable trait in a leader in a school faculty, yet such a trait might be considered highly undesirable in their leader by a group of counterfeiters.

After examining 124 studies on the relationship of personality factors to leadership, Stogdill in an early publication summarized the evidence as follows:[10]

A person does not become a leader by virtue of the possession of some combination of traits, but the pattern of personal characteristics of the leader must bear some relevant relationship to the characteristics, activities, and goals of the followers. Thus, leadership must be conceived in terms of the interactions of variables which are in constant flux and change.

Stogdill found that the only conclusion which received even fair

---

[10] Ralph M. Stogdill, "Personal Factors Associated with Leadership. A Survey of the Literature," *The Journal of Psychology*, 25 (1948), 64.

support in the studies examined was that leaders excel nonleaders in intelligence, scholarship, dependability and responsibility, activity and social participation, and socioeconomic status. Similar results were found by Bird, Jenkins, and Myers.[11]

Because support for the trait theory was lacking, the conclusion was reached that leadership as a generic function does not exist. Some writers went so far as to say that leadership is a function of a specific situation, including the particular activity of a group at a particular time.[12] Others suggested that other frames of reference be used in the study of leadership phenomena.[13]

More recent research findings indicate that the conclusion drawn from earlier studies were too extreme in their emphasis upon the importance of the situation and their tendency to downgrade the importance of the personality and competencies of the leader. If was found that a leader who is effective in one situation tends to be effective in similar situations. Furthermore, it was found that general characteristics, as opposed to specific traits, are typical of leaders in a variety of situations. The current view is that not only are both the leader and the situation important in leader effectiveness, but that they interact, with the leader affecting the situation, and the situation in turn affecting leader behavior.

After reviewing studies conducted between 1948 and 1970 on leadership traits, Stogdill wrote:[14]

The leader is characterized by a strong drive for responsibility and task completion, vigor and persistence in pursuit of goals, venturesomeness and originality in problem solving, drive to exercise initiative in social situations, self-confidence and sense of personal identity, willingness to accept consequences of decision and action, readiness to absorb interpersonal stress, willingness to tolerate frustration and delay, ability to influence other persons' behavior, and capacity to structure social interaction systems to the purpose at hand. . . .
The characteristics considered singly, hold little diagnostic or predictive significance. In combination, it would appear that they interact to generate personality dynamics advantageous to the person seeking the responsibilities of leadership. The conclusion that personality is a factor in

[11] Charles Bird, *Social Psychology* (New York: Appleton, Century, 1940), p. 379. W. O. Jenkins, "A Review of Leadership Studies with Particular Reference to Military Problems," *Psychological Bulletin*, 44, no. 1 (January 1947), 54-79. Robert B. Myers, "The Development and Implications of a Conception of Leadership for Leadership Education," (Doctoral dissertation, University of Florida, 1954), p. 107.

[12] Jenkins, "A Review of Leadership Studies," p. 75.

[13] William E. Martin, Neal Gross, and John G. Darley, "Studies of Group Behavior: Leaders, Followers, and Isolates in Small Organized Groups," *Journal of Abnormal and Social Psychology*, 47, no. 4 (October 1952), 842.

[14] Stogdill, *Handbook of Leadership*, pp. 81-82.

leadership differentiation does not represent a return to the trait approach. It does represent a modification of the extreme situationist point of view. . . .

The various factors describing leaders in fifty-two studies published since 1945 were analyzed by Stogdill. Those factors which appeared in nine or more of the studies are shown in order of frequency in the following table.

Leadership Factors Appearing in Nine or More Studies[15]

Rank Order	Factor Name	Frequency
1	Technical skills	18
2	Social nearness, friendliness	18
3	Task motivation and application	17
4	Group task supportiveness	17
5	Social and interpersonal skills	16
6	Leadership effectiveness and achievement	15
7	Emotional balance and control	15
8	Administrative skills	12
9	General impression (halo)	12
10	Intellectual skills	11
11	Ascendance, dominance, decisiveness	11
12	Willingness to assume responsibility	10
13	Ethical conduct, personal integrity	10
14	Maintaining cohesive work group	9

As Stogdill emphasizes, the frequency shown in the table relates to the number of studies in which a factor appears and does not necessarily indicate the frequency with which such factors are characteristic of leaders. The factors reflect the interests of the researchers in deciding what items to study as well as the leadership phenomena themselves. Nevertheless, despite its limitations, the table does shed some light on the factors associated with leadership.

Of the factors in the table, only the first one relates specifically to competence in the organizational task. The human dimension is represented by numbers 2 (tied with number 1 in terms of frequency), 3, 4, 5, 7, 11, 12, 13, and 14. More general factors which conceivably relate to either the organizational task or the human dimension are numbers 6, 8, 9, and 10. Thus, the table calls attention to the importance of the human as well as the task dimension in the practice of effective leadership.

Taken as a whole, the research findings suggest that both the trait

[15] Data adapted from a table in Stogdill, *Handbook of Leadership,* p. 93.

and the situational approaches to leadership are too simplistic. Leadership appears to be a complex phenomenon involving infinite numbers of interactions among people, tasks, and other situational elements. While the consideration of individual human traits has not proved to be productive in the study of leadership, more recent research demonstrates that there are indeed human characteristics which relate to leadership effectiveness.

Dimensions of Leadership

Of the numerous research studies which have been conducted relative to leadership, many have explored the task and the human dimensions and their relationships to one another. A number of the early research studies, such as those conducted at the University of Michigan, assumed that the employee-centered and production-centered aspects of leader behavior constituted a single dimension, that as leaders became more person oriented, they would be less production oriented, and *vice versa*. However, it was discovered that an inverse relationship between the two aspects of organizational life did not always hold, that a supervisor might be high or low on both production and person orientations. Thus it was found that task and human considerations do not represent the opposite ends of a continuum, but rather that they represent two different dimensions. An administrator can be concerned about both organizational tasks and people.

Much of the recent research on leadership has centered around these two dimensions, and the findings are informative. Before some of the findings are considered, however, it should be noted that the two terms and their synonyms cover many different types of behavior. Thus, person-oriented leader behavior may include "democratic, permissive, participative, follower-oriented, and considerate patterns of behavior," and work-oriented leadership may include "autocratic, restrictive, distant, directive, and structured" behavior.[16] These different types of leadership represent different concepts and different types of behavior. These differences need to be kept in mind in relation to research findings and discussions concerning the task and human dimensions of leadership.

Early explorations identified two fundamental dimensions of leader behavior: Initiating Structure and Consideration.[17]

---

[16] *Ibid.*, p. 403.

[17] Andrew W. Halpin and B. J. Winer, "A Factorial Study of the Leader Behavior Descriptions," in *Leader Behavior: Its Description and Measurement*, eds. R. M. Stogdill and A. E. Coons (Columbus, Ohio: Bureau of Business Research, Ohio State University, 1957).

Initiating Structure refers to the leader's behavior in delineating the relationship between himself and members of the work-group, and in endeavoring to establish well-defined patterns of organization, channels of communication, and methods of procedure. Consideration refers to behavior indicative of friendship, mutual trust, respect, and warmth in the relationship between the leader and the members of his staff.[18]

These two dimensions correspond to (but are not identical with) the *task* and the *human* dimensions which appear under various appellations in a variety of organizational theories and models.

When studies utilizing the Leader Behavior Description Questionnaire (LBDQ)[19] were conducted with reference to the leader behavior of aircraft commanders, it was found that commanders who were rated high on both dimensions were evaluated as high in overall effectiveness as judged by their superior officers. In addition, those who rated high on both dimensions tended to develop more favorable crew attitudes than those who scored low on both dimensions. However, it was also found that in weighing the two dimensions, the commanders' superiors placed relatively more value upon Initiating Structure, while the crews placed relatively more value upon Consideration.[20]

In another important early study, Hemphill used the LBDQ to measure leader behavior in eighteen departments in a liberal arts college. He found that almost without exception the departments with above-median reputation were those whose chairmen scored high on *both* the Initiating Structure and the Consideration dimensions.[21]

In another study, the leadership behavior of school superintendents was measured.[22] One of the interesting findings of this study is that superintendents, staff members, and school board members all characterized an "Ideal" superintendent as one who scores high on both Consideration and Initiating Structure. At the same time, the board members tended to emphasize Initiating Structure whereas the staffs preferred less structure than the superintendents believed they should initiate.

[18] Andrew W. Halpin, *Theory and Research in Administration* (New York: The Macmillan Company, 1966), p. 86.
[19] For a critical analysis of the LBDQ see W. W. Charters, Jr., *Teacher Perceptions of Administrator Behavior* (St. Louis: Cooperative Research Project, no. 929, U.S. Office of Education, January, 1964), pp. 176–89.
[20] Halpin, *Theory and Research*, pp. 91–94.
[21] John K. Hemphill, "Leadership Behavior Associated with the Administrative Reputation of College Departments," *The Journal of Educational Psychology*, 46, no. 7 (November 1955), 396.
[22] Andrew W. Halpin, *The Leadership Behavior of School Superintendents* (Columbis, Ohio: College of Education, The Ohio State University, 1956).

Research has found that teacher satisfaction is positively related to Consideration and Structuring behaviors of principals, as perceived by teachers.[23] In another study, it was found that school principals rate themselves high on responsibility, authority, and delegation when they perceive their superiors as being high on Consideration.[24] Other studies have found that if there is too much emphasis on production, the result will be a decline in production or an increase in worker dissatisfaction, or both.[25] Research shows also that employees prefer a leader who can respond to situational needs and demands with behaviors which may be either in the nature of Consideration or Initiation of Structure.[26] It has been found that Technical Specialists, Social Specialists, and the Underchosen tend to engage in either task-oriented or human-oriented behaviors but not both, whereas the Stars (older and highly rewarded individuals who had experienced career success) engaged in both task- and human-oriented behaviors, with an expressed preference for being with people.[27] Through these and other research findings, the importance of both Consideration and Initiation of Structure in effective leader behavior appears to be well established.[28]

The Best Style?

Although the importance of both the Initiating Structure and Consideration dimensions might seem to imply that transactional leadership is always best, this view has not been substantiated by research findings. Instead it appears that the type of leadership needed varies in accordance with the particular situation.

Research findings seem to indicate clearly that to be effective, leadership style must be appropriate in relation to the situation. Thus, a research study found that participative decision making in a

[23] R. G. Fast, "Leader Behavior of Principals as it Relates to Teacher Satisfaction" (Master's thesis, University of Alberta, 1964).

[24] Herman J. Bowman, "Perceived Leader Behavior Patterns and Their Relationships to Self-Perceived Variables — Responsibility, Authority, and Delegation," *Dissertation Abstracts*, 25 (1964), 3340.

[25] Robert C. Day and Robert L. Hamblin, "Some Effects of Close and Punitive Styles of Supervision," *American Journal of Sociology*, 69 (March 1964) 499–510. Nancy C. Morse and Everett Reimer, "The Experimental Change of a Major Organizational Variable," *Journal of Abnormal and Social Psychology*, 52, no. 1 (January 1956), 120–29.

[26] Andrew W. Halpin, "The Leadership Behavior and Combat Performance of Airplane Commanders," *Journal of Abnormal and Social Psychology*, 49, no. 1 (1954), 19–22.

[27] David Moment and Abraham Zaleznik, *Role Development and Interpersonal Competence* (Boston: Division of Research, Graduate School of Business Administration, Harvard University, 1963).

[28] Stogdill, *Handbook of Leadership*.

factory in the United States resulted in greater productivity and decreased resistance to change;[29] however, when the research was replicated in a Norwegian factory, no significant difference was found between the productivity of work groups which had and those which had not been involved in participative decision making.[30]

Another significant research discovery concerns the general trend of findings in a single study. Thus, a study by Likert found that of seven *high-producing* sections in industry, six were under employee-centered supervisors while only one was under job-centered supervision; and of ten *low-producing* sections, only three were under employee-centered supervision, whereas seven were under job-centered supervision.[31] These findings have been interpreted to mean that employee-centered supervision is best, yet as has been pointed out elsewhere,[32] the exceptions to the general trend suggest that there is no universally superior leadership style.

Perhaps the most telling evidence comes from a study by Korman, who, after reviewing twenty-five leadership studies utilizing various measures of effectiveness, concluded that:[33]

> . . . Despite the fact that "Consideration" and "Initiating Structure" have become almost bywords in American industrial psychology, it seems apparent that very little is now known as to how these variables may predict work group performance and the conditions which affect such predictions. At the current time, we cannot even say whether they have any predictive significance at all.

Taken as a whole, research findings have not substantiated the notion that there is a single leadership style which is best for all situations. Though the research has often been limited by using the single criterion of productivity, the evidence available seems to suggest that different types of situations call for different types of leadership style.[34]

[29] Lester Coch and John R. P. French, Jr., "Overcoming Resistance to Change," in *Group Dynamics*, eds. Cartwright and Zander, pp. 336-50.

[30] John R. P. French, Jr., Joachim Israel, and Dagfinn As, "An Experiment on Participation in a Norwegian Factory," *Human Relations*, 13, no. 1 (February 1960), 3-19.

[31] Rensis Likert, *New Patterns of Management* (New York: McGraw-Hill Book Company, 1961), p. 7.

[32] Paul Hersey and Kenneth H. Blanchard, *Management of Organizational Behavior: Utilizing Human Resources*, 3rd ed. (Englewood Cliffs, N.J.: Prentice-Hall, Inc., 1977), pp. 129-30.

[33] Abraham K. Korman, "'Consideration,' 'Initiating Structure,' and Organizational Criteria—A Review," *Personnel Psychology: A Journal of Applied Research*, 19, no. 4 (Winter 1966), 360.

[34] For a summary of the relevant research see Hersey and Blanchard, *Management of Organizational Behavior*, pp. 68-73, 84-89. William J. Reddin, *Managerial Effectiveness* (New York: McGraw-Hill Book Company, 1970), pp. 35-38.

Situational Elements

The indications that the most desirable type of leadership style depends upon the situation have led to a search for the situational elements which have implications for leadership style.

A major attempt to identify situational elements has been made through the research efforts of Fred E. Fiedler and his associates.[35] These attempts grew out of Fiedler's concerns about perceptions and the ways in which errors in perceptions of group members about each other affect accomplishment of group tasks. After studying a number of variables, Fiedler came to the conclusion that the most promising variable for study was Assumed Similarity of Opposites (ASo). To obtain a score on this variable, an individual was asked to rate his most preferred and least preferred coworker on sixteen items on an eight-point graphic rating scale, such as the following:

Friendly : : : : : : : : : Unfriendly
Cooperative : : : : : : : : : Uncooperative

For each pair of adjectives, a score representing the difference between the rating for the most preferred and least preferred co-worker was obtained, and from these difference scores, the ASo was computed.[36] Thus the scale measures the capacity of an individual to differentiate between most preferred and least preferred coworkers on task-related items.

After a good deal of research using this scale with formal leaders in formal organizations, Fiedler came to the conclusion that the capacity of the leader to differentiate among workers on task-related items (those in the scale) is related to group productivity or effectiveness,[37] provided that the leader is accepted as a desirable coworker by the group and, in some cases, that the leader strongly endorses key subordinates.[38] Subsequent findings led Fiedler to the research conclusion "that the appropriateness of the leadership style for

---

[35] Fred E. Fiedler, *A Theory of Leadership Effectiveness* (New York: McGraw-Hill Book Company, 1967). From *Leadership and Effective Management* by Fred E. Fiedler and Martin M. Chemers. Copyright © 1974 by Scott, Foresman and Company. Reprinted by permission.

[36] The ASo score was later replaced by the Least Preferred Co-Worker score (LPC), which is computed from ratings of the least preferred co-worker and which has been found to correlate with ASo scores. See Fiedler, *A Theory of Leadership*, p. 43.

[37] A high ASo score represents relatively *similar* ratings for most preferred and least preferred co-workers. The findings were that group effectiveness correlates negatively with ASo scores.

[38] Fiedler, *A Theory of Leadership*, p. 73ff.

maximizing group performance is contingent upon the favorableness of the group-task situation."[39] These findings led in turn to the development of Fiedler's Contingency Model.

The Contigency Model asserts that "leaders who are primarily task-motivated perform best under conditions that are very favorable or very unfavorable for them. Relationship-motivated leaders perform best under conditions that are of moderate favorableness."[40] According to the model, favorableness of the group-task situation depends upon three factors: 1) leader-member relations ("the interpersonal relationship"); 2) task structure ("the degree to which the task requirements are spelled out"); and 3) leader position power ("the right to direct, evaluate, reward, and punish those he is asked to supervise").[41]

Fiedler's work is based upon the assumption that the task and human orientations are at opposite ends of a single continuum, but as has been indicated previously, the research evidence indicates otherwise. This faulty assumption has sometimes led to misinterpretations of Fiedler's data.

While a definitive statement based on present research findings is not possible, some tentative inferences can be drawn from Fiedler's findings. The findings seem to indicate that when situations are highly favorable or unfavorable to the leader, greater psychological distance from coworkers is useful. In situations of high favorability, the group is ready to work at the task and, with the assistance of the leader, to assume appropriate roles. In situations definitely unfavorable to the leader, more direction appears to be useful, for without such direction the work would not be done effectively and the leader would be seen by the workers as being ineffectual. In situations of moderate favorability, the situation is neither so bad that substantial psychological distance is essential to keep the organization intact and functioning (at even a low level), nor is it so good that modification of appropriate roles has become a critical element in maintaining an outstanding level of performance. At the intermediate level of favorability, reduction of psychological distance may be necessary in order that the leader may maintain the mild acceptance of staff members, initiate structure with the staff on problems about which the leader has no more knowledge than the group members, and save his position power for use in critical situations.

These inferences are highly tentative and will doubtless necessitate revision if substantial research findings relative to the Fiedler model

[39] *Ibid.*, p. 147.
[40] Fiedler and Chemers, *Leadership and Effective Management*, p. 81.
[41] *Ibid.*, pp. 64–69.

become available. In making these inferences, the author has attempted to avoid the misinterpretations of Fiedler's data which have sometimes resulted when the research findings in the field as a whole have not been taken into account.

The Hersey-Blanchard and Reddin Models

The attempts to identify situational elements that impinge upon leadership have led to two other models of remarkable similarity, one developed by Hersey and Blanchard, and the other by Reddin. In both instances, leader effectiveness is taken into account.

The model developed by Hersey and Blanchard is called the Tri-Dimensional Leader Effectiveness Model. This model is based upon the basic leader behavior styles shown in the following figure.

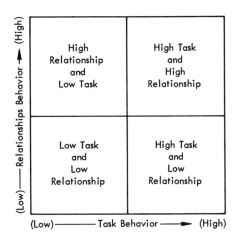

Basic Leader Behavior Styles.*

*Paul Hersey and Kenneth H. Blanchard, *Management of Organizational Behavior: Utilizing Human Resources,* 3rd ed., p. 103.

The lower left corner in the figure represents zero for both task- and relationships-orientation. As one proceeds horizontally to the right, he moves in the direction of leader behavior style characterized by high task-orientation, and as one proceeds vertically, he moves in the direction of leader behavior style characterized by high relationships-orientation (people oriented behavior). The corner at the top right represents leader behavior style with both high task- and high relationships-orientation.

Because leaders may be effective or ineffective depending upon how they interrelate with the situation, regardless of whether or not they are relationships-oriented or task-oriented, an effectiveness dimension was added to the model. The resulting Tri-Dimensional Leader Effectiveness Model is shown as follows.

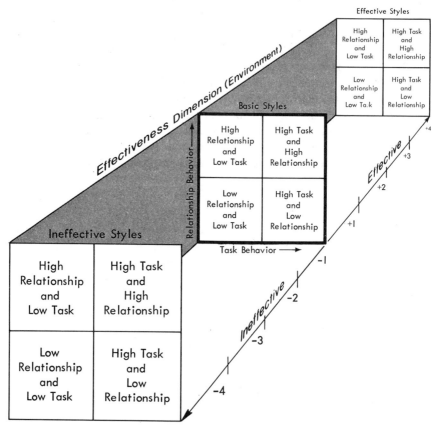

Tri-Dimensional Leader Effectiveness Model.*

*Paul Hersey and Kenneth H. Blanchard, *Management of Organizational Behavior: Utilizing Human Resources,* 3rd ed., p. 106.

The Reddin model, which is similar to the Tri-Dimensional Model, was developed to represent Reddin's 3-D Theory. This theory is based upon the four basic styles of managerial behavior as shown on the following page. The styles are essentially the same as those of Hersey and Blanchard but have been given different names.

The 3-D in Reddin's title refers to the third dimension in the model, effectiveness. The resulting 3-D Model is also shown on the following page.

Both Hersey-Blanchard and Reddin have considered the situational

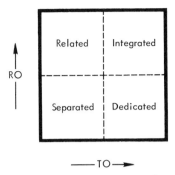

Four Basic Styles of Managerial Behavior.*

*William J. Reddin, *Managerial Effectiveness,* p. 12.

Adding the third dimension. Any of the four basic styles may be more or less effective.*

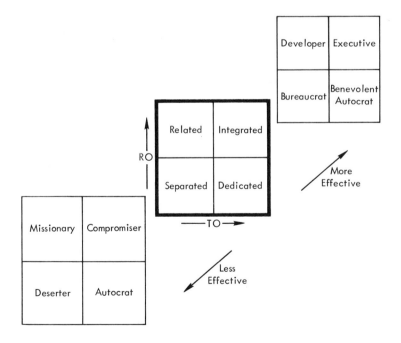

*William J. Reddin, *Managerial Effectiveness,* p. 13.

elements which influence leader effectiveness. Once again the similarities are striking.

Environmental Variables[42]	*The 3-D Situational Elements*[43] (which make demands on the manager's style and affect managerial effectiveness)
Leader	
Style	
Expectations	
Superiors	Superior
Styles	Style
Expectations	Expectations
Associates	Coworkers
Styles	Styles
Expectations	Expectations
Followers	Subordinates
Styles	Styles
Expectations	Expectations
Job Demands	Technology
Organization	Organization
Style	
Expectations	
Other Situational Variables	

Both models are based upon the assumption that leader behavior is influenced by the situation, and both specify interacting situational elements or components which have implications for leadership.

Emergent Leadership

Because the type of leadership needed varies with the situation, a group which is not rigidly structured tends to employ a variety of informal leadership resources in relation to varying situational demands. Ideally a group at any given moment in time will turn for leadership to the individual with the necessary competence. Although no group can be expected to reach this ideal, many groups do utilize the different individuals in the group as leadership resources.

Groups tend to prefer as leaders, persons whose behavior conforms to the norms, values, and objectives of the group. While a leader who is well liked may at times deviate considerably from the group norm, research results indicate that the closer an individual's behavior is to the norms of a group, the higher will be his rank in the group.[44] The informal leader is the one who most completely embodies the norms

---

[42] Hersey and Blanchard, *Management of Organizational Behavior*, pp. 133–34.
[43] Reddin, *Managerial Effectiveness*, p. 65.
[44] Stogdill, *Handbook of Leadership*, p. 262.

of the group.[45] The group believes that it can count on the informal leader to behave in a manner which the group members consider appropriate. Perhaps for this reason, a leader usually receives greater acceptance by a group if he identifies himself with the group rather than with external reference groups.

The group purpose or goal is the predominant group norm when a group is functioning as a rational or work group, and the nonrational behaviors are the predominant norm when it is functioning as a nonrational or a basic-assumption group.[46] Because every group functions at times as a work group and at times as a basic-assumption group, it needs two different types of leadership. As a work group, the group members will look for a leader who is perceived as being someone who can help the group to accomplish its task. A competent individual will be selected in preference to one who is incompetent, and the individual who is perceived as most able to help the group in task accomplishment will rank highest in the group. On the other hand, as a basic-assumption group, group members will want a leader who is somewhat paranoid, who perceives and continually calls attention to real or imagined external dangers threatening the group.[47] Such a leader tends to legitimize and sometimes to heighten anxieties already existing in the group. These two different kinds of leadership may be vested in the same person, though it is not unusual for a group to rely upon a number of different leaders, each of whom performs a specialized leadership function for the group.

In addition, group members tend to look for leadership from a member who occupies a focal position in the group. A member who is chairman of a committee, or one who is responsible for a particular activity, or is the leader in an informal social group, or is a key person in a communications channel, is in a strategic position for leadership. Findings in this area seem to some extent to validate the advice frequently given to individuals who want to get into a school administrative position: "Volunteer for everything."

Finally, groups tend to perceive as leaders those persons who participate actively. A person who talks a great deal, unless verbose, tends to be seen as a leader, and the individual who talks early or late in a discussion is more likely to prevail than the one who talks during the middle of a discussion.

---

[45] J. Rabow and others, "The Role of Social Norms and Leadership in Risk Taking," Sociometry, 29 (1966), 16-27. A. P. Bates, "Some Sociometric Aspects of Social Ranking in a Small, Face-to-face Group," *Sociometry*, 15 (1952), 330-42.

[46] This inference is based upon the theory set forth by W. R. Bion, *Experiences in Groups* (New York: Basic Books, Inc., 1959).

[47] *Ibid.*, p. 67.

EFFECTIVE EDUCATIONAL LEADERSHIP

Leadership can be most effective when knowledge and learned behaviors are used along with intuitive insight in sensing needs and providing leadership in a given situation. Leadership as a phenomenon is so complex and yet so critical to the improvement of organizational life, and indeed of society as a whole, that it constitutes a major challenge to even the most able leaders.

Situational Analysis Elements

Effective leadership is possible only through an analysis of the situational elements in a particular system. There are no simple rules which can be followed to assure effective leadership. Such leadership is possible only through sound judgment and professional competence.[48]

As research has shown, the type of leadership that is most effective differs in many respects from one situation to another. Situational elements such as 1) superiors, 2) associates and coworkers, 3) subordinates and followers, 4) job demands and technology, and 5) the organization itself, need to be taken into account. While psychological distance is probably necessary for effective leadership in any organization, greater psychological distance seems to be necessary in situations which are especially favorable or unfavorable for the leader. The needs and values of the community or society as a whole impinge upon the organization.

Three of the five situational elements affecting leadership effectiveness relate to the people in the situation, suggesting that leadership can be maximally effective only when it is appropriate in relation to the people. Situational elements come into play whenever a school principal decides to provide leadership for a school faculty by involving the faculty in participatory policy making. Some examples are illustrated in the following paragraphs.

1. Superiors

Participatory policy making illustrates the importance of superiors in the organizational hierarchy, for such policy making fares best when the administrative superior is willing for it to succeed. The leader who wants to initiate participatory policy making needs to

---

[48] For an anthropological approach see Margaret A. Ramsey, "The Administrator-Observer as Policy Maker," *Educational Administration Quarterly*, 11, no. 1 (Winter 1975), 1-10.

have at least implicit assurance that higher administration will not be strongly opposed to cooperative policy making.

In a large urban school, a principal initiated cooperative policy making with the school faculty without bothering to obtain administrative approval. Subsequently, he experienced administrative constraints which tended to vitiate the policy-making plan. The school superintendent would insist that the principal put his own recommendations on school matters in writing irrespective of faculty decision, and often purposely required a recommendation on such short notice that the faculty could not be consulted.

Upon hearing that a school principal wants to involve the staff more deeply in policy making, some administrators will be pleased; others will be cautious; some will want to be kept informed as planning goes forward; some will be initially opposed; some may be adamant in their opposition. The way in which an administrator is approached depends to considerable extent upon the administrator's personality.

Because of differences in viewpoint and personality, there is no one best way to proceed. When a school principal wants to obtain administrative support, he may approach his superior directly, may discuss the general idea with him over a period of time before making a specific proposal, may try to link the proposal to some motive or purpose of the superior, may make a point of giving the superior official the credit for any ideas which he has contributed, may try to help the superior to grow in his knowledge and understanding, or may insist upon the right to go ahead regardless of the skepticism of higher-level administration.

2. Associates

Similarly, an administrator's associates may or may not favor organizational change. There are instances in which units of parallel status in an organization have effectively killed an innovation in another unit because of their bitter opposition and their capacity to mount sanctions against the offending unit.

In a large school system, the board of education (upon recommendation of the school superintendent) decided that one of the new high schools should be an experimental unit. Nationally known consultants were brought in to help in the planning, and upon completion of the building, the school staff and principal were carefully selected. At first the school functioned well. Faculty members participated actively in policy making, there was a loose organizational structure which was liked by both faculty and students, and experimentation with new procedures and materials was so extensive that there was a steady stream of visitors. However, problems arose when the school began to negotiate with the other high schools over such matters as allocation of resources, transfers of staff, use of system-wide personnel and equipment, scheduling of sports events, and other joint acitivities. The experimental school was increasingly singled out for disadvantageous treatment. When the principal resigned to take another position, the individual selected to be the new principal was one of the traditional principals in the school system. He was specifically instructed by the central office to scuttle the experimental programs (which had been developed through teacher participation) and to make the school more traditional.

The approach to associates in promoting change needs to vary in accordance with their positions concerning proposed changes, their attitudes, and their individual personalities.

3. Subordinates

Like administrative officials, school staffs have varying reactions to participatory policy making. While it might seem that a school faculty would welcome such participation, there have been instances in which even a highly professional faculty has voted overwhelmingly against an offer from the administration that it help to make policy. Such opposition frequently stems from suspicion of administrative motives. Whatever the reason for opposition, the type of leadership provided needs to be different in a faculty opposed to participatory policy making as compared to one enthusiastic about it, and the personalities of individual faculty members need to be taken into account. In the former instance, the administrator might insist that faculty members accept appointments to policy-forming committees. In the latter instance, the administrator might move rapidly in granting to the faculty, extensive policy-making authority including the right to create and appoint necessary committees and task forces. An administrator is well advised to provide a different kind of leadership for a faculty with a few strong leaders as compared to one without such leaders.

4, 5. Job Demands and the Organization Itself

The type of leadership which is effective is contingent not only upon the people in the organization, but also upon job demands and the organization itself.[49] To be effective, leadership related to routine jobs may need to be highly directive, whereas leadership related to professional or other creative tasks may need to be far less directive and more in the nature of assistance and support.

[49] Robert Dubin and others, *Leadership and Productivity* (San Francisco: Chandler Publishing Co., 1965).

Growth as an Educational Goal

Although situational elements have implications for the type and style of leadership which will be effective, there is a constant factor in effective educational leadership, and that factor is the central goal of education, namely, the promotion of human growth. It is useful to remember that the human and task dimensions can strengthen each other in a reciprocal relationship. Nowhere is this possibility more real than in education. The task of learning the subject matter should be accomplished in a manner which contributes to the development of the individual, and conversely, an individual may desirably seek to develop his human qualities in a manner which increases his capacity for learning. It is sometimes useful for practical purposes to think of the learning of subject matter as being task-related and to think of self-growth as being human-related, yet actually the two types of growth can and should be mutually reinforcing.

Because of the interrelationship of the task and human dimensions in education, no task of educational leadership is more important than the creation of an enabling climate, that is, a climate which enables people to function with increasing effectiveness. It is in this way that the leadership in an educational organization can provide for greater task accomplishment and continuing personal growth. Climate is an encompassing dimension in a school, and educational leadership is effective only to the extent that it serves as a force for improving school climate.

The Organizational Environment

Conditions in the community and the larger society are intertwined with educational goals. Leadership necessitates a vision of what the community can become and of the place of education in helping the community to progress. It must sense that to be meaningful, the goals of education must be derived from the goals of the larger society. Schools exist to meet community needs, and the interpretation of those needs as a basis for the school program is crucial to the success of the school enterprise. Similarly, the interpretation to the community of the school's program is crucial to the support which the schools will receive from the community.

The aspect of leadership which has been most neglected in current research efforts concerns boundary functions, that is, the management of transactions which cross school and school system boundaries. Yet these functions are an important aspect of leadership. In fact, the Tavistock group believes that they are the very essence of leadership.[50] In education, as in other types of organizational endeavor, such transactions pose a major concern for responsible leadership. They necessitate the development of free and open communication between a school or school system and the people and organizations which make up its environment; cooperative relationships and endeavors with other community organizations; continuing analysis of student, community, and societal needs, and evaluation and revision of the school program in relation to those needs; and growth in understanding of education on the part of both professional and lay persons.

Moral Leadership

The urgent need in contemporary society is for moral leadership. Such leadership is needed from the entire school staff and from the whole education profession. But school administrators have a special responsibility. Administrators can continually renew their educational vision and moral sensibilities through identification with their own profession and through the growth opportunities which it offers. Yet an administrator must finally take an individual position if he or she is to exert moral leadership. This position needs to be expressed in both words and behavior. An administrator needs *verbally* to oppose discrimination and also *to take administrative action* to reduce it. An administrator needs not only to talk about the importance of ecology, but also to help the school system move toward greater conservation and development of human and physical resources. The administrator needs not only to stress human values verbally but to provide leadership in the development of more humane schools in which students can learn effectively and at the same time experience acceptance and respect. Administrators need to learn to demonstrate consistency between what they say and their own behavior: to prize education and growth for themselves; to be self-disciplined; to be doing and caring persons.

Moral leadership involves helping people move forward from where they are. If the goal is too far distant or the movement toward it too fast, the resistance created will move people away from the goal rather than toward it. The problem for an administrator is thus to develop a vision, a vision of a better society made possible through education, and to translate the vision into educational goals which

[50] A. K. Rice, *The Enterprise and Its Environment* (London: Tavistock Publications, 1963). See also Ronald E. Hull, "A Research and Development Adoption Model," *Educational Administration Quarterly*, 10, no. 3 (Autumn 1974), 33-45.

can be understood as being both achievable and difficult, and eminently desirable as the moral and educational aspirations of a free people.

SUGGESTED READINGS

Bennis, Warren, "The Sociology of Institutions or Who Sank the Yellow Submarine?" *Psychology Today*, 6, no. 6 (November 1972), 112-20.

Bennis, Warren G., Kenneth D. Benne, and Robert Chin, eds., *The Planning of Change*, 2nd ed. New York: Holt, Rinehart and Winston, Inc., 1969.

Cartwright, Dorwin and Alvin Zander, eds., *Group Dynamics: Research and Theory*, 3rd ed., Part 5, "Leadership and Performance of Group Functions." New York: Harper & Row, Publishers, 1968.

Goodlad, John I., *The Dynamics of Educational Change: Toward Responsive Schools*. New York: McGraw-Hill Book Company, Inc., 1975.

Hare, A. Paul, Edgar F. Borgatta, and Robert F. Bales, *Small Groups: Studies in Social Interaction*, rev. ed., chap. 12, "Leadership." New York: Alfred A. Knopf, 1966.

House, Ernest R., Thomas Kerins, and Joe M. Steele, "A Test of the Research and Development Model of Change," *Educational Administration Quarterly*, 8, no. 1 (Winter 1972), 1-14. Clark, David L. and Egon G. Guba, "A Re-examination of a Test of the 'Research and Development Model' of Change," *Educational Administration Quarterly*, 8, no. 3 (Autumn 1972), 93-103. House, Ernest R., "A Response to Clark and Guba: The Logic of Revisionism," *Educational Administration Quarterly*, 8, no. 3 (Autumn 1972), 104-6.

Knowles, Henry P. and Borge O. Saxberg, *Personality and Leadership Behavior*. Reading, Mass.: Addison-Wesley Publishing Company, 1971.

"Leadership: Psychological Aspects; Sociological Aspects; Political Aspects," *International Encyclopedia of the Social Sciences*, 9, 91-113.

Levinson, Harry, *Executive Stress*. New York: Harper & Row, Publishers, 1970.

Netzer, Lanore A. and others, *Education, Administration, and Change. The Redeployment of Resources*. New York: Harper & Row, Publishers, 1970.

Owens, Robert G. and Carl R. Steinhoff, *Administering Change in Schools*. Englewood Cliffs, N.J.: Prentice-Hall, Inc., 1976.

Selznick, Philip, "Leadership in Administration," in *Readings on Modern Organizations*, ed. Amitai Etzioni. Englewood Cliffs, N.J.: Prentice-Hall, Inc., 1969, pp. 185-90.

Stogdill, Ralph M., *Handbook of Leadership. A Survey of Theory and Research*. New York: The Free Press, 1974.

Zaleznik, Abraham and David Moment, *The Dynamics of Interpersonal Behavior*, Part 4, "Leadership and Change." New York: John Wiley & Sons, Inc., 1964.

CONCLUSION 11

Human beings have been able to achieve their preeminence among all earthly creatures, indeed have been able to survive among stronger and faster adversaries, because they have proved themselves to be superior in intelligence, in their capacity to learn better ways of adapting to new conditions. Human beings have become what they are because of their ability to utilize and strengthen their own resources through education.

In this period of rapid change, the need is for more informed attention to the human aspects of education. In a technological society, technological changes in education will inevitably come. Progress in the use of technology in education — the increasing use of films, educational TV, tapes, computers, and other such aids — seems assured. But can a technological society survive, and is it worthwhile, unless its human foundation is strong?

Society the world over is plagued by social problems which represent inadequate functioning on the part of human beings. Crime, juvenile delinquency, drug addiction, prejudice, serious marital discord, unethical business and professional practices, corrupt government, and the international use of force — these and other deleterious forms of behavior occur all too frequently in the modern world. Yet such behaviors typically are not the result of inherited tendencies, organic defects, or illness. They are simply instances of poor functioning which stem from the incapacity of individuals to meet their needs in ways which are responsible to themselves and others. The desperation which individuals feel in their inability to satisfy basic needs is reflected in exaggerated means to achieve need satisfaction. Exaggerated needs for love, safety, significance, and belonging are expressed in a wide variety of forms of antisocial behavior. If education is thought of in its true sense as including not only formal schooling but also education which takes place in the family, neighborhood, and society as a whole, then the social problems of interpersonal relationships stem from a single basic cause — and that cause is miseducation.

It has become increasingly popular for commentators, politicians, and others to say that nobody really understands the causes of social problems, that nobody knows why some people become addicted to drugs or alcohol, that no one can account for the excessive crime and corruption in our society. This ostensible lack of understanding provides a good alibi for inaction, for if the causes of social problems are a mystery, nothing of a preventive or ameliorative nature can be done.

One of the hallmarks of a professional is the capacity to develop and maintain perspective. For an educational administrator, maintenance of perspective means the capacity to develop an understanding of what a democratic society can become, and to view the vicissitudes of the society not only in terms of day-to-day events but also in broader more holistic terms in relation to the society's potential.

It would of course be futile to deny that many social phenomena are still puzzling to behavioral scientists. The study of human behavior is still in its infancy, and vast problem areas need to be explored. Nevertheless, despite the shortcomings of present knowledge, a great deal is known about human behavior. Scientific findings have advanced to the point where a prescription for wholesome personal development could be agreed upon by most informed persons. The prescription would include a child's living in a stable family where individual autonomy is the life style, where communication is open, sharing of chores is common, and action responsible to self and others is the norm. It would include experiences in a neighborhood with social institutions such as the church in which all persons, including minorities and children, would be respected. It would involve learning in a school with an open climate and individual performance goals which each child could meet if and only if he or she really tried. It would involve growing in citizenship through participation in community activities and governmental processes in which integrity could be rightfully assumed and in which the goals were directed toward assuring opportunities for a better life with justice for everyone.

Much is known about the elements associated with personal development. Unfortunately, however, the knowledge available has generally not been applied to the problems of educational administration. Despite verbal statements to the contrary, many educational administrators run the schools by using bureaucratic forms of management at the expense of individuality.

Administration is justified only to the extent that it contributes to the capacity of an organization to fulfill its primary mission. In the field of education, administration is justified only as it contributes to the capacity of the schools to help children and youth grow toward responsible adulthood. Such growth implies recognition of the importance of intrinsic motivation and emphasis upon the realization of individual potential through personal creativity.

Individuals in every school need to be enabled to identify their own motivations and to discover their own resources for moving toward self-actualization. Individuals need to be enabled to learn to function autonomously, to make their own decisions, to invest their lives as they so desire, to develop in a manner which is uniquely their own. Each person must learn to meet his or her own basic affectional needs and to move toward others in ways that are satisfying and genuinely strength giving. By learning to respect themselves as persons and to be unafraid to stand alone, individuals can develop the courage which will enable them to be open and to develop ever-deepening communication with others. Such openness may lead to conflict, but conflict which can be constructive rather than destructive in its methods and consequences.

Paradoxically, autonomous individuals grow in the realization that they cannot achieve their purposes in isolation. Autonomous functioning thus leads directly to organizational responsibility and constructive citizenship—not to the compliance desired by some administrators, but to responsible action on the part of individuals in enabling an organization or group to define and achieve its purposes. Commitment can then be based upon the development of individual responsibility rather than upon selfish interests or blind allegiance.

Since learning is best promoted by teachers who are effective persons in their own right, educational administration can realize its potential only as it nurtures growth through intrinsic motivation on the part of the school staff. Attempts to force staff members to grow have run into the difficulties which so often attend means which are not compatible with desired ends. What is often forgotten is that it is natural for people to want to grow. However, people grow in their own ways—not in the uniform ways which many administrators try to require. The efforts of administrators to help teachers grow in understanding are conditioned by the level of understanding of the administrators and staff development specialists themselves.

The tendency of many administrators to adopt bureaucratic methods to the neglect of individuality can be ascribed to the fact that structural forms which assume uniformity are easier to administer than are those which assume individual differences. There is nothing about education which requires that administrative purposes be different from the purposes of individuals in the organization. There is general agreement that the mission of the schools is to provide opportunities for each person to grow and develop. Constraints on the schools in carrying out this mission develop from disagreements as to means rather than as to the mission itself. This situation is different from that in the business community where, although there is growing recognition of the social responsibilities of business, it is generally agreed that a central purpose of business in a capitalistic system is to make a profit. One can readily understand why the purposes of the organization and the individual worker in a business are so often in conflict.

This type of conflict, which grows out of the organizational mission and appears to be inherent in business, is not present in education. To be sure, conflict between group and individual purposes is inevitable in some respects whenever a group or organization exists. However, conflict between organizational and individual purposes in schools cannot be attributed to the nature of the school's mission. Much of this type of conflict can be attributed only to lack of knowledge and insight.

A relatively untapped store of knowledge about human behavior in schools, though incomplete and doubtlessly inaccurate in many respects, is available. The great need is for teachers and administrators who can develop a depth of insight in utilizing this knowledge to promote learning on the part of individual persons and groups.

A number of models based on behavioral science findings have already been developed. The time for the schools to change in accordance with theory and research findings on the nature of human behavior is now, and the responsibility of every administrator is to take whatever forward-looking steps are possible, however small such steps may be.

The utilization of behavioral science findings will not give definitive answers to educational and administrative problems. The problems will change, and disagreements over ways of coping with them will persist. What the utilization of behavioral science findings can do is to help eliminate practices and disagreements based upon ignorance and misconceptions. Without specifying what should be done, scientific findings can point the way toward improved educational and administrative practice.

The thrust of this book is its emphasis upon the human dimension in educational administration. However, if individual students are to learn to cope in the modern world and are to become competent citizens, both the task and the human dimensions of the school and its administration must receive attention. That these two dimensions are inextricably interrelated is illustrated whenever a person tries to identify his own motivations. Motivation is a human attribute; yet a person must be motivated to do something, and that something is in the nature of a task. Whenever a school tries to help a student to identify career goals, both the task and the human dimensions come into play. Whenever an administrator works with a staff to develop performance goals, both staff purposes and the tasks to be performed are involved. If the task dimension is neglected, performance goals are likely to be low, and if the human dimension is neglected, standardization and coercion are likely to be employed in such a manner that motivation and growth are stultified.

The challenge to every school administrator, and the great opportunity, is to provide for educational experiences through administration which takes account of both the task and the human dimensions of the educational organization. Such educational experiences can help to assure that the human foundations of our society will not disintegrate, but rather will support a humane technological society in which men and women can live with zest and hope, more capable of fulfilling their vast potential for functioning in a manner which is satisfying and productive, both for themselves and for the whole society.

AUTHOR INDEX

SUBJECT INDEX